Praise for Other Works by Claude Lecouteux

"Claude Lecouteux is the most versatile and wide-ranging of the scholars of the medieval imagination—any book of his is a treat."

RONALD HUTTON, PROFESSOR OF HISTORY AT
THE UNIVERSITY OF BRISTOL, ENGLAND, AND
AUTHOR OF *WITCHES, DRUIDS AND KING ARTHUR*

"*The High Magic of Talismans and Amulets* is the only talisman book you will ever need. In this expansive tome, Lecouteux has unified information never before assembled in one place. This book is a useful guide and a wellspring on the subject, drawing from cultures throughout time and around the globe. Here, given to the readers, are historical examples of famous talismans and amulets, their meanings and origins, and explanations on how to generate them."

MAJA D'AOUST, WITCH OF THE DAWN AND
AUTHOR OF *FAMILIARS IN WITCHCRAFT*

"What are the ancient mysteries of earth and water? Guided by the sure hand of Claude Lecouteux in this erudite and accessible book [*Demons and Spirits of the Land*], we find keys to the recovery and renewed understanding of indigenous European religious traditions concerning land and water. A valuable book—highly recommended."

ARTHUR VERSLUIS, AUTHOR OF *SACRED EARTH*
AND *RELIGION OF LIGHT*

"With the *Dictionary of Gypsy Mythology,* Claude Lecouteux has filled a void long overdue in its need for address. He approaches a mysterious and all too oft misunderstood culture with respect, compassion, and genuine interest. The resulting text is compelling, informative, educational, and practical, as the alphabetical layout lends itself to research as well as reading for pleasure."

VANESSA SINCLAIR, PSY.D., PSYCHOANALYST, ARTIST,
AND AUTHOR OF *SWITCHING MIRRORS*

"Claude Lecouteux's work on the topic of ancient magic spells stands out as a refreshing reminder and example of what real scholarship should be and can be. *Traditional Magic Spells for Protection and Healing* is eminently researched and readable: it features a substantial introduction, chapters organized by topic, several appendices, an index, and a full bibliography. It is a must-read not only for the specialists of ancient magic and medicine but also for the general public."

"Both scholarly and accessible in this translation, *The Secret History of Vampires* is a gem. Lecouteux reveals ancient precursors to the vampire myth that are overlooked by most researchers. These and other theories are backed by a plethora of supporting evidence, including primary sources in the appendices, making this a must-add to any vampire library."

"*The Hidden History of Elves and Dwarfs* explores the transformations through time of the 'little people' of ancient Europe, both as 'elementals' personifying subtle powers of the natural world and as ambiguous projections of our own fears and desires. We have always had uneasy relations with these furtive beings who populate a secret world just out of sight, both close to home and beyond our ken, intimate and alien, a 'hidden folk' who manifest the quiet mysteries of our daily lives. Professor Lecouteux offers a comprehensive and engaging 'unnatural history' of these exotic familiars."

"*A Lapidary of Sacred Stones* has to be the most incredible book ever published on sacred and magical stones. The illustrations are magnificent and worth the price of the book alone. A must-have for historians and anyone interested in the sacred and magical properties of stones. This book is really a magical mystery tour!"

"Once again Claude Lecouteux produces a thoroughly researched, eminently readable, and delightfully entertaining text that blends scholarly ethos with respect for the unknown. Readers with a casual interest in the supernatural will find their knowledge greatly expanded and their curiosity provoked even further. Those already adept in the subject will nonetheless find much to mull over in *The Secret History of Poltergeists and Haunted Houses*."

TALES OF
WITCHCRAFT
AND WONDER

The Venomous Maiden and
Other Stories of the Supernatural

CLAUDE AND CORINNE LECOUTEUX

TRANSLATED BY JON E. GRAHAM

Inner Traditions
Rochester, Vermont

Inner Traditions
One Park Street
Rochester, Vermont 05767
www.InnerTraditions.com

SUSTAINABLE FORESTRY INITIATIVE
Certified Sourcing
www.sfiprogram.org
SFI-00854

Text stock is SFI certified

Originally published in French under the title *Contes, diableries et autres merveilles du Moyen Âge* by Éditions Imago, 7 rue Suger, 75006, Paris
First U.S. edition published in 2021 by Inner Traditions

Cataloging-in-Publication Data for this title is available from the Library of Congress

ISBN 978-1-64411-170-3 (print)
ISBN 978-1-64411-171-0 (ebook)

Printed and bound in the United States by Lake Book Manufacturing, Inc. The text stock is SFI certified. The Sustainable Forestry Initiative® program promotes sustainable forest management.

10 9 8 7 6 5 4 3 2 1

Text design and layout by Debbie Glogover
This book was typeset in Garamond Premier Pro with Gill Sans MT Pro, Myriad Pro, NixRift, and Shango used as display typefaces

To Benoît, Annelise, Perrine, and Mathilde

CONTENTS

Abbreviations of Works Cited

AaTh: *The Types of the Folktale* by Antti Aarne

BP: *Ammerkungen zu den Kinder- und Hausmärchen der Brüder Grimm* by Johannes Bolte and Georg Polívka, 5 vols.

CPF: *Le Conte populaire français* by Paul Delarue and Marie-Louise Ténèze

EM: *Enzyklopädie des Märchens*

KHM: *Kinder- und Hausmärchen* by the Brothers Grimm

Motif: *Motif-Index of Folk Literature* by Stith Thompson

TU: *Index Exemplorum* by Frederic C. Tubach

RELIGION, ROMANCE, AND FABLE

The Middle Ages—a descriptive phrase that encompasses a span of ten centuries and which was invented by the librarian of the pope in 1469—represent a period that is poorly known to most people. The Middle Ages were allegedly "dark"—namely, the so-called Dark Ages. But this period also witnessed the blossoming of oral traditions whose echo can be found in many texts that have come down to the present day. Epics and romances, tales and legends, fabliaux and lays—all were performed aloud, and every minstrel and jongleur had a repertory at their disposal not unlike the one that Elias Lönnrot collected during the nineteenth century when he compiled the Finnish *Kalevala*. These original medieval tales rarely possessed the form in which we might find them today in the versions of Charles Perrault, Madame d'Aulnoye, or the Brothers Grimm. They were most often included in the romances, in which they would constitute an episode, or else were fictionalized. In 1928, Vladimir Propp noted that "the romance of chivalry finds its origin in the domain of the tale." Several medievalists have examined this subject and have managed to find fragments of tales scattered almost everywhere, but considerable research remains to be done.[1]

The tales are hidden in the collections of *exempla*,[*2] in compilations like the *Deeds of the Romans* (*Gesta Romanorum*), the oldest manuscript

---

*[An *exemplum* (pl. *exempla*) is a cautionary medieval tale, often incorporated into a sermon to illustrate a doctrinal or moral point. —*Ed.*]

of which dates from 1342, a collection that Johann G. Graesse did not hesitate to describe as the "most ancient collection of tales" and which was translated into several languages,[3] notably Polish and later Russian. Some of its stories were recast as folklore, and traces of them can be found, for example, in a Caucasian folktale.

The tales are also concealed in historiographies, sermons, farces, fables, and lays. They can be recognized by their structures and by the functions embodied in their protagonists, with everything else being variable. Precisely because they possess an open structure, they are receptive to the interpolations of new elements, and we are often faced with narratives that combine non-native elements.

Legends are constantly adapting to their sociocultural environment; they are rewritten in the style of the times in which they circulate, and, during the Middle Ages, moral and religious considerations played an important role in the transformation process. Legends were most often composed from a primary motif—an event or personal experience—or a notion around which the narrative was crystallized, and one category of legendry is called a *récit de croyance,* a "narrative of folk belief." Finally, these legends all say they are true.[4]

A distinction is made among five types of stories:

- Legends of the dead
- Demonic legends
- Historical legends
- Christian legends, including the legends of the saints
- Etiological legends

The ancient texts, a great many of which were written in Latin, collected oral narrative traditions, but the tales were also transposed into the courtly and chivalrous world. The décor was changed: the activities of the nobility, the medieval courts and their pomp, formed the environment. Yet the marvelous is omnipresent: fairies, dwarfs, and demons haunt this world, giants and magicians—both male and female—serve as antagonists (the female variety having the ability to change you into a dragon or a doe), but deliverance comes in the nick of time, with a few rare exceptions! What Propp called the "magical methods" are encountered in the course of every narrative: elixirs, salves, rings, stones of great virtue,[5] simples, spells—the imagination here seems boundless.

The period of the Middle Ages presents three areas of interest with regard to the study of tales and legends. It first offers us evidence about their antiquity; next, it shows us the dominant themes and motifs on which they were structured; and finally, it provides us with valuable information about the mentalities of the long-distant past, as these stories are riddled with realia borrowed from the civilization in which they are immersed.[6] A major movement for the rediscovery of this ancient literature took place in the nineteenth century, and many stories were translated or adapted. Just under thirty of the Grimms's fairy tales derive from the Middle Ages, while that number increases to thirty-three in the work of Ludwig Bechstein.[7] It was also during the nineteenth century that writers, and even the authors of opera librettos, began incorporating medieval tales and legends into their work, helping to rekindle the public's interest in them.

One of the other merits of the tales and legends that we have chosen to rescue from obscurity is that they show how the romance writers of the Middle Ages recast the popular narratives from oral tradition and how they mined this lode of stories to construct their own tales. In "Frederick of Swabia," one of the forms taken by the classical tale of *Cupid and Psyche,* we find the incorporation of the myth of bird women, a visit to the dwarfs, and the deliverance of a young woman who has been metamorphosed. In "Liombruno" we see the fusion of the story of the child promised to the devil with that of the fairy mistress. The tale of the "magical return," represented by "Henry the Lion," is enriched with that of the "Grateful Lion," and the tale of the woman slandered sees its structure tripled in "Crescentia."

During the Middle Ages the border between tales and legends was both fluid and porous. The two genres are composites and constantly shift in terms of their elements. Modern definitional criteria—the tale is characterized by its happy ending, in contrast to the legend; the latter stands outside of time and space, while the former is well anchored in reality, and so forth—are barely applicable here. Now there are exceptions to these rules. Incidentally, we should note that in many cases the list of tale types includes legends. By trying to stick a label on the whole thing, the historians of literature can be misleading.

Equally vague is the border between *exempla*—religious legends— and folktales. "The Incest of Gregorius" provides a good example of this. Numerous references in the nomenclature of Antti Aarne's and Stith Thompson's motif indexes for folktales line up with those of the *Index exemplorum* (Index of Exempla) compiled by Frederic Tubach. All of this is to be expected because the Middle Ages did not truly seek to distinguish among all these narrative forms, and, depending on the era, the same story could be called a fable, an *exemplum,* a story, or a tale. Take a look at the French lays of the twelfth and thirteenth centuries:[8] the majority of them are tales built on themes that have been clearly noted by the folklorists.

The three major vectors of tales and legends are the religious literature, the romance, and the fable, but traces of them can be found in other literary genres. In the first case, they serve as scaffolding for moralizing or allegorical interpretations; in the second case, they are transposed. The heroes are no longer anonymous; now clothed with chivalric virtues, they live in castles, they go on hunts and participate in tourneys, and so forth. The action is situated in a geographical location, except in those cases when the author is specifically following a folktale. The romances built on the theme of the quest—a quest for identity, for sovereignty, or a bridal quest—are comparable to the initiatory tales exalting the qualities prized by a society: courage, perseverance, generosity, and charity are rewarded. Rescued from the claws of the monster that abducted her, the maiden gives her hand to the hero or gives him the instructions he needs to achieve his quest.

Until 1350 or thereabouts, the majority of vernacular texts were composed in verse, contrary to those in Latin. Versification entailed the use of chevilles* and repetitions. Set within a feudal environment, these texts are characterized by long, stereotyped descriptions of feasts,

---

*[A *cheville* is a word or phrase added to a line to make it metrically balanced but serves no other purpose. —*Trans.*]

clothing, arms, and battles. They are rife with allusions or reminders of courtly values because the poets and romance writers, whose livelihood was dependent on their benefactors, had to present the latter with heroes in whom they could recognize themselves. Furthermore, during the era of manuscript production, the scribes overlooked and sometimes left out passages, or skipped words. This led to the creation of obscure passages, mysterious phrases, and allusions that are incomprehensible to anyone who lacks access to the several different textual variants that may be extant today. To translate these legends in a literal way, word for word, as we have done elsewhere,[9] results in a text that only specialists can appreciate. So we have adapted these stories by tidying them up— in other words, by eliminating the redundancies and summarizing the long descriptions and the constant references to God, and to his Mercy and Omnipotence, except when such elements play an important part in the narration.

In some instances the reader will find two versions of the same story presented, separated by one or two centuries but worthy of note because of the alteration of the essential elements, which thereby document the evolution of the narrative based on the talent of the storyteller. In the appendices, more recent accounts (from the seventeenth to nineteenth centuries) will show the role that the historical era has played in the written obsession with these stories.

After each story, the section marked with the symbol 📖 provides some comparative sources and related literature concerning the tale or legend.

CHAPTER I
ANIMAL TALES

1. The Bat

Once upon a time, the animals declared war on all the birds that had feathers for flying. There was a large and brutal battle that lasted for a very long time, but the outcome was indecisive. Madame Bat, fearing that the birds were on the losing side, did not want to stay with them for long. "With my claws, my muzzle, and my head, I look like an animal," she told herself. Thus, she departed to help her enemies.

However, the eagle had put all his effort into fortifying, rallying, and assisting his troops. He inspired them with so much courage for the battle that they fought proudly and cut down the pride of the animals. They struck their foes so hard and so much that the eagle's troops emerged victorious. The animals dashed forth in large numbers in vain; they were not able to mount any resistance and the victors then dealt with the bat. They plucked out all her feathers, thrashed her, and gave her a good beating for abandoning them. She remained all black and bare, and the whole court condemned her to no longer fly during the day.

MARIE DE FRANCE, "DE VESPERTILIONE,"
FABLES (TWELFTH CENTURY)[1]

The story that inspired Marie de France explains some of the bat's characteristics. It is a part of the group of etiological legends that responds to the questions raised by the people of a bygone day: "Why is the sea salty?" "Why is the crow black?" and so on. It can also be found in the exempla *and in sermons, as well as in historiography.*

AaTh 222 A; TU 501

📖 Albert-Lorca, *L'Ordre des Choses;* Jacques de Vitry, *Sermones Vulgaris,* no. 153; Johannes Gobi, *Scala Coeli,* no. 420; Vincent of Beauvais, *Speculum historiale,* III.

2. The Grateful Lion

Once upon a time there was a knight who was passionate about hunting. One day, a lion came up to him limping and held out his paw in which a thorn was stuck. The knight got down from his steed and pulled it out, treated the wound with some balm, and healed it.[2] It so happened that the king was also hunting by chance in this same forest and held it captive for many long years. One day the knight rebelled against this monarch and sought safe haven in the woods, robbing and killing all those who crossed his path. He was eventually captured, and the king handed down the following sentence: he would be cast to the lion, who would not be given any food so as to increase his hunger. Once in the pit, the knight became greatly afraid while awaiting the hour of his death. But the lion looked at him quite closely, and once he recognized him, he displayed great joy and remained near him for seven days without eating him.

When news of this extraordinary behavior made its way to the ears of the monarch, he was amazed. He had the knight brought out of the pit and asked him: "Tell me, my friend, how is it that this lion has done you no harm?"

The knight told the king about his adventure with the animal, adding: "That is why I believe he is not attacking me."

"Since the lion has not eaten you, I, too, am going to spare your life. Henceforth, you must strive to change your life."

The knight thanked the king, mended his ways, and ended his days peacefully.

Gesta Romanorum, chap. 104[3]

This story shows what happened during the Middle Ages to the legend of Androcles and the lion, which Aesop turned into a fable. It enjoyed huge popularity and provided episodes to many courtly romances; Chrétien de Troyes and his imitators recycled it in "The Knight of the Lion." It is also found in the "Life of Saint Jerome."

📖 Aulus Gellius, *Attic Nights*, bk. XIV; EM, s.v. "Androklus und der Löwe"; Pliny the Elder, *Natural History*, VII, 21, 3–4 (the hero is named Mentor of Syracuse).

3. The She-Wolf

A priest traveling with his servant spent the night in a forest. He had built a fire and was keeping vigil close to the flames when a wolf approached them and said:[4] "Stay calm and do not be scared; you have no need to tremble when there is no cause for fear!" The priest then begged him in God's name to do them no harm and asked him what manner of creature he might be. "Our people were once cursed by a Bishop," the beast answered. "We are forced, every seven years, to exile two persons, a man and a woman, from their land and to alter their shapes. They then take on the appearance of wolves.[5] But when the seven years have passed, if they are still alive, they can return to their country and to their original nature, while another couple will replace them under the same conditions. My companion is gravely ill and living her final moments. Come and give her last rites."

Overcoming his fear, the priest followed the wolf to a hollow tree where a she-wolf was lying. She was groaning and moaning like a human being. She greeted the churchman and asked for last rites, but he hesitated because he was looking at an animal. Then, using his paw as if it were a hand, he pulled back the hide from the wolf's head and unrolled it down to her navel, revealing the body of an old woman.* The priest finished by giving her the communion for which she asked, and the wolf skin immediately covered her again.

In the morning, the wolf led the priest and his servant out of the forest, showed them the safest road, thanked them, and disappeared.

GERALD OF WALES, *TOPOGRAPHIA HIBERNICA*, II, 1[6]

Behind this legend is hidden a belief in werewolves in Ireland that has been clearly confirmed since the twelfth century. Another account offers some information that completes this text: "One day the Irish began howling like wolves against Saint Patrick, who was preaching the Christian religion to them. So that their descendants would have a visible sign of

---

*This reflects one of the beliefs about werewolves: beneath the skin, the person remains human.

their ancestors' lack of faith, the saint asked God to make it so that some of them would be transformed into wolves for seven years and live in the forests like the animals whose appearance they had assumed."[7]

📕 EM, s.v. "Wolfsmenschen" and "Giraldus Cambrensis"; Lecouteux, *Elle courait le garou; Witches, Werewolves, and Fairies.*

4. The Brave Serpent

During the reign of the emperor Fulgentius there was a knight named Zedechias[8] who lived in his empire. He had married a very beautiful but impossibly stupid woman.[9] A serpent lived in one room of their house. The knight participated so often in tournaments and jousting that he became quite impoverished by it. He wept bitter tears and, at the height of his despair, vainly thrashed about not knowing what to do. The serpent took note of his sorrow and, like Balaam's ass[10] from days of yore, started to speak:[11] "Why do you lament? Follow my counsel and you shall not regret it. Give me some sweet milk every day and I will make you rich."* Zedechias was overjoyed and promised to grant him his wish every day. In a short time, he had made a fortune, had beautiful children, and was living in luxury.

One day his wife said to him: "My lord, I am sure that the serpent is hiding great wealth in the room where he dwells.[12] I advise you to kill him so we can steal it from him." Following his wife's advice, at the same time Zedechias brought the snake the saucer of milk, he took a hammer to kill it. When he saw the milk, the snake stuck his head from his hole to drink it as usual. The knight raised his hammer to crush him, but the serpent spotted it in extremis, pulled back his head, and the hammer only hit the saucer.

Shortly after this attempt, Zedechias lost his children and all his goods. His wife then said to him: "Oh, what bad advice I gave you! Go to the snake's hole and make your mea culpa in every possible way so that, maybe, he will forgive you."

---

*Sent by Balak, King of Moab, to curse the Israelites, Balaam suddenly heard his ass speak to him.

The knight obeyed his wife and went weeping to beg the serpent for his forgiveness so he could regain his former wealth. But the beast responded: "I now can clearly see that you are a fool and you will always be one. It is impossible for me to forget that you tried to kill me, just as it is impossible for you to forget that I killed your children and took possession of all your riches. Thus, there can be no peace between us."

Deeply troubled, Zedechias replied: "I promise you that I shall never undertake anything at all against you, if only you will forgive me."

"My dear friend," said the serpent, "be satisfied with my words, for I will never forget your hammer blow and treachery. Get away before something worse happens to you!"

Greatly stricken, the knight left and told his wife: "What a misfortune it is that I followed your advice!" And from that time on they lived in perpetual poverty.

GESTA ROMANORUM, CHAP. 141[13]

This tale features a household spirit in an ophidian shape, a common guise of this creature in the folk beliefs. The well-being of the house always depends on the way this spirit is treated. As a general rule, the owner of the premises concludes a tacit pact with the serpent: he will enjoy a life of wealth and ease in return for food. But if the contract is broken, the spirit will take its revenge or leave, and misfortune will move in.

AaTh 285 A

📖 Lecouteux, *The Tradition of Household Spirits.*

5. The Field Mouse

The field mouse, which looks quite a bit like a house mouse, was formerly so full of pride that it refused to take a wife from his kindred or fellow field mice. "I will never marry," he said, "unless I find someone to my liking!" He started by addressing the sun, because it was the highest, most powerful, and hottest of all things. "Go farther," the sun answered him, "to the cloud that covers me in shade. I can no longer show myself when he hides me."

"You are so powerful," the mouse declared to the cloud, "that I aspire to your daughter's hand."

"Go farther," the other responded, "and you will find one more powerful than me: the wind that scatters me with its breath."

"I will go find it; keep your daughter."

The field mouse thus visited the wind and said to it: "The cloud sent me to you because you are, according to him, the most powerful of all and your might is boundless. You drive away all creatures and destroy them by blowing. I want to marry your daughter because nothing can resist you."

"You are mistaken," replied the wind. "You shall not find a wife here because there is something more powerful than I, someone who makes a fool of me. It is a large stone tower that remains solid and whole. I have never been able to demolish it or weaken it; it repels me so strongly that I no longer dare attack it."

"I don't want your daughter," exclaimed the field mouse, "a woman of low estate! I shall wed one that brings me great honor. I will therefore go see the tower."

He went and asked for the hand of his daughter, and the tower looked at him while answering: "You are fooling yourself and have not paid enough attention. The one that sent you here must be making fun of you, methinks. You will find someone even more powerful than I, someone with whom I could never compete."

"Who is it then? Who is stronger than you in the world?"

"The mouse. It makes its nest and lives in my walls; there is no mortar, hard as it might be, that she cannot pierce. She digs beneath me and through me; nothing can stop her!"

"What? That is sad news! The mouse is kin to me, and I have gone to all this trouble for nothing. I thought I was raising myself up, but I must go back down."

"Such is your fate. Go back home and make sure to remember that you must not despise your own nature. The one who wishes to climb very high above his own rank has only the further to fall. No one should scorn their own rank, as long as it is not dishonorable. You can travel a great distance, but you will never find a wife who is better suited for you than the mouse."

MARIE DE FRANCE, "DE MURE UXOREM PETENTE,"
FABLES (TWELFTH CENTURY)[14]

📖 Transmitted by Johannis de Capua (*Directorium Vitae Humanae*, V, 8), the *Pañcatantra* (III, 13), and the *Liber Kalilae et Dimnae* (IV, 109), this folktale of Eastern origin can be seen, most nostably, in La Fontaine's "The Mouse Changed into a Girl" (*Fables*, IX, 7) and, later, Bechstein's *Neues Deutsches Märchenbuch*.[15]

6. The Resuscitated Horse

Once upon a time there was a valiant knight who was hospitable and generous. At the beginning of the fast of Quadragesima, which is commonly called Lent, he found that he was low on food supplies; it so happens that on this day he customarily held a feast.[16] He ordered one of his servants to discreetly slaughter a good horse that he owned and have it cooked. The servant obeyed his master's orders.

The next day, the squire went out to groom and currycomb the horse. Fearing that people would find out it had disappeared, the knight tried to prevent him from entering the stable. Using all manner of pretexts, he kept him outside, but finally the squire heard the horse whinny. He entered and brought out the animal totally alive.

GERVASE OF TILBURY *OTIA IMPERIALIA,* III, 100

Beneath its Christian overlay, and even though Gervase of Tilbury chose not to reproduce the important details of the traditional narrative, we can recognize in this folktale one of the final vestiges of a shamanic belief, which holds that a slain animal can be revived by reforming its skeleton. One of the oldest examples of this belief can be found in the Eddas.

While he was traveling in his cart drawn by goats, the god Thor came to the home of a farmer who offered him hospitality. Thor killed his goats, they were cooked, and everyone sat down to eat. Then "Thor placed their hides between the fire and the door and told the peasant and his folk to place the bones on top of them, but Thjálfi, the farmer's son, kept the thighbone of one of the goats and split it open with his knife so he could get at its marrow." In the morning, the god took his hammer, brandished it while reciting incantations over the skins, and the goats came back to life, but one of them had a limp in one of its back legs.

The Miracles of Saint Germain *as well as the story of* "Saint Germain and King Benli," *preserved in the* Historia Britonum,[17] *both tell of some similar events; Stephen de Bourbon used this as inspiration for one of his works (no. 217). The detail of the broken bone is missing from the* Golden Legend *of Jacobus de Varagine.*

A narrative deriving from the same shamanic sources can be found in the stories collected by the Brothers Grimm ("Brother Lustig"):

St. Peter, who was accompanying a soldier, resurrected a dead princess: "He cut off all of the dead girl's limbs and threw them in a pot of water, lit a fire beneath the kettle, and cooked them. And once all the flesh had fallen away from the bones, he took the small pretty white bones out of the water, placed them on a table, and arranged them in their natural order." He then invoked the Holy Trinity, and the princess rose up in good health.

The same procedure is present in an Irish folktale from Donegal—here the miracle worker is a young man dressed in red; he reassembles the bones, has them boiled, then places the head back on the torso. And in two Russian legends we have the intervention of God in one and Saint Nicholas in the other.

AaTh 750 C; TU 2533

📖 Afanasyev, *Narodnye russkie legendy,* no. 5; BP I, 422–23, and II, 157, 162; CPF IV, 131–33; EM, s.v. "Gervasius von Tilbury"; Hyde and Nutt, ed. and trans., *Beside the Fire,* 148–53; Lecouteux, *Witches, Werewolves, and Fairies;* Sichler, "Légendes russes," 90–94.

CHAPTER II

ODDITIES AND WONDERS

1. The Bell of Justice

Charlemagne was the best judge of all time. When he traveled about, he would have a pillar topped by a bell erected everywhere he stopped so that every person seeking justice could ring it even when he was having a meal. It so happened that one day the bell rang for the first time, and his servants were not able to find anyone near the rope. It rang again. The emperor ordered his servants[1] to go back at once to learn who had rung it: "If you don't bring the person who rang it back to me, I shall slay you!"

They still saw nothing and returned, full of dread, to Charlemagne, who made all manner of threats to them. The bell rang a third time, and they then saw a large snake pulling on the rope. Stunned, they told Charlemagne of what they had seen, and he got up at once to show justice to the animal just as he would to any man. The serpent was allowed to enter, and the emperor forbade anyone from harming it. After respectfully bowing before Charlemagne, the snake informed the servants that they had to follow it. The servants did so, and it led them through an orchard to its nest, hidden in a thick bush, where a monstrous toad was sitting on the serpent's eggs. They brought the toad back with them and reported what they had seen to Charlemagne. He condemned the toad to death, and it was stabbed with a spear.

NATURRECHT[2]

This legend, which is known as "the bell of justice," can be found (without any connection to Charlemagne) in the Gesta Romanorum *and in the exempla. This text was modified in 1723 by J. J. Scheuchzer, from where the Brothers Grimm took it (cf. German Legends, no. 453). The connection between this legend and one we have included elsewhere in the book ("Love Spell") is based on the snake's stone, which was brought to the court like this:*

"Several days later, the serpent returned to the court, bowed, turned to the emperor's table and lifted the lid of a goblet that was sitting there. It took a precious stone from out of its mouth, placed it inside, bowed again, and left. Charlemagne gave the gem to his wife,[3] whom he loved dearly. This stone had the secret virtue of never allowing her to be absent from his thoughts; when she was away, he pined for her. When she was dying, Charlemagne's wife hid the stone beneath her tongue, knowing full well that if it fell into the hands of anyone else, the emperor would soon forget her. So she was buried with the stone, and Charlemagne did not want to part from her."

AATH 207 C

📖 EM, s.v. "Glocke de Gerechtigkeit." *Gesta Romanorum,* chap. 150, "De campana et iudicio serpente"; Klapper, *Erzählungen des Mittelalters,* no. 133; "De iustitia et virtute gratitudinis exemplo serpentis"; Pasquier, *Les Recherches de la France,* IV, 33 (in *Les œuvres*); Scheuchzer, *Ouresiphoites Helvetica,* III, 381.

2. The Dead Guest

A drunkard once lived near a churchyard that he crossed through every evening when he was besotted with drink. One day, when making his way home by his usual path, he found a skull. He addressed it kindly:

"Poor skull, come home with me to share a meal!"

"Go ahead, I will follow you!"[4] replied the skull.

Terrified and sobered by these words, he returned home, his whole body trembling, and took a seat next to the fire. He had the door to the house shut and, when he went to sit at the table, he ordered his servants, if they valued their lives, to not let anyone, no matter who, come in. Suddenly there was a knock at the door by someone saying that the master of the house had invited him. Petrified by fear, they remained speechless; only one dared answer that the master was absent, but the stranger replied: "Tell him to open the door, for I know he is there; otherwise I will force myself in as I am more than capable of doing." The master of the house pleaded for divine mercy and had the door opened. Everyone there then saw a dead man enter. It was a skeleton upon which nothing remained but skin and tendons; all the flesh had disappeared. A nameless terror seized the household. The dead man washed his hands and took a seat between his host and his wife without any invitation. He neither ate nor drank, he spoke not a single word, and his dreadful appearance plunged them into dread.

At the end of the meal, he stood up and took his leave, saying: "I had no need of the food you offered to me. If you had not made fun of me with your crazed words when you were drunk, I would have not shown up in this abominable form. Farewell! But in eight days, come to me at the same time when you invited me, and I will prepare a meal for you. You must come whether willingly or not." Then he vanished.

The host and his entire family, frightened as they were, sought advice from people with experience so they could learn how to escape this danger. "Put your affairs in order, take confession and repent of your sins, take communion, and, thus protected, wait for God's judgment at the appointed hour," was the only advice he was given.

On the appointed day he made his way to the meeting place with all his relatives. Suddenly a strong wind gently carried him, causing him no harm, to where he could see a superb castle—which was deserted. He entered and found a table containing a variety of delectable dishes. Then the dead man loomed up, bearing the same appearance he had before, greeted him amicably, and bid him to take a seat, while he himself sat down in an ill-lit corner at a dirty table covered with a soiled tablecloth on which some black bread had been placed. Then, looking as if he were weighed down with interminable sorrow, he gazed at his guest sitting at the fine table but unable to eat a thing because he was stunned and frightened. Finally, the dead man stood up and said to him:

"Have you nothing to ask me?"

"Knowing not what my fate shall be, I do not dare; however, I would like to know what fate has in store for me."

"Do not be scared; nothing is going to happen to you. God has arranged things this way to make you a better person. If you had not invited me so rashly, none of this would have happened. As for me, know this: I was once a judge in your town; I neglected my religious duties and led a life of gluttony. Because I was a fair judge, God took pity on me. This is the penitence He has imposed on me: I live in this abandoned castle and, as punishment for my debauched ways, I have nothing but this poor, stained table. Nothing is going to happen to you; return home and atone for your sins with pious works."

At that very moment, the wind picked him up and brought him back to the spot from which it had first taken him.

His family was still there, and they were in mourning for him. When they caught sight of him, they fled because of how much he had changed. The nails on his hands and feet had transformed into eagle claws. The terror he had felt had turned his face black and deformed. Although his absence had been no more than an hour, it had felt like a thousand years.[5] He hailed his relatives, told them of his adventure, and they praised God once they heard it. From that point on he led a virtuous life that ended peacefully.

This is the oldest version of what would later become the legend "Don Juan, or the Feast of Peter" as it appears in the play by Tirso de Molina,

El Burlador de Sevilla *(The Trickster of Seville, ca. 1620). This tale was widely published throughout Europe and could be found even in the twentieth century, notably in Ireland in 1938. Depending on the country, the dead man was the great-grandfather or grandfather of the drunk or libertine. In the Brabant and in Italy, this latter man is named Leonce[6] (Leontius). There are many variations. A bone sometimes takes the place of the skull (Slovenia, ballads of the southern Slavs); sometimes the dead man eats (Croatia); the meal served by the dead man consists of snakes, frogs, and toads (Spain); and in the Brabant the dead man is described as a skeleton wearing a white robe. Quite often the story ends with the death of the drunkard (France, Italy, and among the southern Slavs); the dead man breaks his skull against a wall (Netherlands), drags him into his grave for supper and the man never comes out (Ireland), or else he dies eight days after he returns (France, story collected at La Celle-sur-Nièvre in 1819). In Brittany, "Le Carnaval de Rospordern"[7] speaks of three young people, but only one of them behaves badly and dies. This branch of the tradition is remarkable because of the use the impious young man makes of the skull: he turns it into a mask that he dons to frighten the villagers. The story is given a locale in various places—Reims, Rennes, and so on. Paul Sébillot noted yet other variants, and in the version found in the work of Adolphe Orain (1834–1918), the "hero" invites a skull to his wedding. "When the lid was removed from the soup pot that had been placed before the bride, a skull popped out that began leaping about the table between the plates and the serving dishes"; when the groom went to bed, "he recoiled in horror: his fingers had come to rest on the frozen, cold skull of the dead man." Contrary to the other accounts, this skull has come with good intentions and it saves the husband from certain death, for his wife is a diabolical murderess. The edifying intention remains visible in all the texts that carry warnings against impiety and drunkenness, and some Dutch versions have as a title "Exemplary Song on the Punished Impiety of a Free Thinker."*

A Spanish tradition collected in Chili stands out from others because of one important detail: following the advice of a priest, the young man accepts the dead man's invitation but carries a nursing baby there with him beneath his cloak; when the dead man tries to compel him to eat some

repulsive dishes, he pinches the baby, who starts to cry, and the deceased
person spares his guest.

AaTh 470 A

📖 Cifuentes, *Romances Populares y Vulgares*, 116; EM, s.v. "Don Juan"; Orain,
Trésor des contes du pays gallo, 379–81; Petzoldt, *Märchen, Mythos, Sage*, 157–93;
Petzold, *Der Tote als Gast*; Röhrich, *Erzählungen des späten Mittelalters und ihr*
Weiterleben in Literatur und Volkdichtung bis zur Gegenwart, II, 53–204; Sébillot,
Le Folklore de France, IV, 132–33; "Voorbeldig lied van gestrafte Goodloosheid
eens Vrijdenkers," a broadsheet published with no date in Bergen op Zoom.
Another title: "Un terrible récit: d'un homme qui invita une tête de mort,"
Amsterdam, 1727.

3. Alexander and the King of the Dwarfs

One day Alexander and his retinue came to an immense forest where
they marched for twenty-nine days before coming upon a beautiful
meadow in the middle of which a spring was flowing. They stopped
there. Later, when walking about by himself, the king met a dwarf who
was riding a horse of many colors.[8] When Alexander asked him who
he was, he answered: "I am King Antalonia.[9] With my people, I am
bringing a fiancée to the home of her in-laws. The Macedonian, who
could not see anyone except the dwarf, was greatly amazed. "Each of
my people is holding in their hand a stone that makes them invisible,"
explained the dwarf. "I showed myself to you to give you a warning,"
and while saying this, he gave Alexander one of these stones.[10]

"What do you wish to warn me about?" asked Alexander.

"Among your servants, you have more than one enemy who wishes
you dead.[11] Let us meet again tomorrow near the spring, and I will point
out the criminals."

This they did, and at noon a servant brought King Alexander his
meal. The dwarf, who was invisible, struck the man violently. The man
thought his master was responsible for hitting him and asked him why.
"It wasn't me who hit you," Alexander replied. The same thing happened to a second servant, who blamed the first, and so on, leading
to a big uproar. The sovereign took note of the two whom the dwarf

had struck and the following day relieved them of their duties and sent them back to Egypt.

Sefer Alexander Moqdon (twelfth century)[12]

This passage from the Hebrew "Journey of Alexander of Macedonia" can also be found in German historiography in a more or less developed form (of 251 to 524 verses) and as an independent text as well. One of the Hebrew manuscripts includes another encounter: Alexander enters the land of the dwarfs and Antalonia offers him gold and silver, but the Macedonian asks him for simples and is given the herbs of the seven planets.

📖 *Alexander und Antiloye* (ed. Haupt); EM, s.v. "Alexander der Grosse"; Ross, "Alexander and Antilôis the Dwarf King; Ulrich von Etzenbach, *Alexander* (ed. Toischer), vv. 18,958–19,208.

4. The Venomous Maiden

When Alexander was born, a neighboring king, who wanted to seize Philip's lands, learned the child's future through his diviners. They told him that when the child was grown, he would triumph over him. He therefore mused on ways that he could cause the child's death. He had an attractive young girl of high estate kidnapped and had her fed on poison in a remote location. She grew up to be an intelligent and beautiful maiden. She learned to play the harp. When she reached the age when it was possible for her to know a man carnally, she was so poisonous that her breath corrupted the air and killed any animal that approached her.

A more powerful sovereign than this king declared war on him and laid siege to his fortress. One night, the besieged king had the maiden go out with two other young women who were not venomous. They arranged that they could appear before the monarch who was the head of this army. When he saw the very beautiful maiden, he desired her at once, and when night fell, he brought her into his tent. As soon as he kissed her, he fell down dead, as did a number of knights who came too close to her. That night, the forces that had been besieged made a sortie and crushed their adversaries, who no longer had a leader. This was how the king got rid of his enemy. He had the maiden kept under guard and fed with the purest poison.

This king learned that Alexander had begun his conquests and that his name was now feared and dreaded throughout much of the world. He ordered that four maidens along with the venomous damsel—the most beautiful of them all—be made ready and, together with five young men, given to Alexander as a present and sign of their allegiance. He also sent silver and jewels, the better to hide his treachery.

When he received this beautiful gift, Alexander was enchanted and wanted to kiss the maiden, but Aristotle, a clerk of his court, and Socrates, his teacher, prevented him from doing so, and he dared not contradict them. Socrates had two serfs brought in and ordered the first of them to kiss the maiden. He obeyed and fell to the ground dead. The same thing happened to the second serf. Alexander knew this way that his teachers were right, but he did not stop there: he asked the maiden to touch dogs, horses, and other animals, all of whom perished instantly. He then had her decapitated and, on his orders, her head was burned very far away.

Dialogue of Placides and Timeo
(END OF THIRTEENTH CENTURY)[13]

The philosopher Aristotle was the tutor of the powerful king Alexander, and he taught him everything he knew. Because the renown of this sovereign had even made its way to the Queen of the North, she had fed her daughter on poison from the day she was born. When she reached the age of reason, she was so beautiful and offered such a charming appearance in the eyes of everyone that more than one among them became confused and aroused.

The queen sent her to Alexander to be his concubine. When he saw her, he fell in love with her on the spot and wished to take her then and there. Aristotle saw this and told him: "Give her up or die! She has been fed on poison since she was an infant; I am going to prove it to you. There is a criminal here who has been condemned to death; have him lay with her, and you will see that I speak the truth!" It was no sooner said than done. The man kissed the maiden in everyone's presence and died immediately. Seeing this, Alexander warmly praised the philosopher for sparing him from certain death, and he sent the girl back to her mother.

GESTA ROMANORUM, CHAP. 288
(THIRTEENTH–FOURTEENTH CENTURY)

Taken from an Indian tale, this legend made its way into the West by way of the translations of an Arab text, the Kitab Sirr-al-Asrar *(The Secret of Secrets) in Latin by John of Seville at the beginning of the twelfth century and by Philip of Tripoli around 1234, and in Hebrew by Judah-al-Harizi (died 1225). It can be found in the entire tradition of the* Secret of Secrets, *and later in the works of Roger Bacon and Filippos de Ferrara.*

Depending on the texts, the maiden can kill with her gaze (Latin), her breath (Italian), her kisses or her perspiration (Hebrew), by her bite (Dutch, German), and through coitus (Italian). According to Avicenna (980–1037) and Rhazes (865–925), her saliva is deadly. In the Latin and Hebrew versions, the antagonist is the queen of India, whereas in the Arab text, she is the mother of the king of that country.

AaTh 507 C

📖 Bacon, *Secretum secretorum cum glossis et notulis* (ed. Steele), I, 21, 60; EM, s.v. "Giftmädchen," "Alexander der Grosse," "Basiliskummädchen"; Filippo of Ferrara, *Liber de introduction loquendi* (ed. Vecchio), chap. 106.

5. King Gontran's Dream

Gontran, the king of the Franks, was a peaceable and sensible man. I would like to tell you of a remarkable event from his life that is never mentioned in the *History of the Franks*.

One day when he was out hunting, his retinue scattered as they always did, and he remained alone with one of his men, the most loyal of them all. He suddenly felt quite weary, laid his head on his companion's knees, and fell into a deep slumber. A small animal, a kind of serpent, slid out of his mouth and sought to cross the stream that was flowing nearby. The man who accompanied the king drew his sword from its scabbard and used it to form a bridge so the little animal could reach the other bank. The snake then threaded its way into a hole in the nearby mountain, came back out a short time later, crossed back over the stream using the sword, and reentered the mouth of Gontran. When the king woke, he said: "I had a strange dream; it seemed as if I crossed a river over an iron bridge and entered a mountain where I saw an enormous quantity of gold." His servant then gave him a detailed description of what he had seen. Immediately, they began to dig at the indicated spot and found a treasure of considerable size there,[14] one that had been there since the days of antiquity.

PAULUS DIACONUS, *HISTORIA LANGBOBARDORUM*, III, 34
(EIGHTH CENTURY)[15]

Paul the Deacon (ca. 720/730–797/799) recorded this strange scene, which corresponds to the description of a manifestation of a "double," with the animus, *or soul, externalized in the shape of an animal. This legend is found throughout Europe in varied forms. It can be seen in the work of Aimoin (born circa 970) and Vincent of Beauvais (based on Hélinand of Froidmont), but the adventure was experienced by an archbishop of Reims, the animal is a white weasel, and there is no treasure involved. In the* Gesta Romanorum—*one of the most popular texts during the Middle Ages[16]—the motif of the missing bridge and the treasure is handled differently: The spirit of Guy took the shape of a weasel to scale a mountain. The two friends decided to set off on adventure. They found a dead dragon with a belly filled with gold and a sword on which was written: "With this sword, the knight Guy shall defeat his enemies" (chap. 194: "De duobos militibus Guidone et Tyrio").*

The important study by Vera Meyer-Matheis makes it possible to see that the most frequent forms of the alter ego are the mouse—which is sometimes red—the scarab, the dung beetle, the bumblebee, the cat, the toad, the bird, the spider, or the fly. The Brothers Grimm republished this document in their German Legends. *Paul the Deacon tells a second anecdote (VI, 6), which follows the same direction:*

When Cunincpert, the king of the Lombards, was deliberating with his high squire on ways to kill Aldo and Grauso, he saw a large fly on the window. When trying to swat it, he severed one of its legs. The fly flew away. While Aldo and Grauso were on their way in response to the summons of the king, they met a lame man who was missing a foot. He told them that Cunincpert was determined to kill them. The two men took sanctuary in a church. Furious, Cunincpert promised to spare their lives if they revealed the name of the person who had betrayed him. Aldo and Grauso told him of their meeting with the lame man, and the king realized that the fly whose foot he had removed was an evil spirit.

AaTh 1645 A

📖 EM, s.v. "Guntram," "Traum vom Schatz auf der Brücke"; Grimm, *German Legends,* no. 428; Lecouteux, *Witches, Werewolves, and Fairies;* Lixfeld, "Die Guntramsage (AaTh 1,645 A)"; Meyer-Matheis, *Die Vorstellung eines alter ego in Volkserzählungen,* 65ff., and texts cited in the appendix, 56ff.; Vincent of Beauvais, *Speculum naturale,* II, 108.

6. The Water of Youth

A king stricken with an incurable disease learned from his doctors that the sole remedy was the water of youth, because it could cure any disease. He summoned his sons and implored them to travel the earth to try all the waters, promising his kingdom to the one who brought the remedy back to him. After being given money, they divided the world between them: the eldest son followed the rivers, the middle son traveled across the plains, and the youngest son traveled over the mountains.

Finally, the youngest son met an old man in a forest who told him how to get to the fountain of youth and explained the dangers that lay in wait for him. "Don't go there if you don't think you have the strength to face them!" he said. "You must first slay a serpent, then you shall meet a choir of damsels, but do not look at them! Next you shall see knights and noblemen bearing all manner of arms: but accept nothing from them! Finally, you shall come to the door of a palace where there is a young maid who has the key to the fountain. The door is covered with bells that ring if you brush past them." The old man gave him a sponge to muffle their sound.

Despite all of this, the young man set off on his journey. The serpent attacked him, but he easily killed it with his spear. He then entered a meadow where beautiful women surrounded him, but he covered his face and passed by them without saying a word. He came before a magnificent castle where noblemen and knights offered him all manner of weapons and fine steeds; he turned down these offerings with disdain and headed toward the palace. He muffled the bells with the sponge, entered, and saw a splendid woman whom he humbly begged to show him the fountain of youth. "My father told me that I would wed the knight who overcame all the trials set on his path and reached me safe and sound. You are that knight: you shall get the water of youth, and I shall be your wife," she told him.

After they wed, he returned to the home of his father, who handed his kingdom over to him.

JOHANNES GOBI, *SCALA COELI*, CHAP. 538

(FOURTEENTH CENTURY)[17]

Here we have one of the oldest known texts of tale type 551 ("The Water of Life"), the sons in quest of a wonderful remedy for their father, distributed during the Middle Ages by means of the exempla. *It was very widespread throughout Europe, and one of its variants can be seen in the work of the Brothers Grimm (KHM, no. 97), which presents a very similar tale (AaTh 550, "The Gold Bird").*

AATH 551; TU 5214

📖 CPF, II, 347–64; EM, s.v. "Verjüngung"; cf. Lecouteux, "Lebenswasser."

7. The Dolphin Knights

A ship was sailing one day on the Mediterranean Sea, accompanied by numerous dolphins.[18] A young sailor shot an arrow and wounded one of them. Immediately, a storm blew in that was stronger than any ever seen before. The sailors were about to give up all hope when a horse arrived, walking over the waves and bearing a man who looked like a knight. "If you would have your lives spared," he told them, "surrender to me the one who wounded the dolphin." After much hesitation, the guilty one thought it best to sacrifice himself for his companions; he mounted the horse behind the man, who swiftly bore him away, crossing across the sea as if it were dry land until they came to a remote land where the sailor found the knight he had wounded in the form of a dolphin lying in a bed. This knight ordered him to remove the arrow; he obeyed and healed the wound.* He was swiftly returned to his boat, where he told his companions of his adventure.

GERVASE OF TILBURY, *OTIA IMPERIALIA*, III, 63

Some animals have always fascinated men, the latter often believing that they were human beings who possessed the power to change into animals and back again. Dolphins and storks are the most common examples in the Middle Ages. The dolphins here are the masters of the water and command the weather.

8. Albert the Leper

Near the Rhine River there once lived a peerless knight named Albert, who was nicknamed "the poor" as misfortune seemed to beset him continuously. He was rich and quite dashing but was entirely devoted to the vanities of knighthood; to save him the Lord therefore decided to test him and struck him with the repugnant disease of leprosy. Like a new Job,[19] Albert bore this punishment with patience and gave blessing to God.[20] But when his servants and his relatives fled at the sight of his disfigured face and because of the foul odor that wafted from him, and his friends mocked him, treating him like a new Job and appropriating his possessions, he felt disgust and horror at their doings. He used his remaining money to give to doctors, but when that ran out, the doctors disappeared as did his last friends. He could no longer stand the sight of those close to him, and he retired to a remote place where he spent fourteen years. One day, a physician showed up and said: "If the poor man had any money, I would be able to cure him." The leper promised him as much money as he wanted because he counted on his relatives and his few remaining friends to give it to him if he visited them with the doctor and, in truth, they agreed to do it. The physician examined poor Albert and said: "This

---

*Here there is a magical notion: only the person who caused the wound is able to heal it, just as only the caster of the spell can lift it.

illness can only be cured with the blood of a pure person who will accept death wholeheatedly."[21]

A poor maiden, whose father had sometimes brought her back clothes from Albert's castle, was present. She remembered all his charitable deeds and asked: "What will happen to my lord Albert?"

"He has leprosy," she was told. "It horrifies everyone, and only the blood of a person ready to die for him can save him."

The young woman rushed in to see the ailing man. "Lord," she cried, "I remember well the clothing that you used to give my father for me. As a sign of my gratitude, I am ready to die so that you can recover your health." Overjoyed, the leper went with her to the doctor's home, and the doctor then prepared the containers in which he would collect the maiden's blood. At the sight of this, Albert cried out: "I do not wish to be saved by the cruel death of such a faithful young girl! I would rather die and this virtuous maiden remain alive than see her die in such a dreadful manner." He then told the doctor to leave.

The following night, God appeared to him, healed him, and showed him a place where his parents had hidden a treasure. This treasure permitted Albert to buy back all his possessions and more besides. He then married the young woman who would have sacrificed her life for his and, after a long and happy life, he left this world as a Christian.

PULCRUM DE LEPROSO CURATO (1485)[22]

The plot of this tale is the story of Job, who was able to tolerate the ordeals God imposed on him. But in the Bible, God allowed Satan to test Job's faith. Before it was changed into an exemplum, *this pious narrative was the subject of a famous story, "The Poor Henry" (circa 1520) by Hartman von Aue.[23] It was rediscovered by the Brothers Grimm in 1815. The story was made into a ballad by Adalbert von Chamisso (1839), a poem by Henry Wadsworth Longfellow ("The Golden Legend," 1851), and an opera by Hans Pfitzner and James Grun (1895). In 1902, Gerhard Hauptmann made it into a five-act play, and in 1905, Dante Gabriel Rossetti adapted Hartmann's text into English under the title*

"Henry the Leper." The blood cure of this story can be found in other narratives—namely, "Amis et Amiles" and "Amicus et Amelius," written around 1090.

   📖 EM, s.v. "Amicus et Amelius."

9. The Ship in the Air

On one feast day in England, at a time when thick clouds covered the sky, the people leaving a church after Mass found a boat's anchor hooked to the gate of a tomb. Its rope was hanging from the sky. In fright they were discussing this even when the rope began moving as if someone was pulling up on it to disengage the anchor. Then a sailor came climbing down the rope. The crowd there grabbed him, but he died in their hands, suffocated by the humidity of our air as if he were drowning in the sea. When their companion did not rejoin them, the sailors above cut the rope, leaving their anchor behind. It was used to manufacture the ironwork for the door of the basilica where everyone can see it. This marvelous fact proves that the upper sea is located above us.

GERVASE OF TILBURY, *OTIA IMPERIALIA,* I, 13

(EARLY THIRTEENTH CENTURY)

This story, presented as something that actually happened, reflects the cosmogony that is visible in Genesis 1:7 when "God created the firmament and separated the lower from the upper waters." It also reflects the notion that a communication is established wherever the sea touches the clouds. It was thus believed that when sailing, it was possible to continue one's voyage on the sea of clouds. Another text by Gervase of Tilbury states explicitly that this contact is established at the borders of the ocean. Earlier, Agobard, the Bishop of Lyon (778–840), talked of vessels sailing on the clouds that came from a land called Magonia (Magonia, ex qua naues ueniant in nubibus).

   📖 Agobard of Lyon, *De grandine et tonitruis,* II (in *Agobardi Lugdunensis Opera Omnia,* ed. Van Acker); Gervase of Tilbury, *Otia imperialia* I, 13; Lecouteux, "Le radeau des vents."

10. Hippocrates's Daughter

Because people truly like to hear about wonders, I shall tell you about one. Hippocrates's daughter lived on the island of Kos in the form of a dragon. It was said that she measured one hundred rods.* The residents of the island regarded this transformed woman as their sovereign. She lived in a cave under an old castle, from which she emerged two or three times a year. However, she never harmed anyone on these occasions except those who aroused her anger. It was thought that she had been a beautiful maiden before being transformed into a dragon by the goddess Diana. It was also believed that she could regain her human form if a knight was bold enough to kiss her on the mouth,[24] but it would cost him his life shortly afterward.

One day a knight from the Order of Saint John on the nearby island of Rhodes galloped up to her lair in search of adventure. The monster stuck out her head, and the knight and his mount were so terrified by this horrible vision that the horse bucked its rider into the sea.

There was also the young lad who made landfall on Kos for amusement and to take on fresh water. He knew nothing about the dragon. Arriving at the foot of the old ruined rampart, he saw a very beautiful young woman who was adorning her hair while beholding herself

---

*[A rod is the equivalent of six feet. —*Trans.*]

in a mirror. He mistook her for a prostitute lying in wait for men so she could earn some money. Seeing him in her mirror, she asked him: "What do you want?"

"I would like to be your lover," he answered.

"Are you a knight?"

"No!"

"Then it is impossible! Go back to your companions, have yourself knighted, and come back tomorrow morning. I will come to meet you changed into a dragon. Kiss me then on the mouth, and I will be freed and entirely yours. My treasure and the entire land shall belong to you. Don't be scared when you see me in that form; I will not do you any harm because I have been bewitched and cannot be freed any other way."

The young man left, was dubbed a knight, and returned to the cavern the next morning. When he saw the maiden coming out in the horrible form of a dragon, he grew frightened and fled. The beast pursued him, screaming, and the faster the man fled, the more plaintively the dragon cried. The knight did not live long after this encounter.

The Travels of Mandeville, chap. 9[25]

This legend was widespread throughout the entire medieval West through the translations of the Travels of Sir John Mandeville. *It is an adaptation of a story whose traces can be found almost everywhere and has the merit of providing the start of an explanation for the death of the maiden freed in the same way in* Seyfried von Ardemont.

📖 Huet, "La Légende de la fille d'Hippocrate à Cos."

11. Mercury and the Woodsman

God shows his favor and benevolence to the good men, but he punishes the wicked.

A carpenter was cutting wood by the side of a river so he could build a temple for the gods. While he was doing this, his ax fell into the water. He began to cry and asked the gods for their help. Mercury took pity on him and went to him.

"Why are you sorrowing?" he asked him, and gave him a golden ax. "Is this yours?"

"No," the man answered.[26]

Mercury showed him one made of silver.

"Is this one yours?"

"No!"

Seeing that the carpenter was a good man, Mercury pulled his ax out of the water and gave it back to him with some other things.

The carpenter told his companions the story of what had happened. One of them went out to cut wood and let his ax fall into the water. He began weeping while begging the gods for their help. Mercury appeared and showed him the golden ax.

"Is this the one you lost?" he asked.

"Yes, dear Lord, that is mine!" the man replied.

Upon seeing the malice of this villain, Mercury did not give him that ax or any other and left him crying, because God, who is good and just, rewards the good in this world and in the other world punishes the wicked.

JULIEN MACHO, *LA XII.*

FABLE FAIT MENCION D'UNG CHARPENTIER (1480)[27]

Before it became a tale, "Mercury and the Woodsman" was a fable taken from Aesop. Enjoying wide distribution, it can be found in China and Japan. La Fontaine used it for writing his story "The Woodchopper and Mercury" (Fables, V, 1).

AaTh 729

📖 EM, s.v. "Axt: Die goldene A. des Meermannes."

12. The Skull

Once there was a prince who was particularly fond of hunting. One day, when he was indulging his favorite passion, a merchant happened to take the same path by chance. When he saw this nobleman, he felt a surge of admiration for his impressive bearing and luxurious garments. He then told himself: "How God must love this man! Isn't he handsome and vigorous? And his companions are also dressed so elegantly, aren't they?" With these thoughts racing through his head, he addressed a servant: "Tell me, my friend, who is your master?"

"He is ruler over a number of lands," the valet replied. "He is a powerful sovereign who is rich in gold, silver, and vassals."

"God must be pleased with him, for he is handsome and quite wise, compared to all those I've met before," the merchant concluded.

The servant repeated these words to his master. On his return to the palace, the prince invited the merchant to be his guest for the night. The merchant dared not refuse and followed the prince. Once he was in the castle, he saw such a profusion of wealth and so many rooms highlighted with gold that it stunned him with amazement. When dinnertime arrived, the prince gave him a seat next to his wife. When he saw the grace and beauty of this lady, he almost lost his mind and said to himself: "Merciful heaven, the prince has all he could desire, a beautiful wife, sons and daughters, and servants in large number."

While these thoughts were coursing through his mind, the serving platters were conveyed to the table. The most delicious dishes were brought out and served to the princess inside a human skull,[28] while the other guests were served on silver plates. When he saw the skull before him, the merchant shivered in fear and told himself: "Woe is me! I fear I shall lose my head here." When she perceived his agitation, the princess tried to reassure him as best she could.

Once night had fallen, he was brought to an imposing chamber where there was bed prepared for him, surrounded by curtains. There was a large lamp in the corner. After he got into bed, the servants shut the door and left him by himself. When he looked toward the light, he saw two dead men hanging by their arms. A state of indescribable anguish seized him, which prevented him from sleeping. The next day when he got out of bed, he thought to himself: "I fear I could be hung here today alongside these other two."

Once he was up, the prince summoned him and asked: "Dear friend, was my home to your liking?"

"I liked everything, except that the meal was served in a human skull, which alarmed me so greatly I was unable to swallow. And I was hardly in bed when I saw two young men hanging in the corner of the room. This scared me so much I did not get a wink of sleep. For the love of God, I ask you to grant me leave."

"My very dear friend, you saw my splendid wife and the skull in front of her. Here is the reason for that. It was the skull of a noble prince who seduced my wife and slept with her. I surprised them in bed, grabbed my sword, and slit his throat. Since that day, I have placed his skull in front of her to give her shame and to ensure that her sin remains constantly before her eyes. The son of the dead man killed the two men currently hanging in the chamber, who were my relatives. I therefore go to gaze upon them every day so as to sharpen my desire for revenge. When I think of my wife's adultery and the death of these two lads, all joy flees me. Go your way in peace, my friend, and do not judge without knowledge."

The merchant made his farewells and resumed his journey.

Gesta Romanorum, chap. 56[29]

This story is a variation on a theme that was very popular during the Middle Ages.

📖 Di Maio, *Le Cœur mangé.*

13. The Messengers of Death

One night, a woman gave birth to a child. Her husband received a visitor whom he asked to be the child's godfather, adding: "Tell me your name, so that I can recognize you in the crowd."

"I am Death,"[30] the other responded, "and I bring many fears to the earth, both day and night."

"Ah, take pity on me and let me live for a long time."

"I promise, dear friend. Before I come to get you, I will send you messages,[31] of that you can be sure." With these words, Death left.

The man lived for a long time and saw many harvests, then he fell ill. Afterward Death appeared before him and said: "Come, comrade, I have come to take you."

"Oh! You didn't keep your promise!"

"Just remember!" Death replied. "One day you felt a stitch in your side and asked yourself, 'What is this little pain?' That was my first message. When your ears began to ring, your eyes to water, and your eyesight grew weak, those were two other messages. When you suffered from toothache and your cough was worse than usual, and your memory became untrustworthy, that was three messages. When you began walking more slowly and your skin began to wrinkle, your voice became hoarse and your beard became gray, I was sending you four. So you see, my friend, I have kept my word. Let God concern himself with your soul and let it leave your body."

And the good man died.

HUGO VON TRIMBERG, *DER RENNER*
(EARLY FOURTEENTH CENTURY)[32]

This story was very popular from the Middle Ages into the eighteenth century, and La Fontaine echoes it in his "Death and the Dying Man" (Fables, VIII, 1). Hugo von Trimberg (ca. 1230–1313) was the first one to record it. It is also present in an exemplum *by John Bromyard (died circa 1390) and numerous sixteenth-century authors. See appendix 2.*

AaTh 335

📖 BP I, no. 267, 171–72; III, 293–97; EM, s.v. "Boten des Todes"; Röhrich, *Erzählungen des späten Mittelalters,* I, 80–83 and 258–62.

CHAPTER III

DEVILTRY, SPELLS, AND MAGIC

1. The List of Sins on the Cowhide

The devil is cunning! When the faithful are in church, he worries them and leads them to sin in a thousand ways. He then writes down their sins on a parchment of cowhide that he carries back to hell for his master, Lucifer. He writes everything that the people say during Mass—unfortunately, they rarely keep quiet.

One day, Saint Martin was reciting the Mass with a deacon, and the deacon saw the devil[1] sitting behind the altar,[2] holding a cowhide on which he was writing down everything he heard. He recorded on it every word and sin, and the hide was soon covered. The religious contemplation of the faithful was so superficial that the Evil One soon had no space left on which to write. He then took the hide between his teeth and claws to stretch it out, but this knocked out a tooth, and he violently slammed his head against the wall. The deacon burst out laughing and Saint Martin saw it. After the holy service, he asked him the cause of his hilarity, and his deacon told him what he had seen. Saint Martin informed his flock of this and told them: "Refrain from gossiping and other sins in church! Whoever prays to god with just his lips when his thoughts are elsewhere, would do better to keep quiet."

Von der vnutzen zungen[3]

Widespread throughout Europe thanks to preachers, this exemplum, *whose first confirmed appearance is due to Jacques de Vitry (died before 1240), is also found, for example, in the* Scala coeli *(chap. 25), compiled by Johannes Gobi between 1323 and 1330, and in the historiography. It continued to be handed down into the twentieth century! Lutz Röhrich has compiled a dossier of texts that document the evolution of this subject.*

ATH 826; TU 1630 A

Crane, ed., *The* exempla *or Illustrative Stories from the* sermones vulgares *of Jacques de Vitry,* no. 239; EM, s.v. "Sündenregister auf der Kuhhaut," "Johannes Gobi junior," "Jacques de Vitry"; Röhrich, *Erzählungen des späten Mittelalters,* I, 113–24; Vincent of Beauvais, *Speculum historiale,* VII, 118; Wildhaber, *Das Sündenregister auf der Kuhhaut.*

2. A Visit to Hell

When he died, Louis the Iron* left behind two sons, one of whom, Louis,† succeeded him. He was much more pleasant and affable than his father. One day he issued this proclamation: "The one who shall obtain for me incontestable news about my father's soul will be rewarded with a fine domain." When he heard this news, a penniless knight spoke to his brother, a cleric well versed in black magic, who told him in response: "I sometimes conjured the devil so he could tell me what I wanted to know, but I have long since stopped having discourse with him, just as I have ceased the practice of magic."

The knight persisted: "Think of my poverty and the promised reward!" The cleric finally acquiesced to his wishes, summoned the Evil One, and told him: "I apologize for not having any dealings with you for such a long time, but today I beg you to tell me where the soul of my lord, the late count, is residing." In response the devil swore him a terrible oath in which he promised that he would guide him to that soul, at no danger to his life.

---

*Louis II (1128–1172), landgrave of Thuringia.
†Louis III, nicknamed the Mild or the Pious (1151/52–1190).

In an instant, the cleric found himself in front of the gates to hell. He cast a glance inside and saw burning places in which sinners were being punished in all possible ways. An abominable demon was sitting on top of a sealed pit; he lifted up the cover and blew a blast on his bronze trumpet, which made such a horrible noise that the cleric thought the entire world was screaming and raging. Burning flames of sulfur burst out of the pit. A short time afterward, the count emerged, surrounded by flames, and revealed himself up to the neck.

"Look! It is me, the unhappy count who was once your lord. If only I had never been born!"

"Your son sent me," the cleric responded, "to bring back news of you. If we can help you in any way, please tell me."

"You see what kind of state I'm in!" the dead man replied. "Know that if my sons restore the property of the church"—and he named them—"that I dishonestly misappropriated and bequeathed to my heirs as if it belonged to me, this would be greatly beneficial for my soul."

"My lord," replied the cleric, "can you give me a sign?"

"I shall give you a piece of proof that none but my sons and I know." The cleric received it, and, before his very eyes, the count sank back into the pit.

The devil brought the cleric back home. Although his life had never truly been in danger, he was pale and staggering and almost unrecognizable. He reported to the two sons their father's words and gave them the proof, but they wanted nothing to do with restoring the property.[4]

"I recognize this sign," the young Louis told him, "and have no doubt that you are telling the truth and that you saw my father, so I will give you the reward I promised."

"You can keep it" the cleric replied. "I am thinking now solely of saving my soul."

He gave away all his earthly goods and joined the Cistericians to forget the century and avoid eternal damnation.

CAESARIUS OF HEISTERBACH,
DIALOGUS MIRACULORUM, XII[5]

This legend is part of what is called the literature of revelations, for which there are countless examples. The story compares closely to that of the two friends who decide that the one who dies first will return to tell the other what his fate has been in the afterlife. It can also be found in the Liber de introduction loquendi, *written by Filippo of Ferrara circa 1331–1347.*

TU 4858

📖 Creytens, "Le Manuel de conversation de Philippe de Ferrare O.P. († 1350?)"; Carozzi, *Le Voyage de l'âme dans l'au-delà d'après la littérature latine (Ve–XIIIe siècle);* Dinzelbacher, *Vision und Visionsliteratur im Mittelalter;* Lecouteux, *The Return of the Dead.*

3. The Knight Devoted to the Virgin Mary and the Devil

A young knight, whose friends had urged him to get married, was living beyond his means. He frequented the tourneys and all manner of courtly contests but lost more than he won, and gradually he became impoverished. Happiness and prosperity flew from him as if they had wings. Loath to abandon his horses and his fine clothing, he borrowed money against his inheritance. His property passed into the hands of his creditors and he became so poor that he even went wanting for bread. In his sorry state, he contemplated the means by which he might get assistance.

He had heard it said that "whoever sells himself to the devil and serves him will receive wealth and honors in return." He decided he would go into the woods alone and summon the demon once he was there. The devil came in response to his call and told him: "If you are ready to abandon your God and give yourself to me body and soul, I will bestow you with riches and honors." The knight accepted these conditions, overly elated to see poverty and mockery receding into the distance. He found himself again blessed with abundance, redeemed all his property from his creditors, and lived as he pleased, spending his time dancing and jousting in an atmosphere of joy and magnificence. Any time he needed money, he would find the devil.

One day when he came to make another request for money, the

devil pointed out to him that he had forgotten to renounce the Virgin Mary as well. The devil detested her above all others because her mercy would divert all those who belonged to him in the blink of an eye. "So you must deny the mother of God," he ordered the knight. The latter refused. "You are making a fool of me," shouted the Evil One. "You cannot serve two masters. Decide, or else I shall not give you anything more!" The knight remained firm. The devil shouted: "Woe to her!" The knight cursed him and his riches and now regretted that he had lost the good Lord. The demon stormed off and no longer granted him a thing.

The knight returned home and regretted his apostasy. His enemies, whom he had looked down upon, banded together to humiliate him. They waged war upon him, subjecting his lands to fire and blood and killing or capturing his folk. Every time he tried to correct his situation, he only made matters worse. Forsaken by God, he was the laughingstock of his enemies. They attacked his castle and captured it, after which they demolished it. A ceiling collapsed, killing his wife and child. He was captured and tossed into the dungeon of his castle. The howling mob of his victorious enemies sought booty everywhere, causing such disorder that the prisoner managed to steal away and make his way into the woods.

While wandering in the forest, he met two fishermen carrying sickles and not nets. They captured the knight, stripped him of all his clothes, beat him, and then released him in that state. Dumbfounded, he realized that he was paying for his sin. He groaned and wept and, gnawed by remorse, immediately renounced all earthly goods.

He went into exile. To his great shame, weakness and hunger forced him to beg for his daily bread. He came to a faraway land where no one knew him. One evening, he came to a castle where an old devout count dwelled with his children and ruled over this land. He asked for hospitality, which the old man gladly granted him. He fed him and treated him kindly, as he always did when dealing with beggars.

The next day, when matins was rung, the knight made his way to the chapel before continuing his journey. Thinking himself all alone there, he fervently repented, but the count, who was standing in a corner engaged in contemplative prayer, watched him without being seen. The knight approached the altar, on which was enthroned a beautiful statue of the Virgin and the Child. He beat his breast in contrition, and a flood of tears spilled from his eyes. Several times he cast himself on the ground with his arms crossed, and finally he remained kneeling. He then lifted his eyes toward the statue and invoked the gentle Virgin. He confessed his mortal sin that he rejected Jesus Christ and begged her to intercede with her Son on his behalf and show that she was the Mother of all mercy. "I would rather have died before I sinned," he said. "Without Mary, I would be truly desperate." He wept and grieved until he fell asleep in front of the altar.

The old count's surprise soon changed into wonderment. The statue got up[6] and set down her Son, kneeled before him, and, with hands together, interceded for the sinner whom the devil had taken advantage of but who had never agreed to renounce her. "This poor wretch had chosen another master," the Child answered. "He must therefore serve him and, in conformance with his oath, join him in hell." Mary reminded him of the profound contrition with which the sinner had turned to them and that she was the Mother of mercy, and the knight had appealed to her for this reason. "Take me back in your lap," the Christ asked her. "Out of love for you, I am going to forgive this man if he refrains from all sin in the future."[7] Mary leaned over, grabbed her Child, and reassumed her position on the altar.

The knight awoke and got up but continued to cry and to pray. When he left the chapel to continue his journey, the lord of the manor showed himself. He spoke to him gently and asked him why he was in such misery. The knight confessed everything to him in a flood of tears. The count told him: "Rejoice! The Virgin Mary has obtained your pardon. You must now confess to wash away all your sins." Afterward, the knight devoted himself to serving God and Our Lady.[8]

Marienritter und der tiuvel
(THIRTEENTH CENTURY)

This pious legend is very similar to the first part of the *early fourteenth-century* Dit du Chevalier et de l'Écuyer (*Lay of the Knight and the*

Squire) by Jehan de Saint-Quentin; by comparing it with this text, we can see how the modifications that transform an exemplum *into a legend take place.*

A rich knight, reduced to poverty, falls into despair and decides to leave for foreign lands. In a forest, he meets a squire who seems sad—he, too, has lost his fortune. They decide to travel together. The devil appears and proposes to the two men that they enter into a pact with him: he will grant them riches if they agree to deny God and His Mother. The squire accepts without a moment's hesitation, but the knight, after denying God, refuses to abandon the Virgin. The devil goes off with the squire. On his return, the knight enters a chapel to pray to the Virgin to intercede with her Son on his behalf. The image of the Virgin comes down from the altar to dry his tears and console him. The rich lord of a nearby castle is also in the chapel and witnesses the scene.

📖 EM, s.v. "Teufelspakt"; *Dits en quatrains d'alexandrins de Jehan de Saint-Quentin,* 68–76.

4. The Diabolical Pope

I have heard tell of how a cleric became a pope. He was a gambler who was lacking in all the virtues, but he was quite learned. He knew how to write down everything he was told and knew the Old and the New Testaments perfectly. However, he was poor as Job because he had lost all he had on dice. He decided to improve his lot by giving himself, body and soul, to the devil.

He went to a crossroads, drew a circle around him, and invoked the demon, who appeared right away and was quite vexed at being summoned by this rascal of a cleric. Our man asked the devil to put an end to his poverty. The Evil One offered to make him the master of all Christendom—in other words, the pope. "In return, the day on which you say Mass in Jerusalem you shall agree to let me carry your soul off to hell," he said, and the cleric accepted, thinking that he would make sure to never go to Jerusalem. The devil demanded that he sign a charter with his blood.[9] The cleric pricked his finger and signed the pact.

On the advice of the devil, he went to find the bishop, whose secretary, led astray by the demon, had gotten drunk. The prelate, who happened to have a letter he needed to send, had people look for him, but the Cunning One prevented them from finding him. Annoyed, the bishop let it be known that he would enrich whomever could write a letter for him at once. Our cleric offered his services: "If you put your trust in me, I will write it for you because I am skilled, look at my hand!" The prelate dictated a letter to him that he wrote better than anyone, and the bishop was so impressed with his expertise that he offered to hire him if he promised to quit gambling with dice. The cleric promised to do so, backed up with many oaths, and received clothing cut from the best cloth of Ypres. The new secretary became the most important and respected man of the bishopric.

But he had not abandoned his gambling, and the devil always rolled the dice in his favor.[10] The bishop, who felt a great amity with the cleric, enriched him and, after a year of good and loyal service, sent him to carry a message to Rome. He fulfilled his mission so well that the prelate only liked him all the more and wished never to lose his services.

He sent him to Rome again. When the cleric had been on the road for five days, a messenger caught up to him to tell him of the prelate's death. On the advice of the devil, the pope named him bishop and immediately entrusted him with a bishopric. The secretary, who was now a bishop, was jovial and was beloved by all for his generosity. He lived like this for three years. The Holy Father then died, and, at the instigation of the devil, the young prelate was unanimously elected pope by the patriarchs, cardinals, and princes. He was then enthroned on the seat of Saint Peter just as the devil had promised him.

One day the chaplains came before him and invited him to celebrate the Mass in Jerusalem the next morning, according to custom. The pope was astounded by this request as it was impossible for him to make his way to Jerusalem on the other side of the sea in one night and one day, but they explained to him that it was a small Roman chapel called "Jerusalem,"* where the pope had to give the Mass once a year. He flinched and lamented to himself: "My soul is lost because I must go to that church with the cardinals!" and the hair stood up on his head.

The next day he put on his sacerdotal vestments, climbed over the rood screen,† and summoned four of his valets to his side. He made them swear before all the Christians assembled there to do everything he commanded unless it should endanger their lives. He had a chopping block, a sharpened ax, and a cutlass brought to him, then confessed publicly: "Deceived by the devil, I promised him my soul in exchange for the papacy and, today, I have fallen into his power. I hope that God shall take pity on me. "Cut off my feet," he ordered his valets, "these feet that led me to the demon. Cut off the hands that signed the pact. Cut off my ears and nose, and gouge out my eyes, these eyes that allowed the devil to fascinate them. Tear out my tongue, the tongue that enjoyed speaking to the Evil One and sacrilegiously breaking the holy rules. Then cast everything to the devil!"[11] This was done as he requested. The demons grabbed these limbs that fell into their hands and played ball with them, and then, in front of everyone there in the church, they carried them off to hell. What God did to this pope in the beyond, no one has ever come back to say.

DES TEUVELS BÂBEST (THIRTEENTH CENTURY)[12]

This involves one of the common legends about Gerbert of Aurillac (died 1003), who became Pope Sylvester II. Allegedly, in his youth he had sold his soul to the devil in exchange for the guarantee of a splendid career

---

*In fact, Our Lady of Jerusalem.
†The partition between the nave and the chancel in a medieval church.

that would take him to Saint Peter's throne. According to William of Newburgh (ca. 1136–1198), Gerbert constructed a mechanical head that responded to all questions with a yes or a no. It is supposed to have said "yes" when he asked it if he would become pope and "no" when asked if he would die before saying Mass in Jerusalem. Gerbert therefore decided to never visit this city. . . .

The legend can also be found in the Ci nous dit, *an anonymous collection of moral* exempla *written in northern France at the beginning of the fourteenth century. In this version, a devil tells a discouraged cleric that he will make him a great man on the condition that he give him his soul when he enters a city that is called Moufle. He becomes an abbot and then an archbishop. He fell ill in Gand [Ghent], and the devil came to fetch him, telling him that there was no difference between "gant" and "moufle."**

The tale of a fairy in love with a man is clumsily attached to the legend of this same Gerbert of Aurillac who became pope under the name of Sylvester II, so it will be helpful to introduce the following much more "authentic" text, which was written a century later.

TU 1475 A 8; 3568; 906.

📖 Blangez, ed., *Ci nous dit,* 341, 1–13; Duchesne, ed., *Liber pontificalis,* vol. II, 263–64; Oldoni, "Gerberto e la sua storia"; William of Newburgh, *Gesta rerum anglorum,* §172 (in Howlett, ed., *Chronicles of the Reigns of Stephen, Henry II., and Richard I.,* vol. II).

5. Gerbert and Meridiana

Gerbert of Burgundy, a young man of high birth, good character, and fine reputation, was a student in Reims. Thanks to his efforts, intelligence, and eloquence, he outdid all his fellow students. During this time, all were vying for the hand of the daughter of the Provost of Reims. Gerbert heard tell of her and, as soon as he laid eyes upon her, admired and desired her for himself. He engaged her in conversation and was seduced by her words. He spent his time pleading his case to her with stubborn insistence, but tormented by the certainty that he had no hope. His mental

---

*[*Gant* means "glove" in French, and *moufle* means "mitten." — *Trans.*]

tranquillity abandoned him, and he could no longer manage his affairs or take care of his destiny. He therefore lost his money and, overburdened with debt, abandoned by his servants, and shunned by his friends, found himself all alone in his home, hairy and dirty, unshaven and unkempt.

One day he left the city at noon to take a stroll. Tormented by hunger, he walked deep into the forest. He came to a clearing where he found a woman of unprecedented beauty[13] sitting on a large silk carpet with an enormous pile of money at her feet. In fear that she was a phantom or apparition, Gerbert retreated, but she called him by name* while telling him that he could trust her. Showing that she had taken pity on him, she promised him all the money he saw there, and as much as he could desire,[14] if he scorned the daughter of the provost who had sneered at him and if he truly wished to join with her as a friend. She added: "My name is Meridiana, and I was born to a very noble family. I have always wished to meet someone like me and who was worthy of plucking the first flowers of my virginity.[15] You please me beyond all measure. So long as you give me no reason to become angry, you will be rich and famous, but, once you have recovered your prosperity thanks to me, you must reject the one who made you suffer.† I know that she will regret rejecting you and come back to the one she scorned if she is allowed to do so. If chastity had compelled her to reject your advances, she would have earned divine grace, but by rejecting you with scorn, she could give herself to others without being suspected. Your public defeat masked her depravities. If you always consider that she is unworthy of your embraces, you shall be the greatest of the great on earth. Perhaps you are scared that you are the victim of an illusion and you seek to escape the artifices of a demon succubus in me?[16] You are wrong, for they always demand a commitment or a guarantee,‡ and that I do not ask of you! Take away this money before our union and gradually return to fetch more, in a way to prove that the money you use to settle your debts is not magical in origin. I want to be loved, not as a superior or even as an equal, but

---

*This shows that we are dealing with a fairy. She knows all about him and his situation.
†A prohibition imposed by the fairy in exchange for her favors and love.
‡An allusion to a pact with the devil.

as a servant. You will find nothing in me that is not breathing love."
Desiring what she was offering him, because he wished to get out of poverty at any price, Gerbert kneeled and promised.

Returning home laden with money, he settled his debts little by little so as not to arouse suspicion. He bought furniture, hired servants, and accumulated jewels and money. He fortified himself by eating and drinking, and his happiness in bed at night was great. Every night, Meridiana, who had knowledge of the past, taught him what he needed to do the next day. Gerbert profited from this double teaching of bed and school and reached the highest heights of renown. Meridiana guided him to the peak of glory. In no great time he had become a man without equal, one who was bread to the starving and clothing to the poor, and the savior of all the oppressed.

When she heard people talking of him, the provost's wretched daughter, realizing she had been forgotten, then began burning for the first time with the fires that she had so scornfully rejected. She tried to seduce Gerbert by all possible means, but in vain, and her passion turned into dementia. In the end, an old woman who was a neighbor of Gerbert pulled her out of her torpor and, through a hole in her hut, she showed her the object of her desire walking about by himself in a small orchard. It was hot, and Gerbert had just eaten. After a moment, they saw him stretch out in the shadow of a twisted oak to take a quiet nap. The provost's daughter took off her coat and, wearing only her shirt, slipped beneath Gerbert's tunic, and with her entire body tightly pressed against his, she aroused him with kisses and caresses. She had no trouble obtaining what she wanted from him because youth, the day, the food, and the wine had combined in their various ardors to kindle the fires of love, but he eventually remembered Meridiana. Confused and ashamed, he left to find her and to ask her forgiveness, which she granted him on condition he pay her homage.*

The archbishop of Reims died, and Gerbert was installed in his place. Then, during a trip to Rome, the pope named him the

---

*This is a new prohibition. It seems that the homage involves not taking communion, a detail that appears later in the story.

cardinal-bishop of Ravenna. On the death of the Holy Father, Gerbert was selected to take the throne of Saint Peter. During his entire time in office, he did not take communion when celebrating Mass. During the last year of his papacy, Meridiana told him that he would remain alive as long as he did not say Mass in Jerusalem.* But there came a time when he celebrated the Mass in a Roman church named Jerusalem. Meridiana could not conceal her joy, for she would soon have the pleasure of welcoming him† to her home.[17] When he saw her and at her request he was reminded of the name of the place, before the assembly of all the cardinals, clergy, and people, he confessed publicly, omitting not a single sin of his entire life.

Gerbert spent the little life remaining to him atoning, and he died after a sincere confession. He was interred in the Church of Saint John of Latran. Moisture continuously seeps from his marble mausoleum, but the drops never combine to form a trickle of water except to announce the death of a wealthy Roman.‡ It is said that it forms a stream that falls to the ground at the death of a pope, but when it concerns the death of a noble, the trickle only falls a third, a fourth, or a fifth of the distance, as if to indicate the importance by a larger or smaller flow of water.

WALTER MAP, *DE NUGIS CURIALIUM*, IV, 11[18]

Walter Map (1135/40–1209/10), a cleric attached to the court of Henry II, King of England, collected a number of tales and legends recounting the meeting of a mortal and a fairy. Meridiana, the fairy of noon, grants her love to Gerbert on the condition that he give up the provost's daughter, which is the rationalized form of a Melusine-like taboo. Because the lover broke his promise despite himself, he had to die. The story can also be found in the work of Vincent of Beauvais (Speculum historiale, XXIV, 9)

---

*A new, implicit prohibition that demonizes the fairy.

†Gerbert therefore will rejoin her in the otherworld and live there with her, a typical conception in ancient Celtic literature, an echo of which can be found in the twelfth- and thirteenth-century Old French lays relating to fairies.

‡Oddly enough, this ending makes the deceased Gerbert a kind of *banshee,* a white lady whose appearance always heralds death. When Melusine appears on a tower of the Castle of Lusignan, the castle's lord dies soon after.

and Johannes Gobi (Scala coeli, no. 56, 184), but in the latter's book, a certain Robert takes the place of Gerbert.

6. Love Spell

Charlemagne's love died, and, as he loved her greatly, he had her embalmed because he could not live without her. This was caused by a spell she carried on her person, and he slept with her as a man does with a woman.[19] The only ones who knew were the two chamberlains who had to give her a bath each day.

One day when a bishop was celebrating Mass before the emperor, a dove alit on the altar, carrying a letter that revealed Charlemagne's hidden sin. The prelate read it and condemned the sovereign for not confessing this mortal sin. The emperor denied everything, but the bishop confounded him by producing the missive that had been sent from heaven. "I am in fact guilty of this crime, but it is impossible for me to part from my late wife," the emperor told him. The prelate asked to see Charlemagne's late wife, and the emperor let him enter the room, where he found the dead woman lying in a deep bed as if she were asleep. He opened her mouth, found a stone there the size of a gravel pebble, and took it.[20] Both immediately saw that her body was decomposed, and it then crumbled into dust. "The love I held for her has vanished," said Charlemagne. "She would have made me lose my soul. She stinks as badly as a dead dog! Now I recognize her malice." And he did penance for this sin for the rest of his days.

JANSEN ENIKEL, *WELTCHRONIK*[21]

This legend was woven out of two separate parts, one taken from the Gesta Romanorum *and the other as told by Petrarch (1304–1374). The connection between them is formed by the serpent stone that appeared for the first time in "The Bell of Justice," the text of which appears earlier in this collection. Numerous authors have used it again, including the Brothers Grimm in their collection* German Legends.

   📖 *Gesta Romanorum*, chap. 156 (or 105 in some editions): "De campana et indicio et serpente" (Charlemagne is replaced by Theodosis in this work); Grimm, *German Legends*, no. 459; Petrarch, *Epistola famililiares* I, 3.

7. The Shoemaker and the Malefic Head

In Constantinople there once lived a young shoemaker[22] of low birth whose work surpassed that of all the master bootmakers, and he could make in one day what they could not do in two. He only needed to see a naked foot—be it a club foot or one perfectly formed—and with no delay he would craft a shoe that fit it marvelously. Furthermore, he refused to work unless he had seen the foot. Moreover, because he always won prizes in the contests for spear throwing, fighting, and other tests of strength, his fame had spread in every direction. One day an incredibly beautiful maiden came to his window to ask him to make her a pair of shoes. She showed him her naked foot. The young man took a closer look at the damsel and fell in love with her, first with her foot, and then with her entire person. He abandoned his tools and sold his inheritance to become a soldier. He became distinguished as much among the knights as he once had been among the shoemakers. Deeming himself finally worthy of the young maiden, he took his chances and asked her father for her hand in marriage, but in vain. This setback plunged him into a boundless rage, and he decided to take by force what he was being refused for being a poor commoner. He assembled a large crew of pirates to seek his revenge on the sea for the refusal he had suffered on dry land.

His success made him a figure of dread everywhere. He had gone from one victory to another when he learned of the death of the one he loved. He hastened to the funeral, saw her tomb, and took note of where it was. The following night he returned there by himself, opened the sepulcher, and lay with the dead woman.[23] After he had perpetrated this crime, he got up and heard a voice commanding him to return at the time of the birth so he could take what he had engendered. When the time came, he obediently returned to the tomb. The dead woman handed him a human head and forbid him from showing it except for slaying his enemies.[24] He placed the head, well wrapped, at the bottom of a box, and he then left the sea to conquer the land, holding this monstrous Gorgon in front of him each time he threatened a city or small village. The inhabitants were literally petrified at the sight of this monster resembling Medusa,[25] and no one could understand the cause of this sudden death that left no wounds. In fear of dying, they accepted this man as their lord. Castles, cities, and provinces all capitulated to him, nothing could resist him, and all the knights complained of being so shamefully despoiled without waging battle. Some called him a magician and others a god, but not a single one refused any of his requests.

As he lay dying, the emperor of Constantinople gave him his daughter and heir to be his wife. After several years together, she asked him about the box and would not stop until she learned the truth. Once she was told, she woke him up one day, held the monster in front of his eyes, and he was caught in his own trap. His wife gave the command to take away the petrifying head and cast it into the Aegean Sea with the perpetrator of the crime. Her envoys set sail on a galley, and once they were out on the open sea, they sank the two monstrosities. After they left, the sea began bubbling furiously as if it were trying to show its disgust and was experiencing nausea. After several days of this, the water formed a deep whirlpool: since then, anyone who falls into it, whether by accident or dragged by his greed, sinks without any hope of rescue. Because the name of the young girl was Satalia, it is called the whirlpool of Satalie, or *Gouffre de Satalie* in the common tongue, and everyone avoids it.

WALTER MAP, DE NUGIS CURIALUM, IV, 12

This variation of the Medusa legend appeared between 1181 and 1193 in a book by Walter Map, a Welsh cleric at the court of the English king Henry II. It enjoyed considerable success. Several years later, about 1210, Gervase of Tilbury offered a more specific account: The head of the Gorgon had allegedly been tossed near the reefs between Cypress and Rhodes. Other notable changes include a knight replacing the shoemaker and a queen replacing the noble lady. Gervase ended his story, saying: "Every seven years, the head looks toward the surface of the sea, which puts sailors in great danger."

John of Mandeville (Travels, written between 1355 and 1357) gives us two different versions of these events, thus providing a good illustration of the distortions that arise through the oral tradition. Here is the first:

"When one travels from Rhodes to Cypress, one sails along a land that was once rich and fertile. Its capital was called Satali (Sathalie, Cathalie).

The ocean swallowed it up because of the criminal act of a young man who was said to have loved a maiden. When she died, he opened her grave and lay with the dead woman. Nine months later, a voice told him: 'Run to the tomb. There you will find the fruit that you have fathered. Do not delay, else misfortune will befall you.' When he opened the grave, a horrible head came out of it. It gazed at the city, which sank immediately along with all its inhabitants. Still today, it is terrifying and dangerous to travel near there."

📖 EM, s.v. "Gorgo, Gorgonen"; Gervase of Tilbury, *Otia imperialia*, II, 12; Harf-Lancner and Polino, "Le gouffre de Satalie"; Mandeville, *Reisen; Mandeville's Travels* (trans. Letts), II, 242; Walter Map, *De nugis curialium*, IV, 12.

8. Virgil the Enchanter

A great enchanter named Virgil once lived in Rome; he was a pagan and a child of hell. Here is how he learned magic: Once, while walking through a vineyard, he stuck his hoe deeply in the ground and uncovered a small flask filled with devils.[26] He picked it up and was overjoyed by what he had found. One of the devils imprisoned inside the flask told him: "If you free all of us, we will teach you many tricks of magic." Virgil swore that he would do so on the condition that they keep their promise. They then instructed him in the art of magic, such as is still practiced in Christendom today. So Virgil broke the flask against a stone and freed the demons. He was greatly pleased to acquire goods and honor with no great effort, and he made no delay in experimenting with his art.

In Rome he sculpted the statue of a young woman whose body was depicted with such realism that all the libertines looking for a woman to spend time with hurled themselves on the effigy to fornicate with it.

He also practiced other forms of magic, but I will only tell you of one. He ached for the love of a Roman patrician's wife who did not wish to be unfaithful, even though he was as handsome as Absalom. Despite the threat it posed to his life, he could not forsake her and offered her large amounts of gold and silver. She told her husband about these advances and asked his advice. He was happy to learn of her fidelity and gave her his instructions. She summoned Virgil and complained to him: "My husband is very jealous and hit me quite sorely; he took his horse and rode off in great wrath. I will wait for you to come to me tonight." Overjoyed, the enchanter accepted her invitation. She went on to say: "I will have a basket lowered that you can climb into, then I will pull you up to my chamber at the top of the tower." After night fell, he went to the rendezvous spot and threw a small stone against her window. The woman, accompanied by her husband, heard it and called to the enchanter, who asked her to lower the basket, which she did. Once he was seated inside it, she pulled it back up, but only to the third floor. She then tied the rope tight and left Virgil between heaven and earth.[27] When the sun rose, all of Rome learned of his misadventure. Many people thought him incapable of such an action because he was so wise, but seeing him hanging there convinced them otherwise.

The husband, who had pretended to leave, went to see him, and the enchanter's mind was not really put at rest when the patrician asked him: "What miracle left you hanging here?"

"I wanted this to happen," responded Virgil.

"Who brought you here, along my wall? You must be vexed; your humiliation upsets me," and he lowered him down.

Virgil thought only of vengeance now. He arranged for all the fires of Rome to go out[28] and was so successful that it was impossible to cook anything. Confronted by this predicament, one Roman advised addressing the powerful Virgil, an idea that all found worthy. They went in search of him and upon finding him, told him: "We need your help because as the result of an evil curse, we are suffering from hunger because we are unable to cook any food."

"You might find the solution I propose quite difficult to execute," he replied.

"We shall accept whatever you wish to do, rather than die of starvation."

"Fine. Since you wish it of me, I will reveal where you can find fire. Only the woman who left me hanging along the wall of the tower can save you."

They all raced to her home and badgered her husband so insistently to let her go to meet Virgil, that he reluctantly gave his consent.

The magician gave the lady a warm welcome and asked her: "Are you ready to save the city by following my instructions, or would you rather perish with them?"

"Leave me out of this," she replied. "I have already suffered enough because of you."

"It would be easier to drain the Rhine river dry," he retorted, "than to resolve this problem without you."

She therefore gave her consent, and Virgil revealed this to her: "You have to climb atop a certain stone wearing only your shirt. There you will get on all fours and pull up the behind part of your clothes so that people can once again light their fires. However, if someone tries to transmit the fire to someone else, it will go out. Everyone must light their fire from your burning bottom."

"I would rather die or be exiled than suffer this shame!" she cried.

But Virgil was insistent: "You don't have any choice; it is the sole solution."

Initially, her relatives and even her husband, and who have you, all begged her to obey, but once they realized she preferred death despite their threats and pleas, her husband bound her, undressed her, and set her upon the stone.

Then the Romans came running. The first brought a taper, the second a candle, the third a bundle of straw, the fourth a bunch of leaves, the fifth a beech branch, and the sixth a log, and they all caught fire. The poor woman felt so dishonored that she gave up the ghost.

Then Virgil left Rome and built Naples by using magic. He suspended the fate of the city from three eggs that, if ever broken, would cause the city to sink into the earth and drown all its inhabitants.

Next, he crafted a bronze statue,[29] one hand of which rested over the statue's stomach and the other pointed toward Vesuvius. An inscription in gold letters on this statue said that it would show a treasure. Everyone turned the mountain inside out, but found nothing. One night a drunkard approached the statue and, so that it would no longer mock anyone, knocked off its head with a club so hard that the gold hidden inside it fell out upon the grass. Thus, the treasure was found by the person for whom it was intended.

JANSEN ENIKEL, *WELTCHRONIK*[30]

During the Middle Ages, the great poet Virgil was transformed into an enchanter and a number of magical works were attributed to him. The above text gives only a glimpse of these works. He was renowned for having crafted a bronze fly that drew away the flies of Naples, and for having erected in this same city a bell tower that swayed in rhythm with the bells, and for having a butcher shop built where the meat could not go bad. A large number of authors have provided fragments of his legend—for example, Vincent of Beauvais (Speculum historiale, *VI, 61) and Johannes Gobi* (Scala coeli, *no. 520/9, 383–84).*

📖 Berlioz, "Virgile dans la littérature des *exempla* (XIIIe–XVe siècle)"; EM, s.v. "Geist im Glass," "Vergil"; Comparetti, *Virgilio nel medio evo.*

9. The Talking Statue

At the time when Titus was ruling over the Roman Empire, he enacted a law compelling all his subjects to celebrate the birthday of his first-born son. Anyone who did not honor the birthday and worked on that day would be put to death. Titus summoned Master Virgil: "My very dear friend, I have drawn up a law, but sins can often be committed without me knowing. With your fruitful imagination, find some kind of means that will uncover those who would break my law."

"May your will be done, lord!' Virgil replied. He immediately had a statue with magical powers[31] erected in the center of the city. Every day it told the emperor of all who failed to obey the law, and its accusations led to the conviction of countless people.

At this time there lived in Rome a blacksmith by the name of Focus, who worked without taking any kind of break. Once he lay down in bed, he thought of all the people who had been condemned by the statue. He got up early and went to the site of the statue and told it: "It is your fault that so many people have been killed. I swear by my god that I will crush your skull if you inform on me." Then he returned home.

At the first hour of the day, Titus sent his servants as usual to question the statue to learn if anyone had contravened the law.

"Dear friends, raise your eyes to what is written across my brow," it replied. They clearly saw three sentences:

"Times change and men grow worse.

"They will crush the skull of the one who tells the truth.

"Go to your lord and tell him what you have seen and read."

On being told of this warning, the emperor ordered his soldiers to arm themselves and to take up positions around the statue, and if anyone attacked it, to bring that person to him with their arms and legs bound.

They obeyed and spoke to the statue.

"The emperor orders you to denounce all those who break the law and to tell him the name of the guilty person."

"Seize Focus the smith," the statue replied. "He is the one who threatened me."

They grabbed Focus and brought him before Titus, who questioned him.

"My friend, what is all this I hear about you? Why don't you respect the laws that are in force?"

"Lord, I cannot respect them because I must earn eight silver pennies (*deniers*) a day. How can I earn them if I don't work?"

"Why eight pennies?"

"Every day of the year I am obliged to reimburse two pennies that I borrowed when I was young; I invested two pennies, wasted two, and spent two."

"Explain yourself more clearly."

"Lord, listen to me! I am obliged to give two pennies to my father every day because when I was a child he spent two for me. Now my father is living in poverty so it is normal that I would help him. I have invested two more pennies in the future of my son, the student, so that when it is my turn to become poor, he will return my two pennies just as I have done for my own father. I have wasted two more on my wife, because she opposes everything I do and is stubborn and wrathful. For this reason, everything I give her is wasted. I spend the last two to buy myself food and drink. I cannot survive on less, and it is impossible for me to obtain these pennies without working constantly. These are my reasons. Pronounce a fair judgment."

"My friend, that is a good answer. Go and henceforth work in peace."

Titus died a short time later, and Focus the smith was chosen to be the emperor because of his intelligence. He ruled with great wisdom. When he died, his portrait was painted and hung alongside those of the other emperors, with the drawing of eight silver pennies above his head.

GESTA ROMANORUM, CHAP. 143[32]

A large number of automatons, magical statues, and talismans have been attributed to Virgil. It is said that he was the creator of the Bocca della verità *(the mouth of truth), a mask on one of the walls of the Basilica of Santa Maria in Cosmedin in Rome: when swearing an oath, a person places his hand in the mouth of this mask, which will shut if the person is lying.*

📖 Berlioz, "Virgile dans la littérature des exempla (XIIIe–XVe siècle)"; Comparetti, *Virgil im Mittelalter;* EM, s.v. "Bocca de la verità" and "Vergil."

CHAPTER IV

THE SUPERNATURAL SPOUSE

1. Seyfried von Ardemont

All harken to the story of Seyfried von Ardemont, the son of Cundrie, the sister of my lord Gawain! He distinguished himself early by bringing down a dragon and by slaying some giants. These feats of prowess earned him knighthood and a seat at King Arthur's Round Table. How he met the beautiful Rosemonde, wed her, lost her, and then won her back is the story you are about to hear![1]

As pleasant as life was in the court of King Arthur, Seyfried quickly began to feel the urge to set off in search of new adventures. "I want my fame to grow," he said to himself. The count, Waldin, a young knight, said to him: "Permit me to accompany you on your quest; I swear you my fealty, on my honor." Our hero granted his request, and they formed the bonds of an unbreakable friendship. Well fitted out, they took their leave.

One day they came to a castle that was so well fortified it had nothing to fear from enemy attacks. A town spread out before it, and the two companions went straight to its best inn, where they were given a warm welcome. There Seyfried inquired about the country and its lord and then asked if there was any adventure to be pursued. "My lord here is where civilization ends," the innkeeper replied. "A vast, uninhabited moor extends all the way to the ocean. A terrifying creature dwells there, a serpent of monstrous size. It does no harm to anyone, neither man nor beast, but if someone draws near to it, the moor will go up in flames while a terrifying storm erupts,* a real tempest.[2] I tell you, even if a large army went there, it could not stop from shivering at this sight."

Seyfried decided to go find the serpent the following morning. At dawn he set off with Waldin. They rode all day, and as evening was falling, they saw an abominable monster, the serpent![†] It raised up before them straight as a candle, and the moor all around caught fire. Dark, threatening clouds invaded the sky, lightning flashed, and thunder rumbled. In a show of boldness, the two knights rushed the serpent, and the fire caused them no harm. The beast drew them ever closer to it until they were completely surrounded by the flames. They threw their sharpened spears at it but could not reach it. The fire went out, the storm dispersed, and the sun began to shine. They then saw a handsome column on which an inscription was carved in gold letters: "If a knight shall show proof of enough audacity to remove a hideous toad from the throat of the dragon, a divine secret shall be revealed to him, for the beast will take human form before his eyes."

Seyfried raced toward the serpent and tore the toad[3] out of its throat even though the beast spit at him furiously.[4] Immediately, a beautiful woman stood before him instead of the monster. She lifted her hands toward heaven and enthusiastically said: "Lord, none, not even an angel, can measure up to Your inexhaustible grace! You are the master of the universe and Your power extends from the heavens to hell." Then, turning toward Seyfried, she told him: "You have freed me from the sad fate that weighed upon me. God bless you for restoring me to my first appearance! I am going to die[5] and wish to have a Christian tomb—place a cross upon it!" Hardly had she spoke these words when she collapsed and went pale, and the two companions saw her soul fly off like a white dove.[6] They gave her a Christian burial as she had requested.

Waldin and Seyfried rode for a long time across a wild country, painfully advancing through the thornbushes that hindered their travel.

---

*The description shows that this moor is a separator between the world of men and the otherworld.

[†]In the Middle Ages, "serpent" also meant "dragon."

As their provisions were almost exhausted, they had to eat wild plants and berries and slake their thirst from the clear springs they sometimes discovered.

One day their gaze was drawn toward an object gleaming in the grass, and, when they got a closer look at their find, they saw it was a magnificent crown adorned with gems and precious pearls. They greeted this with amazement, and Seyfried said: "It likely belongs to a powerful nobleman. Whatever way this splendid piece of jewelry found its way here, we can soon hope to encounter people." He placed the crown on his head, and Waldin exclaimed: "Never did a jewel better adorn a knight!"

Three days later, they found a luxurious necklace in the grass. It was gold and set with many precious stones, including rubies, emeralds, chrysoliths, carbuncles, and jacinths,* that all sparkled before their eyes. Waldin earnestly advised his companion to take it, but Seyfried refused outright to do so.

The two knights painfully pursued their route through this deserted region, and, after suffering through three long days, they saw a coat of wondrous splendor. It was so precious that it was worth more than all of King Arthur's treasures. Here again, Seyfried would not touch it despite what Waldin wanted.† "I have no wish to be taken for a thief when we are once again in the company of men," he said.

While pursuing their journey, they saw a mountain of impressive size emerging from the moor. When they came to the foot of it, they discovered that it was surrounded by dense thornbushes. No path cut through them, and the thicket swarmed with wild animals of all sorts— serpents, dragons, and lions.[7] "If we wish to reach this mountain, we will have to fight for our lives," said Waldin. "We are not strong enough to overcome all these monsters. May God protect us!" The audacious

---

*These stones are not there solely for their brightness; they all possess certain virtues and magical properties. For example, the ruby allows the gaining and keeping of domains, bestows devotion, soothes anger and protects against seduction, grants grace and domination over other people, and provides protection against all dangers.

†The discovery of the three objects is a temptation that the hero overcomes successfully: he can therefore continue his journey.

Seyfried asked God for his aid because he wished to know, whatever the cost, what lay beyond the mountain. His confidence breathed fresh courage into his companion, who was now determined to confront all perils, and they went forth.

Paying no heed to the menacing monsters lying in wait in front of their rocky lairs, they boldly pursued their journey with its thousands of hardships, which now included hunger since they only had a miserable pittance of some nuts and berries. Their tenacity was finally rewarded, and they reached the top.

All their cares vanished at the sight of a wondrously beautiful meadow on the other side, in which splendid tents had been set up. Their gaze feasted on the joyous coming and going of knights and ladies. Here some jousted and there others danced; the sound of harps, lutes, and flutes, as well as sweet song, could be heard. Carried away by this marvelous sight, Seyfried cried out: "If this is not the kingdom of heaven, it is paradise at least!" Then while the two knights admired this noble company frolicking before them, the horses of the knights and their ladies were brought forth, trumpets sounded, drums rolled, and an impressive procession formed and readied itself to depart. Consumed with curiosity, Seyfried and Waldin hustled down the mountain and made their way into the meadow. A group of beautiful ladies came to meet them; the prettiest among these women was wearing a crown. She was as entrancing as an angel, and the precious stones on her garments shone and sparkled like the sun. The two companions drew apart to let them pass, but the queen turned toward them, looked at Seyfried, and alit from her horse. Seyfried followed her example. She greeted him with these words: "Lord Seyfried,* welcome to this meadow. Now that you are here, my wishes have come true!" She embraced him and kissed him on the mouth and cheeks. "What joy to find you here!"

"I have undergone many trials," said the knight, regaining his composure, "but they are now far off. How have I, a stranger, earned such an amicable welcome?"

---

*This detail shows that Rosemonde is a fairy. In stories of this type the woman knows everything there is to know about the hero.

Before he got his answer, the queen's retinue approached. The entourage greeted them and brought them two handsome Castilian horses* with caparisons on which they led them to the royal pavilion. Once they had taken off their armor and slipped on the clothing they had been given, the queen took Seyfried aside.

"Noble lady, how were you able to recognize me, a complete stranger?" he asked her. "How did you find out my name?"

"First know who I am. My name is Rosemonde,† and I am of high birth. At my birth, astrologers predicted to my parents that I would wed you in this place or remain a virgin.‡ I have therefore waited for you a long time here. It has been three years since I came to this country by sea, accompanied by the retinue that you have seen close to me."

Rosemonde took Seyfried by the hand and led him into a corner of the tent, where to his surprise he saw the three precious objects that he had found on his way here: the crown, the necklace, and the coat.

"They were placed on your path so they could guide you here.§ If you had taken any one of them, your journey would have ended at that moment. I wish to give you my hand and my kingdom, bold knight!"

"Noble lady, why do you wish to shower me with such gifts when I have never done anything for you and not even broken a single lance in your honor?" our hero replied.

"All your deeds are known to me, from the oldest to the most recent. I am going to entrust you with something, though, that transforms my joy to mourning: you shall not stay but three days in my company, then we shall remain apart for an entire year.§ What misfortune! It breaks my heart."

"Say no more about it, kind lady! What you are telling me is unbearable!"

---

*The horses of Castille were greatly renowned during the Middle Ages.

†"Mundirosa" in the text.

‡This represents an attempt at a logical explanation, one that everyone could understand, for the otherworldly being.

§In French stories and romances, the hero becomes homesick and wants to see his friends and family again after a certain amount of time has passed, whereas in the Germanic world, it is the fairy who asks him to leave.

"It cannot be otherwise. May God bring you back here safe and sound! This is what you must do during this year if you wish to return here and it is your desire that we live together forever: you must never speak of me![9] And if anyone ever praises the beauty of women, never tell them that mine surpasses all. Woe to us if you should forget my words! That would cause great pain for both of us. Our lot would be pain for we would never see one another again and remain apart forever. May God grant you the wisdom to spare us this cruel suffering. If you overstep the prohibition imposed upon you, no one will be able to reunite us."

These three days passed in the blink of an eye, and before they realized it, the hour of their separation had arrived. Before yielding to the prohibition, Seyfried and Rosemonde reluctantly said their farewells.

One of the queen's knights accompanied the two friends and led them safe and sound through the wild lands until they reached the inhabited regions. As he left them, he urged Seyfried: "Keep your promise and you shall rule over many lands! When the year has come to its end, return to the meadow where you met my suzerain and she will find you there. But if you speak of her, there is no sense in returning." He then took his leave of them and went back. Seyfried suggested to Waldin that he go back home to see his family again and to tell them of their deeds. He, meanwhile, planned to return to Caridol and King Arthur's court. Waldin acquiesced, adding: "I will join you soon with several friends."

After spending some time with his family, Waldin went to find Seyfried, who was pining for Rosemonde and wanted to set off in search of adventure while waiting to see her again. One day, they heard of a large tournament to be held in Hibernia, and they decided to take part in it.

While undertaking their journey they met Arbosorans of Cilicie, who was on his way there, too. They decided to travel together, and the knight told them what he knew about the tournament. "The King of Ireland has a very beautiful daughter named Sweet-Love,* and he has

---

*"Duzisamor" in the text.

organized this tourney in her honor. She will give the victor a golden belt and a kiss. If the knight says he knows a woman as beautiful as the princess, he will be given the challenge to prove his words. If he succeeds, he will wed Sweet-Love and receive two large territories. In the absence of proof, he shall lose his life."

When they reached the capital, Gassana, they equipped themselves for the tourney. On the eve of the contest, it was already possible to admire Seyfried's strength and skill, and when the tourney began, he vanquished all his adversaries. The king of Famagusta wished to take his measure. The first attack was undecided, but in the second he knocked him from his saddle. Count Aliers of Crete wished to avenge him, but he met the same fate, and both of them had to submit to our hero. When night fell, everyone returned to their lodgings, where all agreed that Seyfried was the best jouster and the undeniable champion.

The next morning they all gathered in the castle's great hall. Sweet-Love crowned Seyfried and embraced him. Arbosorans then approached the knight and took his hand, saying: "My lord, in all the countries you have traveled, have you ever seen such a beautiful woman?" Then all those there could be heard emphatically lauding the matchless beauty of Sweet-Love. Until this moment, Seyfried had managed to stay quiet, but in reaction to what he was hearing, he told Waldin: "However beautiful she may be, she can in no way compare to the one who is my heart's choice." Count Aliers overheard him and reported this statement to the king.[10] Waldin immediately replied: "Your words are most unwelcome! I hear that you may have brought about your own misfortune." Seyfried then realized what he had done, turned pale, and fainted. When he had slightly recovered from this brutal shock, he exclaimed: "O God, I have spoiled all my happiness and no one in this world suffers as much as me."

The king summoned Seyfried a little later and said to him: "Tell me, valiant knight, where have you seen a woman whose beauty is equal to my daughter's as you just claimed before all? It would be a good idea if you can prove it, otherwise you will regret it bitterly." Waldin came to his friend's rescue: "Since that is the situation, I swear, even if it should cost me my life, that I, too, have seen this lady who is much more beautiful than your daughter. Just as the lily surpasses all the flowers in beauty, hers surpasses that of all other women." These words angered the king, who had the two companions tied and bound. He was prepared to wait for five days for the proof he demanded, for lack of which he would order them to be executed.

This span of time ran out without offering the slightest chance of salvation. The two friends were brought before the king, who said: "You mocked me and caused me pain. This treachery will be your undoing."

"I told the truth," Seyfried replied. "I have never deceived anyone in my entire life!"

During this exchange, the sound of trumpets could be heard; Arbosorans raced out to discover why. He was determined to free the two companions by force if he could find any help. He saw the arrival of an impressive procession—everyone was in mourning and dressed in black—and a lady of incomparable beauty weeping bitterly. It was Rosemonde. He immediately thought, *This must be the woman for whom Seyfried was humiliated,* and he approached her.

"My lady, what is the reason for your grief? Tell me so that I may share your pain."

"I will always remember your loyalty," she answered, "and I beg you to conduct me before the king."

Arbosorans led her into the hall where many noblemen had been quarreling with Seyfried. At Rosemonde's entrance, they all stood to greet her, but she went straight to the king and said: "Your Highness, you should not make such a quick judgment. Your actions are unworthy of you; your crown is swaying and is going to fall off your head! You have shamelessly decided to rob me of my beloved."

The sovereign stared at her and replied: "I cannot deny that I wanted to commit an infamy, but I am going to compensate for it by making him the king of two countries." He signaled to his men, and the two friends were freed from their bonds. Seyfried immediately bowed before Rosemonde and begged her to pardon him.

"Day after day, I pined for you and could not think of anything but you," he said. "It is only out of my love for you that I failed to keep my word, and if I must lose you for that reason, then I would rather to never have been born."

"If it were possible, I would forgive you, but it cannot be any other way,"[11] Rosemonde replied. "What misfortune! We must now part forever, but I beg you, show your courage for love of me and never forget me!"

"My sweetheart, listen to me and be confident! Since you are forced to disappear, I will never abandon my search for you, even if I must travel across the entire earth. I will find you or die! I have trust in divine charity that it will help me find you again and restore my joy."

Rosemonde handed him the three objects that had led him to her, saying: "May these constantly remind you of my life! All the joy the world holds will not be able to console me for losing you." These were her parting words.

Before he left, Seyfried advised Arbosorans to marry Sweet-Love. The court approved the match, and the betrothal was celebrated with great pomp. Everyone rejoiced except for our hero, whose grief was immense. There was nothing to keep him in Hibernia any longer, and Waldin, who shared his pain, accompanied him. They returned to Ingerland, where Waldin was crowned king on the suggestion of his friend. Then Seyfried left, accompanied only by a manservant leading a warhorse that carried a treasure of gold, precious stones, and, most importantly, Rosemonde's three objects.

After wandering through many lands, he dismissed his servant* and decided to make his way to the flowering meadow where he had met his beloved for the first time.

For a long time he rode at random and eventually came to a very high mountain. He scaled it using almost impassable paths that were obstructed with boulders and uprooted trees. He came finally to the meadow, where only the pavilions remained. While looking for traces of Rosemonde, he found a cave behind a large linden tree in which a hermit† was praying. When the hermit saw him, he first feared for

---

*When trying to win back the fairy, the hero must always be alone.
†The hermit is the first helper whom the hero meets in his quest.

his life. However, he mastered his fear and, standing up, greeted the stranger.

"My lord, what miracle brings you to me? I have lived here for a very long time and only one man has visited me. This was the time when a young and beautiful queen was settled here with an impressive retinue; but it has been three years and three months since they left. I heard the lamentation of the lady concerning a young knight for whose love she came here. I heard her say that he had disappointed her greatly. She prayed to God each day to rid her of her grief."

"Show me the direction from which the queen came," Seyfried asked him.

"She came from the place where the mountain falls into the sea that extends into infinity, and she left by the same path."

"It is me who is the knight whose treachery she regretted so. Now that I know the way, I am going to follow her, get as close to her as I can, and die. Whether I get there by swimming or walking, I intend to go to where she lives, and no one can make me change my mind!"

"Fie, then! What a gloomy speech," said the hermit, losing his temper. "Would you lose all chance at heavenly bliss?"

"There is no joy left for me on this earth, so I want to try."

Seyfried bid him farewell and began racing toward the water, but the old man, moved by such distress, wrapped him in his arms to hold him back and then told him: "If you wish to race off to your ruin, at least hear my counsel. Even if it is no help to you, it will be better than what you are planning. A griffin often comes here. In this deserted land, no movement can escape its sight, and it always finds its prey. I am going to sew you inside the hide of your horse; perhaps it will carry you beyond the sea."[12]

Before sealing him inside the hide of his steed, the hermit gave him the three objects, some nourishing plants, and his sword; then he left him on the bank.

A griffin soon came, seized this prey, and flew off. Seyfried couldn't tell how long the journey lasted. Finally, the bird deposited him in its nest at the top of a tree.

While the monstrous bird frisked about in the neighboring forest, the knight split open the hide and climbed down the tree, carrying Rosemonde's gifts and his good sword.

Hardly had he touched ground, when he saw a wild man of terrifying appearance.* This was Althesor, who dwelled in this solitude.

"My lord, tell me, what brings you here?" he asked. "I am very surprised to meet you in this place where no one has ever come before."

"If you wish me well, I am happy to see you," Seyfried answered.

"If I can be of any help to you, I will gladly give it to you, but tell me what land you are from."

"A griffin carried me here."

"It is God who came to your aid," said Althesor, dumbstruck. "I am at your service," he added.

"Where am I and who rules here?" asked Seyfried.

"This land knew great renown," Althesor sighed, "but a wicked lord is oppressing it along with its queen. No one is equal to her in beauty, but, by the fault of a valiant knight who abandoned her, her joy has departed. A certain Count Girot claims that she promised to wed him. He challenges to single combat all those who would deny him full right over my mistress. A gentle maiden has picked up the gauntlet[†] and hopes, with God's help, to avenge this sacrilege. May she place Rosemonde, our queen, out of danger! The meeting will take place in less than three weeks in Ardemont.[‡]

"If I could be sure I will not regret it, I would entrust you with something," Seyfried ventured.

"I solemnly swear to never betray your secret," Althesor answered.

"If you agree to hold your tongue for as long as necessary, I will place my fate in your hands. I am the knight whom your sovereign went in search of in foreign lands. My love robbed me of my reason, so much so that I violated her prohibition and spoke of her; our separation was inevitable."

---

*This figure is one of the variables of the fairy tale; he sometimes takes the form of a hermit.

†This means that no man has dared defend her.

‡*Ardemont* means "Mont Ardant," the Burning Mountain, a name that has connotations of the otherworld.

As proof, Seyfried showed him the three objects. Full of joy, Althesor kissed him on the lips, cheeks, and hands. "Blessed be this day!" he shouted. "This will be the end of the distress of our country. My lord, make your own decision! I am at your command."

He built a large raft, and, out of fear of the griffin, he covered it with branches so that it looked like a tiny island. They traveled all night and, driven by a favorable wind, in the morning came to a mountain from which fell a torrent that turned into a wide river. Althesor poled the raft alongside the shore, moored it, and then took Seyfried's possessions upon his back. He led the knight to a castle that was located half a league from Ardemont. "The lord of this fortress is loyal and valiant. His counsel is good. You shall see that he deserves your trust and that I have given you the best advice," he told him. Our hero told his tale to his host, who swore fealty to him and placed all he owned at his disposal.

On the morning of the combat, a circle* was marked out and seats were placed around it. Count Girot arrived, accompanied by his family and friends. The maiden who had offered to confront him was also there. Girot entered the circle and said: "If there is a knight here bold enough to replace this young girl, may he prepare himself. I await him!"

"May God grant me his aid!" the maiden said. "My righteousness and your crime give me my strength. I have no fear of you."

At that moment, Seyfried appeared in full armor, drawing the gaze of all with the splendor of his equipment. Once he entered the circle, all there thought they were seeing Saint George arriving to help them. "Here I am, ready to confront you in place of the maiden. My lord, prepare yourself! I am impatient to punish your sacrilege," he shouted at Count Girot.

After two jousts that were indecisive, Girot was finally unhorsed so violently that he remained senseless on the ground and everyone thought he was dead. Seyfried walked over to him and removed his

---

*Trials by combat and duels take place in a space that has been marked off. This is the ancestor of the modern-day ring, which was once regarded as sacred.

helmet. The count regained his senses. "By my faith, I cannot let this affront go unpunished!" he yelled. "I shall get my revenge and do so in such a way that my renown will be no less after the battle than it was before." They once again met in combat, this time with swords, and Seyfried split his adversary's helmet and head.

The combat had barely ended when Seyfried bowed to Queen Rosemonde and left the site without being recognized. She would have liked to know the identity of the knight who had prevailed victoriously for her, but he had disappeared without a trace. Except for the lord who had given him lodging, no one knew his identity.

This latter suggested to Rosemonde that she organize a grand tournament for all to share in her joy. She agreed and sent pages to the four corners of the land to invite the nobles. It took place six weeks later and ended with festivities and dances. She was thinking to withdraw from the world to a cloister where she could mourn for her lost beloved.

Without being recognized, Seyfried appeared at the tournament and emerged the great victor. During the party that followed, Rosemonde remained seated, alone and melancholy. Mingling with the crowd, our knight's heart clenched at the sight of the one he loved suffering so terribly. He slipped out of the hall and returned to his lodging accompanied by his host. There, he put on superb clothes, and one hundred knights organized into a procession to accompany him. At their head, he returned to the royal castle to the blast of trumpets. On hearing this noise, everyone stopped dancing and raced to meet the new arrivals. Rosemonde was leaving the hall in turn when Seyfried approached her. The surprise rendered her mute, and when she saw him appear suddenly before her, she fainted straight away. He stood her back up and led her back to her place. She regained her composure and, looking at him with eyes full of love, said: "My sweet friend! You are most welcome!" In her joy she kissed him a thousand times and gave him a thousand nicknames. "Blessed be the journey that brought me back to you," he answered. "I sought you everywhere through mountains and valleys. My burning desire to see you again is now satisfied."

When the nobles learned of the dangers he had overcome, they congratulated him, and, once he had returned to his host's castle, they held a council. The next morning, after attending Mass, the nobles and knights made their way to the palace to announce to all that they had chosen Seyfried to be king and crowned him on the spot. He granted them fiefs, and a joyous celebration concluded the day. To a loyal burgrave he gave Gentiane, a relative of Rosemonde, in marriage. The union of the two lovers was celebrated for fourteen days with all the necessary pomp, and later Rosemonde gave birth to a son, whom they named Florimont.

Seyfried von Ardemont[13]

Constructed upon a Melusinian theme, this courtly romance attributed to Albrecht von Scharfenberg (thirteenth century) consists of two main parts: the hero's childhood (verses 1–265), with all the standard elements— revelations of the qualities of a future knight by means of battles against monsters, close parallels of which can be found in the German Arthurian romances—and the story (verses 266–519) that we adapted here. The text came down to us through the reworked version by Ulrich Füetrer (died ca. 1495–1496).

📖 EM, s.v. "Martenehe, Die gestörte M."; Lecouteux, *Mélusine et le Chevalier au Cygne.*

2. Liombruno

First Canto

My lords, poverty has caused much bad luck and setbacks to many people who then lose their freedom and sink into terrible misery. Without belying the truth, I would like to tell you the tale of a poor man, who, because of it, had to promise his son to the devil.

He owned neither land nor vineyard, but he did have a wife who was as fresh as a rose and gave sustenance to three children. He was a fisherman who, to his great misfortune, never caught very many fish.

One morning this good man arose and set off in his boat to fish but remained empty-handed, which grieved him greatly. He came to a small isle where he met a very large demon, who asked him: "What will you give me if I provide you some fish?"

"I will give you whatever you ask," he responded. "Ask!"

The demon deliberated with his fellow demons and then came back. "If you bring one of your sons here[14] and promise not to deceive me, I will give you something to eat as well as pieces of gold and silver."

The good man took this quite painfully, but, poor as he was, he accepted. "I will give you my youngest and bring him to this isle," he answered. With no further delay, the devil filled his boat with fish, gave the fisherman much wealth, and told him: "If you try to trick me, I will drown you."

"Rest assured that I will not try to trick you," the good man said boldly before going back home, wearing nice clothes, his boat full of fish, and with the money.

Once he was home, he clad his wife and eldest son in new garments and furnished their house. Despite his pain, he called his youngest son, had him climb aboard his boat, and then deposited him on the isle and said: "Wait for me to come back." He abandoned him with this false hope even though he was only eight years old.

Not wishing to witness the death of his son, the fisherman left and the devil loomed up, determined to carry the little boy away. The boy was greatly confused with no one to give him comfort, but he made the sign of the cross and the devil fled. The boy found himself alone with his terror. Looking up, he spied a young girl with the face of an eagle above him. She drew near and said: "Have no fear, I shall take you away from here!"

"I shouldn't leave," he replied, "because I am waiting for my father."

"I will bring you back to him soon," the eagle replied. She grabbed the young boy and flew so high up into the sky that his hair was scorched.[15]

The eagle pointed out her country from the sky. Her immense castle was four hundred days' journey away and even more, as shown on the maps, but it only took one night to get there. They left the isle at dusk and reached the castle at dawn.

The bird set him down in a magnificent hall. "Now, await my return," she told him. She entered into his chamber and turned into a young girl. People would say that she came from paradise because she shone with a glow that was brighter than the stars and looked like the sun rising into the sky. She wore the nicest cloths, was no older than ten years of age, and her name was Madona Aquilina.* She came to him and said: "Handsome friend, be welcome! It is I who carried you here and freed you from the devil's claws." The boy found the right words to thank her and added: "Madona Aquilina, I am happy and your servant forever."

"Happy," she answered, "you shall be even more."

She was ten years old and he was eight, and she remained a virgin for more than eight years.

During these eight years, she had him study with a teacher, who instructed him in a worthy manner. He taught him to write and to joust, as well as how to handle weapons. No one could withstand his blows, and all the inhabitants of the land said: "He is the son of a count or a baron" because of the fine figure he cut.

Once they both had grown up, he resembled a lily and she a rose. This radiantly beautiful woman told him: "My heart will never find peace until I have achieved my dearest wish: I would like above all else to be your wife. Beloved, I have brought you up and I beg you to be my husband."[16]

"Madona Aquilina," the young man responded, "you took the trouble of educating me, you pulled me out of the sea; I am ready to satisfy your desire."

She then gave him the name of Liombruno.†

He married the lady as ordained by fate. Their powerful castle was

---

*In other words, "Lady Eagle (Aquiline)." Her name and appearance indicate that she is a bird-woman and a fairy.

†This represents a new birth, and she is the good fairy who presides over it.

provided with all they needed. It had two carefully decorated portals that stood tall in the air. No one could enter them without the consent of Madona Aquilina.

Liombruno knew the magic phrase for entering and leaving as he wished. He organized many tournaments and often emerged as victor in all the jousts. His wife beamed with happiness and loved him more every day, for he was handsome, full of grace, and she adored him.

One day when Liombruno seemed to be quite pensive, the beautiful woman asked him: "Dear husband, why are you so sad?"

"Madona, one thought never leaves me; I would like to see my brothers, my father, and my mother again."

"If you want to leave, I would like your promise without any lie that you shall return on the day I set for you. Return before the end of the year!"

"Madona, have no worries!"

She then gave him a ring intended to protect him and told him: "You can ask it for whatever you desire, silver pennies (*deniers*)[17] and clothing. It will obey you.[18] But be on your guard and don't deceive me—you would then not be able to obtain anything more from me! Do not miss this deadline by more than four days." Before his departure, this beautiful and charming woman had him dubbed a knight and girded a sword around his waist without delay. He left and was henceforth called Sir Liombruno.

He would have had to travel for 410 days. Madona Aquilina put him to sleep with a magic spell and then ordered a fairy to transport him promptly to his own country, where he awoke the next morning.

Liombruno arose at dawn and looked around him. The handsome knight humbly thanked God then asked the ring to grant him his wishes. He first obtained a good charger, then rich and handsome garments, such as every knight needs, a chest full of coins as was befitting to his estate, and, lastly, loyal servants.

He returned home where everyone welcomed him with joy and bid him welcome. He gave his mother a dress. They asked him: "Where were you?"

"In truth, I made some successful deals with rich merchants who paid me with clothing and jewels. They also made me a Knight of the Golden Spur."

Liombruno remained with his family for several months. After nine months, he told them: "I should leave, for I promised these merchants to return before the year's end."

"Oh, Liombruno, where do you want to go?" his parents asked. "Don't you know that the king of Granada wishes one of his daughters to wed and is organizing a grand tournament?"

Hearing these words, the young man decided to try his fortune. He immediately wished for a fine charger and a suit of solid armor. All his wishes were realized thanks to the ring. He equipped himself and left his parents weeping.

He rode so swiftly that he soon reached Granada, where everything was prepared for the tournament. The great joust was just beginning. The next day, Liombruno made his way to the field where the crowd was gathered. There was a powerful Saracen there whom everyone already assumed would be the winner. He was so strong and valiant that none dared confront him. Liombruno courteously introduced himself to him.

"You come to me as if you wish to joust," the other responded. "So come into the arena!"

"Gladly," answered our knight, riding boldly onto the enclosed field.

The proud Saracen mounted his horse. Liombruno turned his around to meet him, and both spurred on their chargers, rushing at each other until they collided. Listen to the clash of unrestrained blows! They inflicted deep wounds upon each other. The Saracen's armor was no equal to that of Liombruno, who stuck his lance and sword in his body, killing him. Badly wounded, Liombruno remained master of the battlefield.

The king summoned the knight and said to him: "Valiant knight, as promised my daughter shall be your wife and you shall be her husband."[19]

"Gladly," Liombruno answered. "It will be as you wish, great and valorous king."

But before giving his daughter to the knight, the king asked his barons for counsel.

"What do you think of this knight? Perhaps he is already married? Even if he is valiant and full of courage, he hardly suits me."

"If you wish to follow our advice," they said, "order that each knight boast his merits and supply proof of it." The next day, this then took place.

The first knight boasted of having a beautiful wife; the second, a beautiful house; the third, a good, swift charger; the fourth, a noble falcon; the fifth, a castle with stately towers; and the last extolled his own nobility.

"What is your boast?" the king asked the knight.

"Pardon me, sire, that is what I am about to tell you."

"You are pardoned."

"I boast of having the most beautiful woman in the world. Twenty days from now, I shall prove it!"

"You ask for twenty days?" the king replied. "I shall grant you thirty!"

Liombruno then spoke to his ring: "Bring Madona Aquilina very quickly!" But because he had broken his word, nothing happened. He spent thirty days in trepidation, because he would lose his head on the thirty-first.

On the set day, the lady arrived and landed outside the city. She helped one of her companions to put on her own clothes and sent her to see the king and his barons. When the sovereign saw her, he turned toward Liombruno: "Is this your wife?" But he replied: "No, noble lord."

Another companion introduced herself to the king and his barons. When he saw her exceedingly lovely face, he asked Liombruno: "Is this your wife, noble warrior?"

"No, my lord," the knight responded sweetly, "these two maidens are her companions."

Then Madona Aquilina came in, and her beautiful face shone like a mirror. When he saw her, the king cried out: "Noble lord, please forgive me."

"I forgive you," said Liombruno.

And the lady quietly left.

Liombruno took his leave and raced after his wife, who was waiting for him in a field. He craved her forgiveness, but she replied: "Renegade, traitor! I don't care if you die!" and she went on her way.[20]

Second Canto

My lords, in my first poem, I told you how Liombruno escaped the devil. I told you how he first returned to his father's house in great honor and, following the book, how Madona Aquilina abandoned him, stripped him of his arms and horse, and how he made himself guilty of a great sin. Here is the next part of his adventures.

Three malefactors had robbed and killed two merchants. The stolen money was sitting on a stone in a field, and they were dividing it up while arguing in loud voices. They had drawn their knives and were about to come to blows over a coat and a pair of boots. The first one wanted the coat, the second one wanted the boots, and the third was upset that there was nothing left for him. All three were becoming irate. Liombruno then arrived. The oldest of the robbers hailed him, and Liombruno quickened his step.

"Valorous friend, you can play the role of Providence for us in this matter!" the malefactor yelled to him. "This coat is quite handsome, and these boots!"

"So that I can render an impartial judgment," the knight replied, "tell me about their properties, and then hear my decision."

"You are clairvoyant!" the most astute of the robbers blurted out, while turning to look at him. "Whoever dons this coat shall become invisible,[21] and I will tell you this about the boots: whoever wears them on his feet will acquire the speed of the wind, for they are enchanted."[22]

"I would not believe that unless I tried them on myself," Liombruno replied.

"Slip them on and take a few steps along the path," said the old man.

Without delay the young man put on the shoes and then asked the first thief to give him the coat.

"By my faith, if what you say is true, this is a great treasure!"

"Put it on," the old thief responded, "and you will see!"

Liombruno slipped it on.

"Can you see me?" he asked.

"No," the brigand answered. He then took as many florins as he wanted because the others could not see him.

Clad in the coat and the boots, he slipped away without delay. In a fury, the other two brigands vented their anger on the oldest thief.

"Is that a friend or relative, since you let him leave that way?"

"I don't know him," the other replied. "I have never seen him before, except in this forest."

The others would hear none of it. "You let him get away so you can meet up with him later when you want to!" Consumed by their wrath, the two rogues stabbed him with their swords, and he gave up the ghost. They then turned toward the stone where the money had been set and, seeing that the pile had shrunk, began to quarrel. "You stole it!" said one. They began stabbing at each other with their swords so rashly and violently that they ended up killing one another. Hearing the din of battle, Liombruno turned back at once and took all the money he wanted. There were more than 3,700 coins! He then made his departure, faster than the wind, traveling like lightning, until he came to an inn, which he entered immediately. He found three merchants there who greeted him.

Each gave him a warm welcome and spoke to him amiably: "Pull up a chair, dear lord!" Liombruno spoke to the innkeeper: "Bring us some of your best wine! Pour some wine for these merchants, for I wish to profit from their company!" Once they had drunk, Liombruno said to them: "Venerable merchants, you who know the whole world and all its countries and all its kingdoms—tell me of a land on the other side of the sea where Madona Aquilina resides!"

None of them had an answer for him, but the oldest merchant said: "Even if you travel for a good many long years, you will not find an answer, for only the wind can tell you about it."

"So is there a person somewhere who can tell me where I can find the wind?" asked Liombruno.

"You must scale this mountain," the oldest merchant told him, "and wait. There is a hermit there who gives lodging to more than sixty winds that have assumed human form. But no one has ever managed to climb that high, except for the hermit, who was carried there by the winds. This mountain is so high that if someone—to his misfortune—tried to scale it, he would not get any higher than half a mile before falling back into the plane below and finding his death. This is why no one has attempted to get there. If you do not wish to die, take care that you do not go there!"

The merchant had described the road leading to this mountain in great detail. The sun had not yet gone down when Liombruno set off, after donning the coat and the boots. He wanted to reach the hermit's house before dusk. Thanks to the boots, he lightheartedly traveled until he reached the mountain, whose height did not scare him at all. He came to the hermit's cell and knocked. The hermit opened the door and, very surprised when he did not see anyone, made the sign of the cross.

Believing it was the devil, he was greatly afraid. Liombruno approached him, speaking the name of Christ as he slipped off his coat. For protection, the hermit invoked the immaculate Virgin.

"How did you get here?" he asked. "What way did you take? Until now, no man has ever succeeded in climbing the mountain unless the wind carried him."

"It is out of the love I bear for my wife, because she holds my heart under a spell, that I have come here with the help of my magic boots," the knight replied. "Her name is Madona Aquilina, and she is queen of a foreign land."

"On my life, I have never heard such a tale," the hermit exclaimed.

"I was told that the winds live here,"*[23] Liombruno went on. "In the name of my love, I beg you to have the courtesy of interrogating them when they return."

The West Wind arrived first with the vigorous Gabino right behind, then all at once the winds of the Levant and of Greece arrived with the good trade winds. Then the Mistral, with its devastating fury, and the Austral, the Boreal, and the Tramontane winds, as well as numerous winds from the sea and the caves.

The hermit implored[24] them in the name of the all-powerful Christ; and each responded that it did not know, when one wind suddenly added: "Sirocco has still not come; he might be able to tell

---

*In the Middle Ages it was believed that the winds originated in caves.

you something." Sirocco then arrived and the hermit interrogated him.

"For the love of God, please tell me where the country is in which Madona Aquilina resides, if you know."

"I have been there and will return there early tomorrow morning."

"If you permit me," said Liombruno, "I would like to accompany you."

"You wish to go with me to this faraway land?" Sirocco replied. "I cannot wait for you, my friend. Your words are in vain."

"I will follow you over mountains and valleys," Liombruno replied. "Call me when you set off tomorrow!"

"Understood, you can follow me. But there is no way I will wait for you. I will show you the way."

"Thank you!"

The hermit shared his food with Liombruno, who then went to bed. He did not want to take off his boots so he would be ready when he woke up to follow the wind wherever he went.

At the crack of dawn, Sirocco called him and said: "My friend, do you want to accompany me?"

"I am ready!"

Sirocco showed him the path. "Do you see that mountain in the distance? You will find me there if you can catch up with me."

Sirocco then left in a burst of speed. Liombruno took his leave of the hermit, slipped on his coat, and ran behind the wind. The wind looked back several times, but the knight had already gotten ahead of him. He was first to arrive on the mountain, and the wind found him waiting there. "What kind of man are you that I cannot hear or see you?" the wind asked. "No matter how fast I run, you are quicker than me. I did not think that you would be able to catch up to me. Do you see that mountain far away? If you can get there with me, I will show you the castle of Madona Aquilina."[25]

The wind left first. Liombruno put on his coat and followed it. Sirocco often looked back, calling the knight's name, but Liombruno had already gotten ahead of him. Once he was on the mountain, the young man took off his coat. Sirocco arrived and told him: "I assure you, dear friend, never have I met a faster runner. Stand! There is the castle!" The wind thereupon bid him farewell and resumed his journey. Without any delay, Liombruno made his way there and joyfully entered the palace, where he found Madona Aquilina at the table. Without her noticing, he took what he wanted from her plate.* She was greatly amazed, because she did not think she had even eaten a quarter of what she had been served. This sweet and noble lady took this as a sign that things were going badly for Liombruno and that he was either dead or in distress. "How ill-fated I am! What a huge sin I have committed. I should have been indulgent and not stripped him of both his arms and his steed."

Thanks to the power of the magic coat, the bold knight remained invisible. He still had the ring that Madona Aquilina had given him when he left. The valiant lord remembered it just then and dropped it on her plate.[26] The lady saw it and exclaimed: "It is the wondrous ring that I gave Liombruno when he so gaily left me to go back to his land. My heart will remain ever mournful and my soul filled with grief, as long as I never again see the love of my life." She then swooned on her bench.

Her companions carried her to her bed and caressed her hands and her fair face. She regained her senses and moaned: "Oh, woe is me! Poor me! What shall I do? I would like to know for a certainty where my dear husband has gone. Tonight, I shall know!" The maidens left the chamber on their mistress's orders, and Liombruno slipped inside and drew near his wife, who had fallen asleep in her grief. He lay down next to her and kissed her beautiful face and mouth. She woke up again. He wrapped his coat around himself, and she could not see him. At once she said: "Alas, how I suffer! I thought Liombruno was here. I was certainly dreaming of him; it is a sign that he is dead."

As he remained invisible, she went back to sleep. Liombruno began to torment her again. She turned over so quickly that she caught a glimpse of him before he had a chance to wrap his coat around him totally. Madona Aquilina pretended to go back to sleep. He took off his coat. She quickly grabbed the knight by his hand and caressed it while asking: "Who taught you how to use this charm? Who told you the way to get here?" Liombruno recounted all his adventures to her and told her of the thieves, the coat and the boots, and about the wind that had

---

*Generally speaking, this kind of behavior is a distinguishing feature of dwarfs.

showed him the way. They reconciled, embraced, and each forgot their suffering. They lived in joy and perfect love until the end of their days.[27] In your honor, this story now ends.

LA HISTORIA DEL LIOMBRUNO[28]

*This short, fourteenth-century Italian romance (*cantare*), divided into two cantos of forty-seven and forty-eight verses, is a story of royal initiation for which other Indo-European parallels can be found. It shares many points in common—the Melusinian taboo, in particular—with the French lays of the thirteenth century that feature fairies, and with two other Italian cantari, "La Ponsella Gaia" (which is quite similar to the "Lai de Lanval" by Marie de France) and "Il Bel Gherardino."[29] The latter story goes as follows:*

Having rapidly squandered his father's legacy, Gherardino leaves Rome with his faithful servant, Marco Bello. They both come to a fairy's castle, where they are served without seeing anyone. They go to bed, and a young maiden, the Fata Bianca, comes to sleep next to Gherardino. He lives happily with her for three months but desires to see his country and his mother again. When they part, the fairy gives him a magical glove that will grant him all he desires, and she advises him to not tell anyone of what has happened to him. Gherardino reveals his secret to his mother, and the glove loses its magical powers. After several adventures, the hero weds the fairy.

AaTh 400 A*; 518

📖 BP II, 318–55; EM, s.v. "Martenehe, die gestörte M," "Kind dem Teufel verkauft oder versprochen," "Streit um Zaubergegenstände"; Lecouteux, "Das Motiv der gestörten Mahrtenehe"; Lecouteux, *Mélusine et le Chevalier au cygne.*

3. Frederick of Swabia

There once ruled in Swabia a good and just lord, Duke Henry. He had three sons, Robert, Frederick, and Henry, who had been raised in the best fashion. They learned how to read and write and, when they were old enough, how to handle and break lances, to joust, to hunt, and to shoot the bow.

Henry lived to be 106. When he felt his end was near, he summoned his sons and told them: "My dear sons, fear God; show compassion to the poor, the widows, and the orphans; and have heart especially to be impartial judges. Never commit an injustice to benefit a friend." The three brothers promised and, keeping their word, ruled with charity and equity.

One day, Duke Frederick,* the youngest son, went hunting accompanied by six servants. They flushed a deer, and because Frederick wanted to hunt it by himself, he ordered his companions to wait for him. He tracked the animal until the fall of night, without catching it.[30] He became lost in the forest and, randomly wandering, came upon a castle where he thought to ask for hospitality.

He found the door open, but all seemed deserted and no one came to meet him. He entered the courtyard and alit from his horse. He then tied up his mount and entered a wondrously beautiful hall where he did not see a soul.[31] There he found a table well stocked with meat, bread, wine, and fish. He sat down and eased his hunger while giving thanks to God. Once he was restored, he entered a room where he found a beautiful bed, already made. Tired as he was, he lay down upon it to spend the night.

Hardly had he fallen asleep when someone tousled his hair. He woke up but did not see anyone at all. He was eager to learn what was at

---

*In one of the manuscripts of this romance, Frederick's name is "Wieland," which refers to the famous mythical smith who married a swan maiden.

the bottom of this mystery. He therefore pretended to fall back asleep. Someone approached, whom he grabbed by the hand.

"If you want to stay alive, tell me who you are!" he shouted.

"Duke Frederick, if you assure me that you will not take my life or my honor," a woman's voice replied, "I will tell you everything."

He promised the unknown person that he would not do her any harm. "I trust you," was the response, "so I shall tell you my story. My father is an excellent king. My mother died during my childhood, and I was instructed in all the virtues. The king raised me at court until I was fifteen and then he convened an assembly to discuss what he should do. All urged him to marry again so he could have a male heir. So he married Flanea, but this was not a wise choice as she behaved badly and cheated on him with others. Everyone liked me, because I never committed any evil acts. This vexed my stepmother, especially since everyone sang my praises while looking at her with disdain.[32] I asked her to give up her evil ways and return to the path of virtue. She acquiesced and assured me of her good feelings, but deep down she detested me all the more.

She had a magician for a lover, a man named Jeroparg,[33] to whom she complained that I had humiliated her. "Avenge me or I will kill myself," she told him. "Make it so that Angelburg—that's my name—loses her father's favor and vanishes from my sight forever!" And the magician promised her he would do it.

Thanks to his artifices, he cast an evil spell on my father. As long as he remained in his castle, he could see normally, but once he left it, he was blind and could see nothing of what was going on around him. The doctors could not cure him. He therefore convened an assembly of all the wise men of the region and promised a rich reward to the one who could free him of this evil.

All their attempts were in vain, and no one knew what to do until the magician—who was richly clad and had made himself unrecognizable by magic—stepped forward and promised to help him. He brought my father outside and, as he could not see anything, asked that I be summoned with two of my companions. Once we were before him, he took a ring from each of our fingers and passed them to my father. He recovered his sight at once[34] and granted the magician the rich reward he had promised. Before this, my father had threatened to have the person responsible for his problem killed, and, as he held me responsible, when he was drunk with rage he ordered my death. He wouldn't listen to any of my protestations of innocence, and I would thus have been executed if my stepmother hadn't intervened. She pretended to be compassionate and begged my father to let me live if I was ready to accept the penitence she would impose on me. My only choice was to accept this or die.

"Angelburg," Flanea said, "henceforth you and your two companions* must live in the forest in the form of does;[35] you shall run all day through fields, woods, and hedges. When night falls, you will be able to eat, drink, and find rest and sleep in a house.[36] But in the morning, you will become does again and return to the woods. Nobody on earth can free you from this, except the son of a good prince. Angelburg, he will have to pursue you for an entire day through bushes and thickets until nightfall. Then, in the house where you have found refuge, he must, without ever seeing you, spend thirty nights of the year near you, without touching you or dishonoring you. At the first meeting, he must spend two nights with you. At the end of three weeks, three nights; ten weeks later, five nights; and during your fourth meeting, which should

---

*These companions play a minor role and seem to be included only to add up to the figure three, which is so frequent in fairy tales.

take place fifteen weeks later, ten nights. For the fifth and last time, he must return to you at the end of twenty-three weeks,[37] and when you have again spent ten nights together, you and your companions shall be freed,[38] and you can return to your mother's country.[39] But if you were dishonored, you shall remain does for eternity; even at night. You shall never regain your human shape and will have to feed yourselves in the forest. Never again will you be able to enjoy the food and drink of men.

"If you let him see you,[40] the prince will have to pay the price with the loss of an eye.[41] Then you and your companions will be changed into three white doves and you will fly away to the clearest, most beautiful fountain in the world. It is located on a mountain. When you arrive there, you will regain your human form, and you will bathe there after removing your human clothes. You will put them on again after the bath, when you eat and drink. After the meal, you will turn back into doves,[42] fly aloft, and spend the night. Only the prince, who has seen you, despite the prohibition, will be able to free you. If a noble maiden returns to him the eye he lost, he will be able to find the path to the fountain in which you bathed. If he takes your clothing,[43] he must not return it until after you promise to marry him. This will be the deliverance of all three of you, and you will be able to return to the land of your mother.

"After she had her say, the king found the sentence to his liking and I had to comply. Having heard all, the lords of my mother's kingdom tried to console me by telling me they would hold it for me for thirty years. I had to leave with my two companions and look for a land where we could spend our time in atonement while hoping for deliverance. Of all the ones we came to, it was this forest, where I heard it said that the three best princes lived, which pleased me best. You now know what my fate is. You have entered my bed with no opposition from me; I will sleep on the ground with my companions."

But Duke Frederick refused. He got up and shouted: "I will fulfill all the conditions so that you may be freed."

"Think again on that because, if you make a mistake and transgress the prohibitions that have been imposed, my fate will become worse," Angelburg responded. "I would prefer to remain as we are."

Frederick persisted with his intention and stated: "I would rather die than to see you thrown into such distress." She put her trust in him and lay by his side, and they had so much to talk about that the night passed by in the blink of an eye. At dawn, Angelburg said: "I must resume my shape as a doe and return to the woods." As soon as she left the premises with her companions, the castle vanished.[44] Frederick had to remain in that place until dusk, then the castle reappeared. He could eat, drink, and lie down in the bed where Angelburg joined him.

At the end of the night, she told him: "Respect the deadline and come back in three weeks. You must leave to go hunting by yourself, I shall find you on your path as a doe, and if you pursue me until nightfall, you shall find the castle." Frederick assured her that he would keep his promise. They then parted. She went into the forest, while he took the road back home.

On his return, his brothers questioned him about his long absence and he answered them: "I pursued a doe until evening without managing to catch her. I spent the night in the forest where my horse ate grass while I ate apples and pears. When I was returning the next day, I was caught off guard by a terrible storm. I took shelter in a cave to protect myself from the pelting rain and roaring thunder. I stayed there all that day and the following night." His brothers were satisfied with this explanation, and life went on as usual.

Once the three weeks had gone by and the time had come for Frederick to find Angelburg again, he snuck off to go hunting. Everything took place as planned: the doe leaped in front of him, and he followed her until nightfall; she then disappeared and he saw he was once more in front of the castle he already knew. He drank and ate there and then stretched out on the bed. A short time later, Angelburg joined him. They swore their mutual love for one another. When they parted on the third day, Angelburg bid Frederick to come back in ten weeks: "I beg you urgently to keep our secret safe," she added, "otherwise we shall be struck by great misfortune." He promised her this, and upon his return home he arranged with a loyal friend for the latter to confirm that they had spent the last three days together, so that no one would become suspicious.

At the end of ten weeks, he prepared to meet Angelburg. He commanded a loyal servant to say that he was withdrawing to spend some time alone and would not be seen by anyone. This time he spent five nights next to Angelburg, and, fifteen weeks later, he remained for ten nights. Then he left her to return in twenty-three weeks. On his return, he was asked where he had tarried for so long, but he was so skilled at offering explanations that everyone believed them.

Before this last span of time had passed by, Frederick's brothers held a council in which the counts and knights of the region took part, accompanied by many beautiful women. Seeing them reminded Frederick of Angelburg and his desire to see her again. He ached for her so much that he sank into a deeper and deeper state of melancholy. He had no desire to take part in any of the knightly games and remained apart. His love for Angelburg, which he had not revealed to anyone, tormented him, and his secret pain gnawed at him. He grew weak and became ill.

During this same time, Flanea asked Jeroparg: "What has become of my stepdaughter, Angelburg?"

"A week from now, you shall know," he replied.

Through his magic he learned that Frederick had undertaken the task of freeing her and that he had managed to surmount the major part of the trials. He needed just ten more nights to achieve her deliverance. But he also knew that Angelburg was staying in a forest and that Frederick was sick with love for her. "I shall go pay him a visit," he said, "and lead him into transgressing the prohibition on seeing Angelburg in her human form. I will make it so that their joy turns into torment." The treacherous Flanea started laughing and responded: "If you succeed, that will put an end to the deliverance of Angelburg."

Frederick's illness grew worse; his brothers grew alarmed and looked for a remedy. Doctors could do nothing, for they knew not the cause of his affliction. A foreign mage then appeared at court, claiming that he could definitely heal this patient. It was Jeropang, the magician! At his request, he was left alone with Frederick. He asked for a candle to be brought to him and pretended to examine Frederick before whispering in his ear: "You are racing to your ruin because of a woman. Do you want to die from love?" Frederick, too surprised to deny it, asked the doctor how he knew. "There are signs that never lie, which let me learn the cause of your illness," the man answered. "Tell me everything you have done! I can assure you of my complete discretion."

Putting his trust in the doctor, Frederick responded: "I am pining away for a maiden who lives in the forest. I am forbidden to look at her or speak about her."

"Lord, if you would follow my counsel," replied Jeropang, "you can see her secretly, while she is sleeping next to you. Here is a tinder for light. You can use it to contemplate her at your ease. Afterward, put it out and lie back down next to it."

"Master, your advice pleases me," said Frederick, and the hope the doctor brought to life within him restored his health. He got a little better every day and, once the twenty-three weeks had passed, he slipped away into the forest, pursued the doe, and came to the castle. Angelburg joined him and greeted him lovingly. But she was morose and fearful of some great misfortune. Frederick reassured her and boosted her courage. They talked until dawn; then Angelburg went back into the woods.

During the evening they conversed for a long time, until fatigue forced Angelburg to close her eyes. Frederick grabbed the tinder and made a light. He saw that Angelburg was a thousand times more beautiful than all the women he had ever seen, and it seemed that she shone brighter than the sun. He could not tear his eyes away from her, and he forgot to put out the light at the moment she awoke.[45] "Woe is us!" she exclaimed. "You shall never see me again, and you have plunged us into misery. I never could have imagined this. You shall pay for it with the loss of an eye. And I have lost all hope of ever being freed." Frederick's fear caused him to faint.

"Forgive me!" he said when he came back to his senses.

"My forgiveness shall not help a thing. We would have been reunited forever if only you could have stayed firm for eight more nights. Go back home; I cannot be of any help to you."

Frederick realized the immensity of his transgression, but taking courage, cried out: "I shall free you or die trying!" Having abandoned all hope, Angelburg responded: "Even if the whole world belonged to you, no one could tell you where to find me. I don't even know in what land stands the mountain that holds the fountain where I must stay."

"I will not give up, and I will risk body and soul to free you. Give me a farewell gift that will offer me hope of finding you again, if God wills it!"

"Take this gold ring. There is a stone set in it that will protect you from death if you are threatened by fire.[46] Keep it until the day you die."

Angelburg's two companions arrived and exclaimed: "Alas, my lord, what punishment we shall suffer because of your transgression."

"What are your names?" Frederick asked.

"My name is Malmelona, and I am a prince's daughter," replied the first.

"And I am Salme, the daughter of a count," the second replied. "I believe you are capable of freeing us, and I give you this ring that will confer to you the strength of three men."

Malmelona also gave him a ring with gemstones, telling him: "It will protect you from poison."[47]

"Despite all my sorrow, I will hold you in the bottom of my heart," were Angelburg's parting words.

"Knowing this consoles me, whatever my punishment will be. I will

never give you up! If I break my oath and fail to free you, may God abandon me!" And then his beloved vanished.[48]

When he returned to the castle, Frederick sought out his brothers and told them: "Let us divide up our father's legacy!" Although they were reluctant to do so, he forced them to submit to his will. He exchanged his portion for gold, then set off with thirty faithful servants in search of the clear fountain.[49] Everywhere they went, they asked about it, but in vain. Frederick's money dwindled away until there was little left and he commanded his servants to go back to the castle, and they had to obey. He pursued his route alone.

Penniless and destitute, he came one day to a city, in front of which a powerful army was camped. He asked the inhabitants, who had given him a friendly welcome: "Why is this army prepared for war?"

"My lord, we will lead you to Osann, our queen. She will tell you what you wish to know," they replied.

She was young and had no husband. She gave him a friendly welcome and asked him who he was and where he came from.

"My name is Frederick, and I travel the world in search of adventure. I have already seen many lands and shall continue until I die. If there were great deeds for me to perform somewhere, nothing could please me more. So what is that army before your city?"

"It is led by a cruel and powerful prince named Arminolt," Osann answered. "This traitor murdered my parents and is demanding that I give my inheritance to him.[50] My vassals refused and have decided to defend my kingdom. Arminolt then tried to take it by force and threatened to turn me over to his lackeys if he captured me. He now holds all my lands except for the capital, which he is besieging with his army. He comes to the gate every morning to shout: 'Surrender her to me, else I will put everyone to the sword!' This ignominious threat awoke a mad anger within me, and I have had it proclaimed everywhere that I shall give my hand to whoever will kill him in single combat. Whether the victor is of high or low birth, he shall rule over my country if he brings me back his head. Although many knights have heard my call, none have helped me yet."

"If you give me good armor, I will face Arminolt," said Frederick.*

Osann granted his wish at once. A short time later, Arminolt appeared before the gate and shouted, as customary, that Osann be surrendered to him. Frederick took her by the hand, went to find him, and said: "Give up your shameless claims and return Osann's lands to her. If you do not wish to make peace with us, return here tomorrow at the same time to face me."

As was to be expected, Arminolt chose combat. The next day, the space for the duel was marked off and the two foes rushed at one another. After a brief jousting match, Frederick unhorsed the prince, who remained prone on the ground senseless. Hardly had our hero set foot on the ground when the other stood up and hurled himself at Frederick with a sword in his hand. He was strong and valiant and pressed Frederick sorely, which caused anguish to Osann and her ladies. But casting a glance at the beautiful princess restored the knight's confidence. He remembered the ring that Salme had given him and, drawing on all its power, struck the buckler and breastplate of his adversary fiercely and turned the situation around. Arminolt cried out for mercy, but Frederick would hear none of it. He pounded him with blow after blow until Arminolt begged Frederick to spare him and make him his prisoner. He promised to return Osann her kingdom and to become her vassal. Frederick spared him and handed him over to the lady to do with as she pleased.

Great was her joy; she thanked the victor with her whole heart and

---

*This adventure marks the beginning of the hero's redemption.

offered him her hand and her dominion. "That's impossible," Frederick answered, "for you know full well that I have sworn to roam the entire world as a knight errant. I cannot now break the oath that I have kept during the darkest times, even at the cost of a magnificent reward. I must forswear you and your kingdom." Despite Osann's pleas, he remained firm, and it was much against her will that she agreed to let him leave, for she had fallen in love with him. So he set off, with his purse again well filled.

He traversed many lands, but his quest remained fruitless, and when his money was once again exhausted, he sank into poverty. However, no matter how impoverished he became, he never got rid of his fine armor, forged by the dwarfs, and he hid the rings that Angelburg and her companions had given him.

One fine day he came to the foot of a mountain covered with fir trees. He heard voices and headed in their direction, whereupon he found himself in a meadow in which the beautiful queen of the dwarfs,[51] Jerome, had set up her pavilion. When she saw the stranger approaching, she wondered what he wanted because he was in armor. "Fair lady, I have traveled through many countries in the pursuit of glory, for I have heard tell that it is through this that one can gain wisdom and find adventure." Jerome saw how pale and thin he was and realized that he was suffering from hunger. She invited him into her pavilion and offered him food and drink. Once he was sated, he looked visibly better. Jerome took a closer look at him and found him to be a handsome man. She could see no flaw, save that he was missing an eye, and found him to her liking. She invited him to follow her home and had him given a horse.

"If you are seeking wisdom, your oath shall be fulfilled, but know that I shall not force you to do anything," she told him.

"I will accept your invitation," Frederick answered. He followed her with no mistrust because he had no idea of her schemes.

When they reached the mountain where Jerome and her people lived,[52] Frederick was given a warm welcome, and, a short time later, she confessed her love to him: "I offer you my hand and my kingdom. You shall rule over all the dwarfs, my subjects." Frederick listened to

these words with no pleasure and replied: "I cannot accept, for my heart is already taken." Jerome was overcome by wrath as she felt offended. When he asked her to allow him to leave, she told him no: "You shall remain forever in the mountain," were her parting words.

To his misfortune he remained a prisoner and thought: "Alas, I cannot continue my quest nor keep my promise!" He fell ill, and the amusements offered him by the dwarfs failed to distract him. One of them realized the state he was in. Because he was good and loyal, he offered consolation, and Frederick asked him how he could escape. The other answered: "We don't know; only the queen knows how to open the mountain. We don't know how she does it. If she will not help you, you will never get out of here."

Faced with this situation, Frederick decided to attempt reconciliation with Jerome. He spoke friendly words to her and assured her that he had not intended to hurt her, but it was all in vain. He therefore finally decided to grant her his love. She kissed him and brought him into a chamber where they spent the night together. They made love, and Jerome ended up giving birth to a young girl who took after her father in size and who was given the name of Zipproner.

The queen had no suspicion that Frederick longed to escape, for he concealed his true feelings from her and did not reveal any of his intentions. However, he thought of nothing but his freedom, day and night. He could now move about through the entire mountain alone or accompanied by other dwarfs.

This was how he made his way into a chamber where he found a young maiden in chains, whom he asked: "Why are you a prisoner?"

"I must atone for a serious transgression," she replied. "I was the queen's favorite confidante, and I betrayed her. She owns a gem; if she places it upon the gate of the mountain, it opens,[53] and if one conceals the stone with his hand, it closes again. But this is the thing. The stone that I had to carry for her was heavy, so I suggested cutting it into three pieces. She agreed to my advice and gave me the task of having it cut, which I did, but into four pieces. I gave three back to the queen and kept the fourth. A dwarf prince named Tytrian sought the hand of Jerome, who turned him down. He then came up with a plan to steal her riches by force.[54] He convinced me to open the mountain by promising me a rich reward. At the agreed-upon time, he appeared at the gate with his army. I was wearing men's clothing so as not to be recognized, and I opened the gate with my stone. But only half of his army had entered when Prince Buktzinos arrived. He saw the mountain gaping open and blew his horn to summon Jerome's dwarfs to battle. There was a brutal battle in which he defeated Tytrian and captured him. Seeing that defeat was inevitable, I covered the stone with my hand and the gate closed again; I then hid the stone in a hole next to it and quickly returned to my chamber, where I put on my usual clothes. Tytrian was then given a choice: either denounce the person who had opened the gate, or die. He betrayed me. I am therefore held prisoner as punishment for my treachery.

"Does Jerome know that you kept a piece of the stone?" asked Frederick.

"She knows nothing of it and thinks that I used one of the three pieces she has, but the one I used remains in its hiding place."

"Tell me your name?"

"My name is Syrodamen, and I am the daughter of the powerful Count Sinofel," she replied.

Frederick now knew how he was going to make his escape. He did not change his attitude toward Jerome so that she would not have any suspicions. He sought out the stone in stealth and ended up finding it. He then decided to organize his escape. He wrote a long letter to Jerome in which he revealed who he was, where he came from, and his meeting with Angelburg. He added that he had sworn an oath to set her free and that he had to leave her, even though it caused him pain. He took one last look at his little girl, Zipproner, whom he loved tenderly, then opened the mountain and left, a free man.

When his road took him to the court of King Turneas, he offered his services. On the advice of Count Pirnass, the sovereign promised him a rich reward if he would fight the enemies of the kingdom. In fact, King Nemoras had invaded the land and laid waste to it. Frederick took leadership of the army and caused the enemy huge losses. He confronted the invader and used Salme's ring, for his foe possessed the strength of three men, and forced him to flee, but Nemoras swore he would return to seek his revenge. This victory earned our hero great prestige.

For six years he loyally served King Turneas until Nemoras put his threat into motion and returned to the country with a powerful army while Frederick was absent on a mission. Nemoras subjected the land to fire and blood and came before the capital of the kingdom. Every day he stood before the gates of the city and asked for a knight to come meet him in a duel, but, in fear of his great vitality, none dared to fight him.

Nemoras had just taken the gate when Frederick arrived after the successful completion of his task. He grasped the situation in an instant and ordered his companions to go into the city and announce his return to the king. They also were to tell him that he would not enter the city until he had defeated his enemy. He went to meet him and defeated him after a brutal attack, obliging him to leave the land and make reparations for all the wrongs he had caused.

After Frederick had served the king for ten years, the time seemed right to him to resume his quest for Angelburg. He asked to take his leave and to receive his reward, but Turneas refused to grant it and asked that he serve him for another eight years. Frederick could not get him to change his mind even when the count, Pirnass, stepped in and tried to make the king understand that he would dishonor himself if he did not keep his word and pay Frederick the price for his loyal service. Turneas would not budge an inch and granted Frederick a derisory reward.

"As you no longer wish to serve me, your sole reward will be the hide of a wild beast," he told him. "There is a deer that lives in that forest that my ancestors could never catch, she is yours!"

"You are taking advantage of the situation," replied Frederick, "and I regret having served you so faithfully. I am sure that not a single gentleman of this kingdom will approve of you."

"Frederick, my dear companion," said Pirnass, "if you need money, I will gladly give it to you."

The knight accepted and thanked him: "I will return it to you if I live long enough!" Pirnass provided him with all that he needed, and Frederick departed.

He entered the dark forest and contemplated: "Should I marry

Osann to end my poverty or else return to Jerome?" But the thought of his oath prevailed and he decided to continue his quest.

He suddenly encountered a doe that spoke to him in a human tongue.[55]

"Hail to you, Frederick! I now belong to you for your hard service, for Turneas has saved me. I would be glad if you granted me your friendship."

"You can be of no help to me," the knight replied. "Go where you would, it matters little to me! A doe has brought me much suffering, and I would rather I never met her. Because of her, I have lost my lands, my brothers, and my people. Life is now painful to me. God, when shall my misfortune come to an end?"

"Frederick, believe me, you no longer have any cause for worry. I will help you acquire goods and honor."

"How can I believe you? You are only a doe, even if you speak the language of men. What can I expect of you?"

"If you give ten years of service to me, and restore to me my freedom, I will keep my word."

"I will gladly grant it to you," replied Frederick.

The doe asked him to come near and embrace her. He obeyed, and she transformed into a beautiful maiden.[56] "Frederick, I would gladly give you my hand and all I own, but I know that Angelburg has won your heart. I also know that you have suffered greatly because of her, so I am going to help you. Take this plant! By placing it on your head, you will become invisible. I am also going to give you back your eye,

believe me!" She handed him the plant and he immediately could see from both eyes. "Frederick, do you see that mountain?" She went on to say: "That is where you must go. You will find a stone, and next to it a spring.[57] Sit down beside the stone and place the plant over your hair,[58] and wait there until noon. Three doves shall then come there who will disrobe and bathe in that fountain in human form.[59] Take their clothes and then remove the plant from over your hair so that they can see you. Let them say whatever they like and do not respond to their complaints, prayers, and tears. If they ask you for their clothes, demand that one of them marry you. May love not lead you astray before they have promised, otherwise bad luck and dishonor await you and that will put an end to all hope of deliverance for Angelburg."

When she stopped speaking, the knight asked her: "What is your name?"

"My name is Pragnet, and I am the daughter of King Persoloni. My stepmother transformed me into a doe.[60] If you need help or run into any danger, I promise to give you aid."

The next day, Frederick climbed the mountain and found the stone and the fountain. He sat down next to it, placed the plant over his head, and waited for the doves to arrive. They arrived at noon and changed into women, disrobed, and bathed in the spring. Frederick took their clothing and removed the plant so that they could see him. They grew scared and cried so much that, feeling sorry for them, he was ready to return their clothes to them when, by good fortune, he remembered Pragnet's warning in time.

Because Frederick remained silent, Malmelona said to him: "Dear companion, you should be ashamed for taking our clothes, we have done nothing to you. So give them back!"

"I will give them back if one of you promises to marry me,"[61] Frederick replied.

Malmelona called him a thief, then offered him rich rewards, all in vain. He persisted in his request. "If you don't want to make me that promise, I am going to leave and take your clothes," he said finally.

Because they did not recognize Frederick, they felt great distress, and Angelburg feared being parted from him forever, the man whom she hoped would find her again after all those years. Because they were unable to remain any longer in the cold water and were scared it would be their death, Malmelona responded, at Angelburg's command, that they were ready to grant Frederick's request. The one he chose would take him as her husband. He lay down their clothes and retreated, and, once they were dressed, he chose Angelburg, who was quite miffed about it, but kept her word. When the betrothals were over, Frederick more than happily shouted: "My sweet love, here you are free!" and he swooned from joy. While leaning over him, Angelburg spotted the ring that she had given him before parting on his finger. The scales fell from her eyes, and she recognized her beloved. The transition from the deepest sorrow to complete bliss caused her to lose consciousness. Malmelona and Salme also realized that they were free. With Frederick, Angelburg returned to the Shining Plain,* her mother's land.

There the lords of the land, with the support of the fathers of the two young girls who would have shared Angelburg's inheritance, kept their old promise. In the meantime, Salme's father had discovered the treachery of Flanea and recommended that she be imprisoned and killed. But Frederick knew full well that this latter would be doing all she could to contest Angelburg's right to her mother's country. "Go fetch my brothers so they can come help me!" he said. They gladly agreed, as did Osann of Brabant and Pragnet, to whom Frederick had also turned for aid.

---

*The name is that of an otherworldly kingdom.

The knight's forebodings proved justified. As soon as Flanea learned of Angelburg's deliverance, she complained to her husband: "Your daughter is slandering me," she told him.

"To ease your wrath, I shall send two counts there to claim souvereignty for myself over the Shining Plain," he replied. His emissaries departed but gave thought to the matter during their journey and came to the conclusion that Angelburg was in the right. Because the king was hesitant to take the country by force, Flanea summoned the magician Jeroparg, whose schemes had already caused her stepdaughter and Frederick so much misfortune. He told her: "He will have to wage three battles, one for each of the young women. I will face him myself and kill him thanks to my skill."

It was easy for Jeroparg to get around Turneas, who lived in fear of Frederick's vengeance since he had never fairly rewarded him for his service. On the other hand, Mompolier was hesitant to commit to action against his daughter, but his wife's insistence finally forced his hand. What more is there to say? The battle took place, and both kings were defeated and captured.

Thereupon, Flanea came to the battlefield, wailing and bemoaning the unfortunate situation of her husband. An unknown knight approached her and said: "Hail, gentle lady! Deign to tell me the cause for your suffering. If it is in my power, I will bring you consolation and comfort, or die."

"My husband is a prisoner; I have been accused of murder and treachery. That is the cause of my woe."

"I shall restore your joy for I am going to battle your adversary three times. Who is he?"

"A prince named Frederick of Swabia."

This knight was none other than the magician Jeroparg, who thought he would dispatch our hero easily.[62]

Through his artifices, he had changed his appearance,[63] and on the following morning, dressed as a manservant, he poisoned the drink that Frederick wanted to take before the duel. If it were not for Malmelona's ring that he wore on his finger and which gave him protection against poison, he would have died! Now Jeroparg had no advantage over him.

Their duel lasted until the fall of evening with no victor or loser. The next day, when the duel resumed, Jeroparg had acquired the strength of three men thanks to his magic, but Frederick, on the advice of Salme, was wearing the ring that granted him the same strength! Again this time, the magician was not able to prevail over him. The decisive battle would take place on the third morning.

They broke their lances and then faced each other with swords, breaking apart each other's shields. Jeroparg cast fire[64] at Frederick, who abandoned his spurs and would have perished were it not for the ring that Angelburg had given him. He made himself invisible with the help of Pragnet's plant, until he recovered his strength and vigor. Angelburg's tears gave him enough strength to prevail over his foe. He was preparing to deal his adversary a fatal blow when Jeroparg begged for mercy. "I am ready to confess who is responsible for all of Angelburg's misfortunes, but first you must capture Flanea," he said. She was captured, and the magician told them of all the crimes that both of them were guilty of committing. When he fell silent, everyone demanded that he be burned at the stake with his accomplice. Mompolier could count on Angelburg's generosity, because it was obvious that he had been deceived. She interceded with Frederick on his behalf so that he would pardon him and allow him to leave in peace.

Turneas was then hauled before the court, but Count Pirnass requested: "Frederick, be magnanimous! Think of all the help I've given you."

"We will spare him, if he abdicated," the knight replied. "I will even grant him a county."

Now that all danger had been averted, thoughts turned to the joining of Frederick and Angelburg in wedlock. Many guests were invited to the wedding and the festivities, which lasted for fifteen weeks. The jubilation was at its height when a strange event interrupted it.

Queen Jerome had never found consolation for the loss of Frederick, whom she had loved sincerely. She devoted all her love to giving their daughter, Zipproner, the best education. When the girl turned eight years old, she wanted to know what had happened to her father. At first, Jerome did not answer, but, faced with her child's insistence, she gave her the letter that Frederick had left for her when he fled the mountain. Once Zipproner learned the circumstances of her birth, she asked her mother: "Allow me to go join my father."

"I will grant you that," the queen responded.

Accompanied by twelve thousand dwarfs and twelve giants, richly supplied with gold and precious stones, Zipproner left her mother's home. Once she reached her destination, Prince Buktzinos went to Frederick to tell him that he had brought Jerome's daughter, and he introduced her to him immediately.

"I have come to show honor to you and to Angelburg," said Zipproner by way of a greeting, and she gave the latter a necklace of precious stones adorned with a magnificent carbuncle. She then gave Frederick splendid presents and asked him: "Do you truly wish to acknowledge me as your daughter?" He looked at Angelburg questioningly, who advised him to welcome his daughter with all the love that a child has a right to expect of her father. Full of joy, Frederick clasped Zipproner to his breast and kissed her.

"You are most welcome!"

"I promise to give you all my motherly love and to take care of you," added Angelburg while kissing her.

Frederick rewarded Malmelona and Salme by giving them rich marriages.

Once the festivities had ended, the guests took their leave and each returned home. The dwarfs and the giants went back to Jerome's mountain. Zipproner kept Prince Buktzinos and one hundred of his retainers by her side.

Frederick then ruled by his wife's side over her mother's land, the Shining Plain. They had a son named Henry, but nine years later, Angelburg fell ill and knew that her end was near. She summoned Frederick, her son, and Zipproner to her bedside: "Frederick, grant me one last wish," she said. "Leave the Shining Plain to your daughter; Henry will have my father's kingdom, and you, go back to Jerome's land and wed her, because Zipproner should not be a bastard and live in dishonor." She kissed all three of them and died.

Her husband remained inconsolable about her loss for a long time. His children finally told him: "End your mourning and ease your grief," but in vain. Every day he made his way to Angelburg's grave. Henry and Zipproner put their heads together to find a way to help their father find consolation and marry Jerome in accordance with the last wishes of his deceased wife. "It is not up to me to convince our father," said Zipproner. "That is your role." Henry badgered Frederick about this so insistently that he finally yielded to his arguments and sent Buktzinos to take a message to Jerome.

After receiving this message, Jerome fell prey to conflicting emotions: her wounded pride struggled with the love she still felt. But the love proved stronger, and she agreed to marry Frederick.

Accompanied by Zipproner and Henry, Frederick traveled to the mountain. Once they got there, his children presented themselves to Jerome first while he, completely contrite, followed behind. Jerome gave him her forgiveness, and their wedding was celebrated soon afterward. A son was born to them, a dwarf like his mother.*

The couple lived in joy and harmony, until the day when Zipproner and Henry were of an age to wed. Following Jerome's counsel, Frederick

---

*Whereas his sister is not a dwarf. This should come as no surprise because in its original usage "dwarf" does not connote a particular size for these beings (who, in fact, can adopt whatever size they please); it is a generic term referring to a race of fantastical beings.

returned to his country, where their daughter married a prince and Henry married a princess. Each took possession of the land bequeathed to them by Angelburg, and the son of Frederick and Jerome ruled over the mountain of the dwarfs.

I was able to recopy this tale in the year of the Lord 1478, during Pentecost in the pretty month of May, on the ninth hour, me, Jean, copyist in Geislingen.

FRIEDRICH VON SCHWABEN[65]

Written during the first half of the fourteenth century, this romance is literally exemplary, for it offers a clear model of the transformation of a story, that of "Cupid and Psyche," through a change of scenery (the world of chivalry) and by the introduction of elements taken from other tales and legends (Jerome's dwarfs, the bird-women, the magical objects). Nevertheless, the structure has not shifted, nor have the primary roles of the characters.

AaTh 400; 400 C; 401 A; 425 A

📖 BP III, 406–17; EM, s.v. "Martenehe, Die gestörte M," "Friedrich von Schwaben: Verwünschung; Schlangenkuss"; KHM, no. 193; Lecouteux, *Mélusine et le Chevalier au cygne;* Velten, "Le Conte de la *fille biche* dans le folklore français."

4. Aeneas, the Swan Knight

A very courageous young man* was crowned king on the death of his father. He married a beautiful woman who, to his great regret, remained childless. One day they were riding on a tour to comfort themselves by looking at their excellent lands, full of trees heavy with fruit and echoing with birdsong. They then caught sight of a poor woman who was going to baptize her twins.

"How is it possible for a woman to give birth to two children, without having known two men?" asked the queen.[66]

"By divine grace, a woman can conceive seven children with her husband at one time," the poor woman replied.

---

*He will be named later.

The following night, the king engendered six sons and a daughter.

The next day, while they were on their way to Saint Vincent Church, the king told his wife: "Rejoice because you are pregnant! God has granted our wishes." They listened to the Mass, and each of them placed a gold ring on the saint's altar and then gave alms to the poor when they left.

When the time came, Beatrix gave birth to six boys and a girl,[67] each wearing a silver chain around their necks. Her mother-in-law, the treacherous Matabruna,[68] who was highly versed in magic,[69] kidnapped them at once and left seven puppies in their place.[70] The midwife shrieked: "Oh, princess, what has happened to you! You gave birth to seven puppies. They must be taken away and buried to save your husband's honor!" Beatrix wept and wrung her hands in such a way that it would have moved a stone, but Matabruna shouted at her violently, accusing her of adultery, and then left the room. She summoned her faithful servant, Marc, and entrusted him with the seven babies, telling him: "The silver chains around their neck means they will become robbers and murderers; you must therefore hurry up and drown them." Marc wrapped them in his coat and made his way into the forest to slay them. But when they smiled at him, he took pity on him and left them there, entrusting their fate to providence. He returned to court, announced the death of the newborns to Matabruna, and she promised him a rich reward.

The diabolical Matabruna alerted her son to the monstrous birth, and he was terribly tormented by it: "I thought there could be no wife more faithful than she," he said. His mother recommended that she be bound and whipped, then cast into a marsh. He gathered his counselors to ask their advice. Some said that Beatrix should be burned at the stake and others wanted her imprisoned. Oraint followed this last advice because he still loved his wife.

During this time, the seven starving children began wailing at the top of their voice in the forest. A hermit heard them, found them, and brought them back to his hermitage, but he did not know how to feed them. A white doe arrived and offered her breast to the children, who nursed on it greedily. She came back every day until they were ten years old. Bareheaded and barefoot, dressed in leaves, the children ran through the woods.

A year later, Mauquarré,* a forester who was very close to Matabruna and the executor of all her vile deeds,† entered the hermitage and saw the seven children wearing silver chains around their necks. Once he was back in Bellefort, he told Matabruna what he had seen. She greeted this with surprise and guessed that they were Oriant's seven children under the protection of God. She immediately told him: "Return to the forest quickly, kill the children, and bring me back their seven chains as proof. If you fail to obey me, you will pay with your life; if you follow my orders, you will be richly rewarded." He returned to the forest and headed to the hermitage. Matabruna summoned Marc and asked him about the fate of the children; he confessed that he had not slain them. Mad with rage, she then gouged out his eyes.

Mauquarré reached the hermitage. The hermit and one of the children were absent. He drew his sword and cut the chains off the children's necks. They immediately transformed into white swans and flew away.[71] He brought the six chains back to the old queen, who hid them in a chest.

---

*The Latin text glosses Mauquarré with *malefactor*.
†The Latin text speaks of evil spells.

The hermit returned soon after with the young boy and grew alarmed when he did not find the other children. They looked all day with no success and returned home suffering greatly. The next day, the young boy went out to look again. He came to a pond in which six swans were swimming. They glided up to him and accepted his bread. From that day, he went to the pond every day to feed them.

Matabruna asked a goldsmith to melt the chains to make a goblet. When he melted the first chain, the silver began to multiply,* and so much so that it was enough for two. He gave one of the goblets and the other five chains to his wife to put aside and swore her to secrecy. He then brought the other goblet to the old queen, who exclaimed: "Now all my wishes have been granted! I have nothing else to fear!"

She then went looking for her son, and when she found him said: "You cannot remain in this position. Your cursed wife must be judged, otherwise you shall lose your honor. Condemn her to death; you will then be able to marry a lady of noble lineage. If not, fear my curse!" Oriant therefore convened a criminal tribunal.

Now let us return to the old hermit. When he was praying one night, he received a visit from an angel[72] who revealed the identity of the children's parents to him, and their abduction ordered by Matabruna, Marc's role, and the theft of the chains by Mauquarré. The angel then told him that Beatrix would be burned at the stake the following day, unless her son hastened to her aid.

"How could he help?" the hermit responded. "He does not know how to handle arms, ride a horse, or wield a sword."

"Don't worry," the angel replied. "Virtue always triumphs over evil."

The hermit could not sleep a wink that night from worrying about the boy, but placing his trust in the divine power, he woke up the child at dawn and told him: "You must go to the city and find weapons so you can protect your mother." Taken aback, the boy demanded an explanation, and the hermit shared the angel's revelations with him. "Before you go to battle, have yourself baptized and ask that you be given the name of Aeneas," he replied before leading him to the city. "Here is the

---

*One of the proofs of the supernatural ancestry of children.

place where your father lives and where your mother is undergoing great torment," said the hermit. "After you have been baptized, arm yourself and put your trust in God," and then he left.

When the people who had gathered to watch the execution saw the lad clad in leaves, his hair all shaggy, and carrying a staff in his hand, they thought they were seeing a madman. He saw the king on his horse and asked him innocently: "Lord, tell me what is this beast that carries you, for I have never seen anything like it." Oriant started laughing.

"It's a horse!" he said. "What is your name?"

"Handsome Son," the boy replied.

"What an astonishing answer! It distracts me from my cares."

"Tell me, what is the cause of your suffering?"

"My wife has committed a crime that she must pay for at the stake. She gave birth to seven puppies, ten years ago."

"My god!" exclaimed the lad. "That woman should not die, she is innocent. I am ready to fight against all those who claim otherwise."

Stunned, Oriant found it hard to believe his ears because the child looked more like a simpleton than a warrior.

The perfidious Matabruna arrived at this moment, driving Beatrix before her with blows from her whip. Oriant informed her of the boy's intention.

"My son, how can you believe the tall tales of this lunatic, this pauper?"

"I am not what you say I am, lady," the child replied. "I want to fight for the queen."

Matabruna, losing her mind, hurled herself on the lad and pulled out more than one hundred of his hairs, but the court and the people all yelled to Oriant that the trial by ordeal should take place and they wrested the boy out of the hands of the wicked old woman.

"Mother, now we shall see if you may be defending a bad cause," the king said.

She went off to find Mauquarré, ordered him to get equipped at once, and then knighted him. She turned toward her son and said: "My champion is ready. You will see that he defends a just cause, and I fear as much for his head as I fear for the dress that I am wearing."

The king asked the lad what he intended to do. "Sire, if I was ruler, I would cast your mother into the flames of an oven as punishment for her evil spells. My cause is good, but have me baptized so God can grant me his aid." Oriant therefore summoned a priest. At that very moment all the bells in Bellefort began to ring spontaneously and all gave thanks to God for this miracle. The child was baptized and named Aeneas.[73]

The wicked Matabruna said to her son: "Fool! Do you think this churl will have the strength and courage to fight? Before the day ends, you will see him without his head!"

"Perhaps," Oriant replied, "but if he defeats Mauquarré, you shall be burned."

The boy asked for armor and weapons, and two squires went off to fetch them. When they entered the armory, they stumbled upon a white shield hanging up, which was covered with gold and precious stones and bore a red cross in the center[74] with this inscription: "This shield is intended for the child Aeneas; it will protect and defend him as long as he carries it."[75] Oriant handed it to Aeneas with a smile and gave him a charger named Feran.[76]

During this time, Matabruna said to her champion: "You will easily bring me the head of this simpleton."

"Whether or not God wills it," Mauquarré replied, "he shall die an evil death at my hands!"

He struck Aeneas's shield, but a flame burst out of the cross that burned so hot he fell to the ground in a daze. Aeneas turned away from him, but, under the influence of the devil, his adversary recovered his spirits and, cursing dreadfully, yelled: "Turn around, traitor! Neither Christ nor cross can save you now; I am going to kill you," and their combat resumed. Mauquarré pounded the center of the cross with a mighty blow, but a two-headed serpent emerged from it and wrapped itself around him, tore out his eyes, and vanished. Aeneas realized that God had stepped in on his behalf, and he beheaded Matabruna's wicked minion. Matabruna then leaped upon her horse and fled to Montbrant Castle,* where she prepared it to withstand a siege.

---

*In other words, the Fiery Mountain.

The young boy presented Mauquarré's head to Oriant, who restored Beatrix to her former rank, and then he asked if anyone knew a blind man named Marc. Someone went to fetch him. "Have no fear," Aeneas told him, "for I know full well that you have saved my life," and he blessed him in the sight of all there. Immediately, a miracle occurred! God restored Marc's sight.

Oriant then asked Aeneas who his parents were: "I am your son," was his answer, and he related everything the hermit had told him. The goldsmith was present and heard this tale; he raced home and brought back the five intact chains and, kneeling before Aeneas, returned them to him while describing the evil actions of Matabruna.

With Oriant and Beatrix, Aeneas, followed by a large crowd, made his way to the shore and called the swans, who joined him in a merry beating of wings. He showed them the chains and placed them around the neck of each swan, and they regained their human form.[77] The sixth swan did not have his chain because it had been melted down; he fell to the ground weeping. Oriant and Beatrix were deeply distressed but found solace in the thought that five of their children had returned. They brought them back to the palace, clothed them, and then took them to be baptized. They were given the names of Johann, Oriant, Peter, and Samson, and the girl was named Rosula or Rosetta.

The elderly king—he was two hundred years old—had Aeneas solemnly crowned with the consent of both the gentry and the common folk. Aeneas told them of all of Matabruna's wicked deeds and asked all for their aid in exacting vengeance. They promised him as one.

One of Mauquarré's relatives who was there went to warn Matabruna. After she had heard his story, she drew out her dagger and murdered him. Her nobles observed that this was a detestable crime, but she replied: "Aeneas seeks my death, but if fortune smiles on me and he falls into my hands, I will tear out his heart!"

Aeneas lay siege to Montbrant. When she saw him, the abominable old woman shouted: "Son of a dog, vile rake!" to which he replied: "Thank you! God shall give you over to me. Now, you will not escape me." She only laughed. Aeneas succeeded in breaking into the castle but found himself cut off from his troops; he defended himself valiantly and was quickly rescued. Matabruna then suggested a duel, and he agreed. She opened her treasury and promised riches to whoever could slay her grandson. A man named Henry offered his services, claiming that he would return with Aeneas dead or alive before the nightfall, and he set out from Montbrant. The knight saw him and prayed to God to support his cause. An angel came down from heaven in the shape of a white dove; he comforted Aeneas and warned him of a trap that was being set for him. "Ten warriors are hidden in the woods to kill you." The hero alerted his men, whom he sent to wait in concealment, and then went to meet Henry. During the combat, he cut off his hand. Immediately, Henry's ten accomplices surged out of the woods, but Aeneas beheaded his adversary and then turned to face his attackers. He stabbed their leader through and then his own reinforcements arrived. Matabruna sent other sergeants against him, but only a few escaped death. Hot on their heels, Aeneas entered the castle and went into the chamber where the treacherous woman was hiding. She hurled herself at him and gave him a wound on his head with a swipe of her sword. He grabbed her by the hair and cast her to the foot of the stairs leading into the courtyard, so hard that she broke two ribs. Once she was captured, she called nobles and churls alike to hear her confess her crimes: "All my life," she told them, "I have never done any good deeds. I have been wicked and mendacious. I love neither God nor His Mother the Holy Virgin, and I have never shown them any devotion. I have brought harm to Beatrix, abducting her daughter and sons, and I wanted her to die. Never has any woman born of the race of Adam perpetrated so many crimes. I will not beg for divine mercy but place myself in the hands of the devil!" She was burned at the stake in the presence of all. Great jubilation then reigned over all the inhabitants, who were happy to be rid of her.

The following night, while Aeneas was in his bed thinking contemplative thoughts, an angel appeared.

"Are you sleeping?" the angel asked.

"No, I am awake. Who is calling me?"

"Me," replied the angel. "God has sent me to share with you His will. He commands you to go to the shore where you will find your brother the swan pulling a small boat attached to his neck. You shall climb into it and let him take you wherever he wishes."

"I am ready to obey, whatever the consequences," Aeneas replied.

He arose early to hear Mass and then announced to the court what God had commanded him to do. He gave the crown to his brother Oriant and told him to take charge of the kingdom and to look after his brothers and his parents. Beatrix gave him a golden horn enameled with niello with this advice: "Make good use of this! As long as you carry it, you will win all battles if your cause is just." She hung the horn around his neck and blessed him.

They all went down to the water's edge, and the swan came pulling a small boat. Aeneas climbed aboard the craft with his arms and enough food and wine for a month, and then, to the sorrow of all, the swan quickly swam away.

De milite de la Cygne[78]

This text, which is noteworthy for its incorporation of the tale of the swan-children into the legend of Lohengrin, as well as for its description of Matabruna, is one of numerous variants of the story of the Swan Knight. Its value lies in documenting the transformation of an old myth—that of the bird-women—into a fairy tale, hence the extraordinary details like the king who is two hundred years old but has an adolescent son. In their collection German Legends, *the Brothers Grimm followed another, more elliptical version of the tale.*

AT 313; 451 IV

📖 EM, s.v. "Lohengrin"; Grange, "Metamorphoses chrétiennes des femmes-cygnes"; Lecouteux, *Mélusine et le Chevalier au cygne.*

5. Helias, the Swan Knight

Once upon a time very long ago, Pyrion and Matabruna, his wife, ruled in Flanders over a kingdom named Lillefort, where the cities of Lille and Douai now stand. They conceived a son named Oriant. One day, while the son was pursuing a deer in the forest, the beast escaped him by leaping over a river, and the exhausted prince sat down next to a spring to rest. A noble maiden[79] then came up to him, who, when she saw his dogs, asked him: "Who gave you permission to hunt in my forest?" Her name was Beatrix, and Oriant was so overcome by her beauty that he declared his love for her and asked for her hand on the spot. She accepted, and he brought her to Lillefort to celebrate their joyful wedding.

His stepmother Matabruna came to meet them but was annoyed at his young fiancée, who arrived with her hands empty and whose lineage was not known to anyone. After some time had passed, Beatrix became pregnant. During that time, one day when she was looking out the window, she saw a woman going to have her twins baptized. She called Oriant to come and asked him: "How can a woman give birth to two children at one time without having known two men?"[80]

"With God's grace, a woman can give birth to seven children at one time," he answered.

A short time later, Oriant had to go off to war. He entrusted his pregnant wife to his mother and left. Matabruna, whose sole thought was how to cause Beatrix harm,[81] came to an agreement with a midwife to substitute puppies[82] for the newborns right after their birth. Matabruna would take on the responsibility for killing the children, then accuse the mother of having shameful relations with dogs.

Beatrix gave birth to six boys and a girl,[83] each wearing a silver chain around their neck. Matabruna abducted them straightaway and left seven puppies in their place.[84] The midwife cried out: "Oh princess, what has happened to you? You have given birth to seven horrible puppies. Let us carry them away and bury them so that your husband's honor remains unblemished!" Beatrix wept and wrung her hands in a way that would have aroused pity in a stone, but Matabruna violently shouted at her and accused her of vile adultery and then left the chamber. She summoned a faithful servant and entrusted him with the seven babies, saying: "The silver chains around their necks are a sign that they will become robbers and murderers, so you must hasten to eliminate them." Marc wrapped them in his cloak and made his way into the forest, where he planned to kill them. But when he saw them smiling at him, he took pity and set them down, entrusting them to providence.

He returned to the court and told Matabruna that the newborns were dead, and she promised him a large reward.

During this time, the now starving children were crying in the forest. Helias, a hermit, heard them, found them, and brought them back to his hermitage, but he did not know how to feed them. A white goat arrived and gave her teats to the children, who greedily suckled them. She came back every day until they were older. The hermit sewed them clothes made from leaves and raised them with the fear of God. He baptized them and gave his name to the one he liked best. Barefoot and bareheaded, wearing nothing but leaves, the children raced about the forest.

Oriant returned home victorious from the war and was greeted by lamentations: his wife had conceived seven puppies with a repulsive dog and they had been slain. His sorrow was great. He gathered his counselors to get their opinions. Some of them told him to burn Beatrix; others wanted to see her imprisoned. Oriant followed the latter suggestion because he still loved his wife. The innocent Beatrix was therefore thrown into the dungeon.

One day, one of Matabruna's hunters saw the seven children with the silver chains around their necks sitting beneath a tree from which they had been picking apples to eat. When they saw him, they fled to the hermitage, and the hermit begged him not to harm them.

Once he was back in Lillefort, Mauquarré told Matabruna what he had seen. She was astounded and guessed they were Oriant's seven children who had found protection from God. She told him at once: "Bring your men and return to the forest in all haste, kill the children, and bring me back the seven chains as proof. If you do not obey me, you will forfeit your life; if you follow my orders, you will be richly rewarded."

The hunter took seven men with him and returned to the forest. On the way there, they crossed through a village where a huge crowd had gathered. He asked why they had all gathered there and someone told him: "They are going to execute a woman who killed her child."

"Ah," said the hunter, "this woman is going to die for one child and here I am going to kill seven! Cursed be the hand that commits such a crime!"

"We shall not do any harm to the children," his companions told him. "We will steal their chains and bring them back to the queen as proof that they are dead."

They reached the hermitage; the hermit had gone out to beg for bread in the village and had brought one of the children to help him. They other six screamed with fear when they saw the strangers. "Have no fear!" the hunter told them. He and his men took the chains from the children's necks. In the space of an instant, they were transformed into white swans[85] and flew away. The hunters brought the six chains back to the old queen and claimed they had lost the seventh. Matabruna then asked a goldsmith to melt the chains to make her a goblet. He took one of the chains to see if it was of good quality. It grew heavier instantly and weighed as much by itself as the six chains all together had before.* He was dumbstruck and gave the five other chains to his wife to set aside. With the chain he had melted, he made two goblets, each one as large as what Matabruna had commanded him to make. He kept one with the remaining chains and carried the other to the old queen, who was quite satisfied with its weight and size.

The hermit returned a short time later with young Helias and became alarmed when they did not find the other children there. They looked for them all day in vain and returned home in great distress. Helias resumed his search the next day.[86] He came to a pond where six swans were swimming. They glided toward him and accepted his bread. Every day after this he returned to the pond to bring them bread. And time passed. . . .

During Beatrix's detention, Matabruna could think of nothing but getting rid of her once and for all. She produced a witness who claimed he knew the dog with whom the queen was alleged to have had relations. This wounded Oriant even more intensely. When the witness offered to prove his tale in a trial by combat,† the king

---

*All of these texts report that the gold began to proliferate, which is a sign of its supernatural origins.

†God's judgment is made evident through legal combat.

swore to execute Beatrix if no knight stepped forth to defend her. In great distress, Beatrix prayed to God, who heard her pleas and sent an angel to the hermit. The angel told him the entire story: who the swans were and what peril their poor mother was in. After hearing this news, Helias made his way to the court of the king—his father— barefoot and bareheaded, clad in nothing but leaves. The tribunal of justice had just assembled, and the traitor was ready to fight. Helias then appeared with his only weapon, a wooden club. He defeated his adversary and thereby proved the queen's innocence. She was freed immediately and was restored all her rights and rank. When the full treachery was made known, the goldsmith who had transformed the chains of the swans was summoned to come at once. He came with five chains and the goblet made with the sixth chain. Helias took the chains, impatient to free his brothers and sister. Suddenly six swans were seen landing on the castle's pond. Oriant, Beatrix, and Helias made their way there, while the people gathered on the banks to watch the miracle.

As soon as the swans saw Helias, they swam toward him. He stroked their feathers and then showed them the chains, which he slipped onto their necks, one after the other. They recovered their human forms in an instant,[87] and their parents hastened to embrace them. When the last swan saw that he remained alone and was not transforming, he began tearing his feathers out from sorrow. Helias wept and urged him to be patient as he consoled his brother. The swan bowed his neck as if to thank him, and all there took pity on him. The five children were taken to the church and baptized immediately. The girl was given the name of Rose, and the four brothers became valiant and pious heroes.

After these extraordinary events, Oriant entrusted his kingdom to Helias and the young king decided that justice should be done. He conquered the castle in which Matabruna had taken refuge and delivered her to the court, which condemned her to be burned. The judgment was carried out immediately.

Helias ruled for some time in Lillefort, but one day, when he saw his brother towing a little boat over the pond, he realized that this was a sign from heaven and that he should follow him in acquiring glory and renown. He called his parents together, revealed his plans to them, and Oriant gave him a horn, telling him: "Guard it well. Nothing will happen to all those who hear it."[88] The swan cried in a strange voice three or four times. Helias made his way to the bank, and the swan flapped his wings as if to greet him. The knight climbed into the little boat and the swan carried him from one river to the next until they reached the place ordained by God.

During this time, Otho I ruled as emperor of Germany, and the lands of Ardennes, Liège, and Namur fell under his authority. Otho held his court of justice in Nijmegen, where any who wished to lodge a complaint about a wrong could do so. The count of Frankenburg came before the emperor to accuse the duchess Clarisse of Bouillon of poisoning her husband and conceiving an illegitimate daughter when he was away on a crusade. The duchy should come to him by rights as he was the brother of the duke. The duchess defended herself as best she could, but the court decided to leave the judgment to God: she had to find a champion who would prove her innocence. She sought a savior—in vain. At that moment, all heard the sounding of a horn. Otho looked out the window facing the Rhine and saw the little boat pulled by a swan, in which Helias was standing armed from head to toe.

The emperor was quite shocked, and when the little boat touched land and the knight got out, he summoned him immediately. Clarisse saw him coming and told her daughter the dream that she had had the night before: "I dreamed that I was in a trial with the count of Frankenburg and condemned to be burned. But, just as the flames were surrounding me, a swan flew above me with water to put out the fire. A fish emerged from this water, which terrified everyone and caused all to tremble. So, I hope this knight will be our deliverance."

The swan-knight greeted Otho and said to him: "I am a poor knight who, seeking adventure, has come to offer you my services."

"Adventures! You are about to have one," the emperor replied. "There is a duchess here who has been condemned to death.[89] Be her champion and you shall save her if her cause is just."

Helias looked at the duchess, who seemed quite honorable to him, and at her daughter who was so beautiful that he secretly fell in love with her. In tears, Clarisse of Bouillon[90] swore to him that she was innocent. The duel took place, and the knight beheaded the count, thereby proving the duchess's innocence. Clarisse abdicated in favor of her daughter, whose hand she gave to Helias. The wedding was celebrated in Nijmegen in great splendor and then the couple returned to Bouillon, where he was warmly welcomed. Nine months later, the duchess gave birth to a daughter, who was given the name of Ida and who later would be the mother of gallant knights.

One day the duchess asked her husband: "Who are your friends and family? What country do you come from?"

"I forbid you to ask me this question,"[91] he replied. "Otherwise I will have to leave you."

She did not question him again, and they lived happily for six years.

Women always like to test a prohibition, however, and this was why the duchess questioned her husband one night when she was lying next to him: "My lord, I would really like to know where you come from."

Stunned, Helias replied: "You know I cannot reveal it to you. I will leave you tomorrow." Despite the tears and the pleas of the duchess and her daughter, he ordered his men to accompany them to Nijmegen and give them over to the care of the emperor, for he would never return. In the middle of this speech, the calls of the swan, overjoyed at finding his brother again, could be heard, and Helias leaped into the little boat.

The duchess reached Nijmegen with her daughter, and the swan soon arrived. Helias blew his horn, presented himself to the emperor, and told him: "I am compelled to leave this land, and I entrust you with my daughter Ida." Otho agreed. After bidding farewell to all and tenderly embracing his wife and daughter, Helias left.

The swan brought him back to Lillefort, where everyone, especially Beatrix, greeted him with joy. Helias's thoughts were dominated by how to free his brother the swan. He summoned the goldsmith and handed him the goblet with the order to make it into a chain like it had been before he melted it down. The smith did as commanded and brought back the chain. Helias slipped it over the neck of the swan, who immediately transformed into a handsome lad. He was baptized and named Aimeri.

DER RITTER MIT DEM SCHWAN[92]

The fairy tale has a happy ending. The end of the story is connected to Ida and clumsily solders the tale to the genealogy of the counts of Boulogne (Bonn in the text!), and the dukes of Bouillon, from whom Godefroy, the king of Jerusalem, is descended. The houses of Cleves, Brabant, and Boulogne claimed the Swan Knight as their ancestor.

AT 313; 451 IV; 762

📖 EM, s.v. "Lohengrin," "Schwanritter," Schwanenkinder"; Lecouteux, *Mélusine et le Chevalier au cygne.*

CHAPTER V

LICIT AND ILLICIT LOVE

1. Hero and Leander

A prince from over the seas had a son named Leander who was particularly handsome and noble. His castle was built on the coastline and, directly facing it, on the other side of this branch of the sea, was the castle of the most beautiful woman ever. She was sixteen years old and her name was Hero; she was so beautiful that no painter had ever managed to capture it: blond hair, dark eyebrows, light eyes, cheeks the color of roses, lips as red as rubies, teeth like ivory, a charming chin, and a throat and chest of dazzling whiteness. Hero and Leander were passionately in love but could only see each other if the young man swam over during the night, guided by the light that Hero placed in the crenels.

Things went on this way for some time, but one day the wind and waves were so strong that Leander did not dare to cross. Hero grew sad and wrote him a melancholy letter: "You can find distraction with hunting, the harp, games, fencing, and archery.* Alas, all I have is my old nanny to whom I talk about you day and night. I ask her: 'Nanny, what do you think Leander is doing at this moment?' 'Like a thief, he is slipping naked through the sea.' Then I ask her: 'Do you think he is halfway?' She gives me comfort and answers: 'He is drawing near!' 'When will he be here?' but she falls asleep and doesn't answer. I often embrace the garment you slip on after swimming, when I am lying in bed unable to sleep, and at dawn, when I finally fall asleep, I have a

---

*A pastime of courtly society.

happy dream—an illusion! I wake up even unhappier. I fear that you no longer love me. Return and dispel my worries."

A fisherman delivered the letter to Leander, who gave a great sigh and turned pale. He answered tenderly: "Hero, my love, my support, there is no joy without you; everything that is playful and happy here is naught to me but torment and grief; the separation seems to be seven years long. My sweetheart, I sorrow all day, and I cannot sleep at night. When I see your signal in the darkness, I wish for the night to be as sweet as the first night we met. I had no fear for my enflamed heart was so resolved that the chill of the waves was no concern. How clear it was that night! When I grew tired from swimming, I would reinvigorate myself by looking at your signal. The sea is certainly bad today, but I can no longer stay away from you and will come the next evening."

As night fell, he dove into the turbulent waters of the sea, but the storm grew harsher, thunder growled, and lightning streaked across the sky. The rain began pelting down more strongly. The swimmer could no longer see the beacon and, pushed by the wind and battered by the waves, he surrendered to the exhaustion that was overtaking his legs and hands and paralyzing his arms. "Woe is me, Hero, I am going to die! I have no fear of death, but I am so sorry that I have to leave you." He consigned his soul to God, and the waves swallowed him.[1]

When Hero learned of the death of her beloved, she collapsed in a lifeless heap, her heart broken, and joined him in death.

Hero und Leander (thirteenth century)[2]

The oldest version of this story is attributed to the Greek poet Musaeus (sixth century BCE). In it, Leander of Abydos has fallen in love with a priestess of Aphrodite in Sestos, and he drowns in the Hellespont. Recast by Ovid ("Heroides" 18–19), the story enjoyed a fair amount of success in the medieval West. Torquato Tasso, Clément Marot, and Christopher Marlowe all published their adaptations of this tale. It is an essentially literary tradition that ended up being transmited orally, and traces of it can be found in folk songs.

AaTh 666*

📖 EM, s.v. "Heron und Leander"; Lachman, *Sagen und Bräuche am Überlinger See,* no. 27, 52; Murdoch, "Die Bearbeitungen des Hero- und Leander-Stoffes"; Rosenmüller, *Das Volkslied.*

2. Zellandine, or the Sleeping Beauty

Once upon a time there was a knight errant named Troylus who was traveling in search of adventure. During his journeys, he came to an island on the Brittany coast and was given shelter in the castle of Lord Zelland. He became infatuated with the lord's daughter, the charming Zellandine, but, because he refused to stay in any one place, he resumed his journey a short time later.

The desire to see her again brought him back to Zellandine's country. Because he would not be able to reach her father's castle before nightfall, he stopped at the home of a noblewoman and learned what had happened to his beloved while he was away. "Lord," the lady told him, "a month ago, when she had retired to her chamber with her cousins after a feast, one of the girls gave her a distaff of linen and she began to sew. Hardly had she begun, when she fell into a deep slumber,[3] and since that time she has not awoken, nor has she eaten or drunk anything. Yet her beautiful coloring has not faded and everyone wonders how it is that she manages to live. It is said that the goddess Venus, whom she has always served, keeps her alive." The lady noted, from Troylus's reaction, that he loved Zellandine, and, because she intended the young woman for her own son, she cast a spell on the knight so powerful that it stripped him of his memory and when he came to Zelland's castle he had lost all his reason.

Zelland was rightly remaining in his palace, surrounded by the best doctors of the land, who were treating the beautiful Zellandine but not managing to find a cure. The castellan's jester noticed Troylus when he entered and examined him carefully, in the way that clowns do. He then told him: "Master, come and sit next to the others, for you shall cure the beautiful Zellandine."

Once he said that, he grabbed his side quite firmly. When Troylus saw that the jester was pulling on him this way, he disengaged himself so quickly that the man fell down. He had barely gotten back on his feet when he began his game again to lead him amid the doctors, who had withdrawn to deliberate.

When the castellan saw the two quarreling and Troylus refusing to obey, he wondered where he had come from and what his jester wanted of him. He heard him tell the stranger: "Come heal Zellandine!" He repeated his order several times and then, weary of this battle, he went to his lord and told him: "My lord, tell the other doctors to leave and take this knght, for he is the one to cure your daughter."

"Away with you!" retorted Zelland, who gave little credence to these words.

"What? You don't believe me!" the jester replied. "Know that none other but this person will be able to cure her, for he alone possesses the remedy."

Irritated by his failure, the jester left the premises. Nevertheless, Zelland went up to Troylus and asked him: "Where do you come from? Where do you live?" Bewitched as he was, Troylus answered with such inanities that Zelland took him for a simpleton and returned to the doctors to learn what they advised. "We know of no remedy for your daughter's illness," they told him, "for it is not of natural origin. Have her carried away and confined in your old tower, and then await the will of the gods whose ways are secret."

Realizing that he would not receive any better counsel, Zelland became quite disturbed by it but followed his doctors' advice. He thus decided to lock Zellandine away so that no living thing could approach her,[4] except himself and his sister. He had her carried up to the highest chamber in the tower and placed on a splendid bed. He had all the entrances walled up with the exception of a window facing east so its light would fill the room. He visited once a day with his sister to see if the gods had shown any pity toward his daughter. But each time, they found Zellandine in the same state, neither better nor worse. For his part, Troylus had remained at the castle without having regained his senses.

One day Troylus and Zelland went to the temple of the three goddesses to pray. Troylus fell asleep, and his companion left him there. At midnight, a female silhouette appeared to him, the goddess of love in person, who touched his eyes and thereby restored his memory and reason. His beloved lady came into his mind at once, his love for Zellandine awoke him, and he decided to set off in search of her.

He made his way to the tower where he learned that she was sleeping. He tried in vain to climb it but abandoned his attempt with a heavy sigh. A page came up to him: "I know that you are Troylus and that, encouraged by Venus, you desire to enter this tower. If you wish to succeed, leave it to me." Seeing that the page could cross a stream without getting his feet wet, Troylus decided to trust him. This page, who was none other than Zephyr,[5] the servant of Venus, ordered him to climb onto his shoulders and he then carried him up to the window at the top of the tower. "Spend the night with Zellandine," he told him, "and I will come to fetch you tomorrow morning." Troylus entered the chamber of the sleeping beauty and lit a candle he found next to the bed. Enchanted by the young woman's beauty, he showered her with kisses, yet she did not stir or wake up.

Encouraged by Venus, he grew bolder and bolder and finally shared Zellandine's bed with her. In the morning Zephyr returned and Troylus had to slip away because the steps of Zellandine's aunt could be heard on the staircase. He quickly exchanged his ring with that of his sweetheart and then set off in search of new adventures. Because she caught a glimpse of his shining armor, the aunt believed that Mars, the god of war, had slept with her niece. She made the bed and left the tower, keeping that secret to herself.

Zellandine continued to sleep in her bed without receiving any other visitors but her aunt. A little goat's milk, which the good old woman dripped between her lips, was her sole nourishment. After nine months had passed, she gave birth one evening to a superb baby boy. This was when her aunt came to see her, as she did every day. When she came to the foot of the bed, she found a handsome baby lying alongside his still sleeping mother and was greatly astonished. When trying to nurse, the newborn seized Zellandine's little finger so hard that he coughed. The aunt was moved to pity at this sight, took the child in her arms, and said: "Alas, little creature, this cough is no surprise because there is no possibility that what you are trying to nurse on will give you any nourishment."

Thereupon the young mother awoke.

"Zellandine, my dear niece, how are you?" asked the aunt. "Speak to me!"

"Dear aunt, yesterday I went to sleep in good health and today I feel sick; I don't know what happened to me."

"No, it was not yesterday; it has been much longer, for you have been sleeping for nine months and you have been carrying this beautiful baby, which you gave birth to today. But I don't know who the father is."

These words plunged her into unspeakable astonishment; she began to weep because she could not remember any man touching her. Sympathetically, her aunt spoke to her: "Don't cry. I am going to tell you the story. The god of war, our ancestor, visited you secretly. He did so to restore your health and to ensure that our lineage does not die out. He conceived this beautiful child[6] who made it possible for you to wake up. So thank him and be grateful! Have no worries; I shall keep your secret."

When Zellandine learned the details of her adventure she wept for a long time. "Don't worry; you can place your trust in me," her aunt said, "because I am going to take your son to a place that is so secret that nobody will ever know any of this until it pleases the gods to reveal all. As consolation, I am going to tell you the story that surrounded your birth.

"Know that you will no longer suffer the wrath of the goddess of fate; she was present at your birth. That same day, your mother had asked me to prepare a chamber for the three goddesses who come following a birth.[7] I set the table and put out food and drink,[8] as is proper, and placed a plate, wine, and bread at the place of each goddess, then sealed the chamber and remained at the door to listen. Lucida, Themis, and the beautiful Venus[9] then arrived, but Themis, who rules our destinies, did not have a knife because it had fallen beneath the table. Thus, she did not eat as well as her companions. When everyone had eaten their fill, Lucida said: "Ladies, we have been given a good welcome, I have therefore made it so this child will be born healthy and grow up, but that depends on you, Themis." "Of course," Themis responded, "but because I had no knife a splinter shall enter her finger when she spins flax for the first time.[10] She will fall asleep and only awaken when the splinter has been removed by suction."[11] When Venus heard these words, she said: "Lady, you are angry and this saddens me, but, through my art, I will make it so that this splinter is sucked out of her finger."[12] Then the three ladies vanished, and I know not what became of them. That, my niece, is what I remember. Take comfort, for you are an heir to Mars!" the aunt concluded while remaking Zellandine's bed.

She then saw a wondrous bird come through the window;* it was a woman from the chest up to the top of its head. Once it had entered the chamber, it went to the bed where the infant was lying, took the child into its arms, spread its wings, and flew away. . . .

PERCEFOREST (LL. 1337–1390)[13]

This is the oldest version of the story of "Sleeping Beauty."[14] It forms only a single episode in Perceforest, *a long, anonymous romance written circa 1340. It is divided into ten books that tell the history of England from the time of Alexander the Great. By sucking Zellandine's finger, the child sucks out the splinter and ends the curse cast by Themis. By comparing this passage of* Perceforest *to Charles Perrault's (1628–1703) version of the story, the long journey that the tale undergoes will become apparent. But Perrault was inspired by "The Sun, Moon, and Thalia," a story from Giambattista Basile's* Pentamerone *(1634), in which we again find the*

---

*It is the sprite Zephyr transformed.

motif of the child nursing on the finger that removes the splinter of flax responsible for the long slumber.

Once upon a time there was a lord who had a daughter named Thalia. He invited all the seers and scholars of the kingdom to draw up her horoscope. All of them were in agreement that the child would face great peril one day because of a splinter of flax. To prevent this misfortune, her father forbade that any flax or hemp, or anything like them, be allowed to enter the house.

One day when Thalia had nearly grown up to be a young woman, she was at the window and saw an old woman pass by who was spinning. As she had never seen a distaff or spindle, she found what the old woman was doing quite attractive. She felt such keen curiosity that she invited the woman to come up to her chamber and then took her distaff and began to roll out the thread. Unfortunately, a splinter of flax went under her fingernail, and she fell down as if dead upon the ground. On seeing this, the old woman tumbled down the stairs. The poor father, when learning of this, paid for this pail of bitterness with a barrel of tears. He then had his daughter taken to a castle in the countryside and sat her on a velvet seat beneath a brocade canopy, after which he sealed the doors, and, so as to forget his misfortune forever, he abandoned his palace for all time.

After a fair amount of time had elapsed, while the king was out hunting, a falcon escaped and perched on a window of the castle. The king went to retrieve his bird and, thinking there were people there, ordered someone to knock at the door. After their knocking went unanswered, he took a harvester's ladder so he could enter the dwelling himself and see what was inside. He climbed up immediately and walked all about and was greatly surprised to find not a single living soul.

Finally, he came to the chamber where Thalia was, as if bewitched. At first glance, the king thought she was sleeping and called her, but he was unable to wake her up, no matter what he did. Because he was smitten with her beauty, he carried her bodily to a bed.* There he left

___
*A euphemism to indicate he slept with her.

her sleeping and returned home to his palace, where he promptly forgot this entire adventure.

Nine months later, the young woman gave birth to twins, a boy and a girl, who were like two jewels. They were raised by two fairies who would enter the palace and place them at their mother's breasts. One day, when they wanted to nurse and could not find her breasts, they grabbed her finger and sucked it so hard that they pulled out the splinter.

Their mother emerged from her deep sleep, saw these two jewels at her side, nursed them, and felt they were as dear to her as her own life. However, Thalia did not know what had happened to her, or why she was all alone in this palace with two infants beside her, or how food was brought for her without her ever seeing anyone. . . .[15]

A<small>A</small>T<small>H</small> 410

📖 BP 1, 434–42; Basile, *Pentameron,* V, 5; EM, s.v. "Schlafende Schönheit," "Zauberschlaf," "Perceforest"; Grimm, KHM, no. 50.

3. Crescentia I

Narcissus, the emperor of Rome, had two sons of his wife Elizabeth and named both of them Dietrich.[16] The parents died prematurely, and the pope decided that the brother who was first to marry would become king. Both became knights and both aspired to the hand of an African king's daughter, the beautiful Crescentia, and the senate gave her the right to choose one of the two brothers. One was gracious, well formed, and called the handsome Dietrich. The other brother, conversely, was swarthy and ugly, and called the unsightly Dietrich. However, it was this latter brother that the young woman chose, and he was crowned king of Rome. He defeated the Normans and then wished to travel across the sea to wage war against another monarch. His vassals advised him to leave the queen in the care of her father, for they feared that his wife would be stripped of the kingdom if he died. Unsightly Dietrich shared this plan with his wife, who told him: "I cannot refuse to go wherever you wish to send me, but I would rather die than suffer the shame of being sent back to my homeland. My father has it in for me because he believes I deserve it for my bad behavior. Lord, abandon this plan!" She then advised her husband to entrust the regency to his brother and to place her under his protection. This was done, and the king left.

The handsome Dietrich, blinded by the devil, aspired for Crescentia's* love, who answered through her tears: "What are you thinking? You know I am your brother's wife. This would be shameful and I would rather die."

"I will get my revenge, if I can," replied the treacherous brother, "for you humiliated me by choosing my brother when I am handsome and valiant. You will pay for that if you don't change your mind, and it shall be you who knows dishonor!"

So Crescentia pretended to accept and commanded him to build a solid tower that would protect her from the wrath of the Romans and to supply it with every necessity, as well as a chaplain and many relics. One night she accompanied him to the tower and had him go in first, and then locked him inside.

"Alas, I am a prisoner," he cried. "Free me so that I don't vanish from the world. I swear I will never attack you! I no longer want you for my wife."

"I pay your oaths no heed. You have bread, wine, a good bed, relics, and everything else you might need. You shall wait here for my husband to return."

No one had any idea of what had happened.

After three years, messengers arrived at the beginning of winter to announce the return of the emperor. Crescentia released her brother-in-law from the tower and promised to keep her silence, and then gave him an official welcome. When asked where he had been all this time, handsome Dietrich responded that he had been held captive far away. She then begged him to go meet her husband.

Handsome Dietrich, the betrayer, gathered twelve of his vassals and promised them money if they helped him. Raising their hands, they promised they would. He then told them what Crescentia had done and

---

*It was Milon who threatened her virtue, and the pope had him imprisoned inside a tower.

beseeched them to confirm everything he would say, as if they had been witnesses.* All of them protested, and the wisest of them urged him to abandon his plan. He was unable to dissuade him, and they resigned themselves to obeying. When he saw his brother, unsightly Dietrich asked him: "How is my dear wife doing?"

"She has behaved very badly,"[17] handsome Dietrich replied, "and I am too ashamed to talk about it. So question these men."

"Brother, can I keep her at my side in honor? If her misconduct is too serious, I do not wish to return to Rome."

"She pushed lust so far that she gave herself to everyone who came to court."

Weeping, the emperor, cried out: "If only I had never met her!"

"Don't be angry at yourself, brother, and turn your thoughts to punishing her. Command her to be hung, stoned, or drowned at the bottom of the sea for her treachery."

"Do with her as you please. I don't care, and I don't wish to see her again."

The traitor therefore immediately sent two sergeants to tell Crescentia her fate while she was outside with her serving women, and all began to lament. The sergeants would have gladly spared her life, but she said: "You must obey your lord. Ladies, cease with your tears!" She removed her headdress and gave it to a serving woman, saying: "Wear this out of love for me! What pleases God must be done." She was bound and cast into the water from the top of a bridge.[18] The current carried her to shore where a fisherman pulled her from the water. Immediately, both the Dietrichs were struck with leprosy and became paralyzed, dumb, deaf, and blind.[19]

The empress told the fisherman: "I am a poor woman. Do you need a servant?" When he returned to the duke's court empty-handed, he was about to be beaten when he explained that he had caught a woman and not fish. He was ordered to present her to the duke, who, though he had met her at court, did not recognize her because she had been transformed

---

*This is in keeping with judicial criteria: an accusation was only valid if twelve witnesses could be produced.

so dramatically by grief. He questioned her, and she replied: "I wanted to go to Rome, but the boat sank." Thinking she must be the victim of a shipwreck, he entrusted her to his wife, who welcomed her kindly and he charged her with the responsibility of teaching their little boy, and even asked for her counsel and entrusted her with the key to the treasury. Jealous of the lady's influence, the vidame of the court thought to himself: "If I can win her over to me, she will get me silver and gold; if she rejects me, I can see to it that she falls out of favor with our lord." He let her know through a serving woman that he desired her. Spurned, he called her a witch before all the other women, and people were hard put to prevent him from abusing her. Seeing that he could not avenge himself this way, he left in a fury with a sputter of threats. Crescentia lamented but, in spite of the advice of the women present, did not tell the duke about it, not wishing to bother him with her troubles. The vidame had a key made for the room in which she slept with the child. Then this dog, this traitor, gently opened the door and took advantage of the noise produced by a strong gust of wind to behead the child with his sword;[20] he then he placed the head in Crescentia'a lap before going to wake up the duke to hear matins. The duke confessed his surprise that his son's tutor had not gotten up in time. So he sent the vidame to fetch her.

The vidame yelled: "Everybody up! The murderess has killed the child, what a pity to see this!" Everyone rushed over and found Crescentia covered with blood. The traitor approached her and struck her on the mouth so hard that she began bleeding, and then shouted at her: "You are going to die and go back to where you came from!"

"You have betrayed my trust," added the duke. "What have you avenged yourself for? Haven't I rewarded you sufficiently?"

"I am lost," Crescentia exclaimed, "but I have no fear of death! I am innocent, although no one can prevent you from doing whatever you please to me, if God so wills."

"How dare you reply!" screamed the duchess. "Let her be drowned at once!"

"Even if we kill her, that will not bring our son back," the duke said. "Let us allow her to leave."

"She must have bewitched you," cried the vidame. "Do with her what you will."

Then, when all were asking for her to be shown mercy, this demon struck Crescentia with his fist, grabbed her by her hair, and dragged her from the room, kicking her before him while shouting: "Vengeance! You will never bewitch anyone again!" Crescentia sighed deeply and called to God: "Lord, receive my spirit, You know that I am innocent." This dog of a vidame hurled her into the river with howls of joy. God punished this injustice: just like the duke, he was paralyzed by gout and stripped of all his senses.

The current carried the empress away and three days later deposited her on a small island. Saint Peter appeared to her over the water, took her by the hand, and led her to the shore without getting his feet wet. He then commanded her to return to the duke and gave her the power to heal everyone who publicly acknowledged their sins.[21] Crescentia therefore returned to the castle that very day; no one recognized her, and she told no one her name. When she was asked if she knew a doctor, she replied: "Take me to your lord, so that I can see if he may be healed." She was led to the duke's bedside and informed: "He has been in this state for three days and doesn't eat; we know that he is alive because he is breathing." Crescentia invited the duke to confess his misdeeds, and he yielded to her request. She commanded him to rise, but it was too painful. "Your sins are are weighing you down," she told him. "It seems that you have not confessed everything to me." Weeping, the duke stated that he had allowed his son's tutor to be cast into the water, and he was healed at once.

He begged her to take care of his vidame, promising her gold, silver, and jewels. "I am not annoyed with him," replied Crescentia. "Let someone take me to him." He refused to publicly admit the murder of the child. Crescentia therefore spoke to the duke.

"He must have wronged you in a way that he doesn't wish to acknowledge."

"What could that be?" wondered the duke. "I have never liked anyone as much as him, and I am prepared to swear that he has never caused me any suffering."

The vidame confessed to killing the child, and, despite the healer's intercession,[22] the duke had him cast into the water.

He then begged Crescentia to heal the emperor.

"Our Lord has sent you to bring us comfort. Heal him and it will be an honor for you."

"Know that God is the doctor," she replied, "and that I draw my power from him."

They left for Rome, where she was warmly received. When Crescentia saw her husband, she burst out sobbing and said: "What did you do? Acknowledge it before all and God shall deliver you from leprosy." Unsightly Dietrich did this, but it was in vain, for he did not speak about his wife. Crescentia urged him to reflect, and he confessed that he had ordered her to be drowned and he was healed at once.

"I have a brother who suffers from the same affliction," he told her.

"Lead me to him!"

Despite the wrongs he had done to her, she ordered handsome Dietrich to confess his sins aloud; he refused at first but then consented and was healed. When they heard his confessions, the Romans wanted to take him to be drawn and quartered, but Crescentia interceded with his brother on his behalf. "I will follow everything you advise," he told her.

The emperor's heart told him that the healer was Crescentia. Once he had promised to grant her everything she asked, she revealed her identity to him. A quick slash of her shirt with a knife revealed a small cross that proved her identity. The sovereign fell to his knees and their joy was great. After a period of eight days, a large feast was organized at the court with all the nobility. Crescentia presented herself before her husband, reminded him of his promise, and demanded they both retire from the world to dedicate their lives to spiritual pursuits and the building of churches and monasteries. Speechless with surprise, unsightly Dietrich still kept his word. Crescentia assumed the life of a recluse in a hermitage, and handsome Dietrich became emperor.

Kaiserchronik (The Book of Emperors; ca. 1150)[23]
AaTh 712; TU 1,898

4. Crescentia II

Emperor Octavian loved his wife above all else because she was faithful, beautiful, and obedient. One night, the idea came to him to go to the Holy Land. The next day, he summoned his brother and the empress and told them: "Beloved, I wish to leave on a crusade and leave the kingdom in your hands, for I have complete trust in you. My brother will help you at every opportunity and, until my return, he shall be at your command." The emperor took his leave and began his journey. The empress then ruled with great intelligence.

Her brother-in-law became violently infatuated with her and felt that he would die if he could not satisfy his desire. One day, when she was alone, he confessed his mad love for her. She violently reproached him, saying: "How dare you urge me to sin, especially as I am your brother's wife?" Peeved, he withdrew, but he continued to bother her day after day. When she realized that he was obsessed and would never give up, she had him tossed into the dungeon, where he remained until the emperor returned.

When the prisoner learned that his brother was coming back, he thought: "If he finds me here, he will ask my wife for the reason; she will not hide the truth from him, and it will be my death." He sent the empress a request to visit him so he could talk with her. When he saw her, he said: "Dearest lady, take pity on me. If my brother finds me in the dungeon, I am ruined. Please let me go."

"Promise me that you have mended your ways, and I will free you," she replied, and he swore to it.

She had him freed immediately and bathed, shaved, and newly clothed. She then told him: "Get on your horse and come with me to meet your lord."

While they were crossing through the forest, they came upon a stag. All the men and women in their retinue set off in pursuit of it, and the empress was left alone with her brother-in-law, who said: "Dearest lady, we are alone; respond to my desire! I wish to sleep with you,"

"I have promised God that no one will ever touch me but my husband," she retorted.

He tore off all her clothes except for a shirt and hung her

from a tree by her hair. He left her that way, took his horse, and went back.

On the same day a duke was hunting in the woods, accompanied by dogs that had flushed a hare. When they came close to the tree where the lady was hung, they caught wind of her smell and came to a stop until their master arrived. Seeing such a beautiful woman hanging there, the duke asked her: "Lady, who are you and what are you doing there?"

"God knows who I am. I am here by the fault of an evil man. For the love of God, free me!"

"Gladly! I shall bring you home with me; I wish to entrust my little girl to you to raise and educate, for you are clearly a woman of noble birth."

Brought back to his castle, she had to share a room with the duke, the duchess, and their daughter. Everyone loved her.

A knight of noble lineage but evil character lived in this castle, for which he was the seneschal. He became inflamed with passion for the lady, offered her all his goods, then revealed his heart's secret to her. She cursed him and cried out: "I swear by God that none shall take his pleasure of me but the one whom God wills." The seneschal felt humiliated by her words and was rankled. From that moment on, his sole thought was how to do harm to the woman.

One night the door happened to remain open to the chamber where the duke, his wife, his daughter, and the lady were. Then, when all had fallen deeply asleep, the seneschal entered the room, slit the child's throat, and put the bloody knife in the hand of the lady, as if he wished to say: "Your hand proves that you are a murderess." He left her hand hanging outside the bed and vanished.

A short time later, the duchess awakened and saw the arm in the light of the lamp that burned every night. In terror, she woke up her husband. He got up and asked his daughter's tutor: "Tell me, did you slay my child?" Horrified, she grabbed the child and discovered her throat had been slit and screamed: "Alas, sire, take pity on me! I am innocent and have no idea who committed this crime without my knowing. God knows how this knife ended up in my hand."

When the duchess realized that her child was dead, she screamed: "Lord, hang her from the gallows for it was she and no one else who murdered my daughter, otherwise she would not be holding a bloody knife!" Turning to the empress, the duke told her: "I shall not do you any harm; take your horse and flee, quickly!" Upset and dejected, she left the room and fled.

After she had been riding for three days, she saw seven men who were leading someone to the gallows. She spurred her horse forward, caught up to them, and asked: "Tell me, what has this man done that deserves hanging?"

"He is a thief and a robber!"

"I will purchase his life from you."

"Agreed!"

She gave them their money, took the man, and then told him: "My friend, I have saved your life; be my loyal servant and you shall be rewarded." He gave her his word. As they were nearing a city, she sent him to find lodging, which he did. The inn he had chosen was pleasant, and she spent seven days there.

In the meantime, a boat laden with precious cloth and merchandise had come to shore near the city. The lady learned of it, and she sent her servant to do reconnaissance. What he saw pleased him greatly, and he informed his mistress about it. The boat's captain presented several objects to the lady. After spending several hours with her, he succumbed to her charms and would have given her his entire cargo if she yielded to him, but he did not betray his feelings at all. After bidding her a courteous farewell, he returned to his boat. The next day, wishing to look at his cloth, the empress ordered her servant to forewarn the captain.

"My friend," the captain told the servant, "I will reward you if you inspire your mistress to come onto my ship in person."

"Pay me and you can rely on me! Once she is there, you can do as you will."

The captain remunerated him richly.

On his return, the servant told his mistress: "The captain begs you to come in person to see the cloth in his boat." Naively she went there. Once she was on board, her servant snuck away. The captain took advantage of a rising wind to hoist his sails and set off. The lady asked him: "What do you have in mind, my friend?"

"I am abducting you so that you can share my bed."

"I will not permit it!"

"You have a choice: either submit or I will throw you overboard."

"Since that is the way it is, make a bed for us where no one will see us."

So the captain had a bed set up at the stern. The empress got down on her knees and begged for help from heaven. A violent storm broke out, breaking the ship in two. Everyone perished except for the lady and captain, who were able to make it to shore by clinging to a spar.

The lady then spotted a cloister in the distance and made her way there. She asked for shelter, and the nuns humbly took her in. From this day on, she lived with them and was liked by all. In a truly short time, she learned the properties of plants so well that all those suffering from illness came to her for healing, and her renown spread across the land.

During this time, all those who had assaulted and humiliated the lady had become afflicted with a variety of ills. Leprosy struck her brother-in-law, then the seneschal came down with gout and became paralyzed.[24] The man she had saved from the gallows became blind and mute, and the captain, who had wanted to rape her, suffered from dropsy and scabies.[25] All of them, having heard tell of the lady's healing skills, showed up one day at the cloister. They did not know the healer was the empress, believing that she was long dead.

When she was summoned to see the emperor, she hid her features.

"Dearest lady, place your hand on the brother who has leprosy," he said to her, "and there are other patients who are awaiting your assistance."

"Lord, I am ready to obey you in all ways, but I warn you that my care can only help those who have confessed everything before those of good heart."

"Who would be mad enough to refuse that!" the emperor exclaimed. Turning toward his brother, he urged him to confess all his sins.

His brother acquiesced, but he said nothing about the crime of hanging the empress by her hair. She then addressed the monarch: "Lord, I am going to administer the remedy to your brother, but it will only work if he makes a complete confession." The remedy had no effect.

The emperor then asked his brother: "Why don't you openly admit what you did?"

"Sire, I cannot do so until you promise not to hold it against me."

"Cursed rascal! What, then, could you have done for you to demand impunity? Tell me, and I promise that you will not have to suffer for it."

Before everyone there, the brother told of what he had done to the empress.

Upon hearing these words, the emperor exploded in rage. "You out-and-out traitor! You told me she had died suddenly in the forest. I regret that I promised you impunity; otherwise I would slay you with my hands. Scoundrel, had you no fear of God when hanging my chaste wife?"

Then the knight who had murdered the duke's daughter confessed to his crime.[26] "My master found a woman who had been hung by her hair and brought her back home with him and entrusted the education of his only daughter to her. I fell in love with her." And he confessed to the murder.

Then it was the criminal's turn to speak. "So when I was about to be hung, a woman riding by herself paid for my life. An ingrate, I handed her over to the captain of a ship."

The captain then acknowledged: "A noble lady was placed in my power. I wanted to sate my desires to possess her, but a storm sank my boat and I was the sole survivor. I do not know what became of her."

After all these confessions, the lady turned to the emperor. "Sire, all these men have openly revealed their misdeeds." She gave them the remedy, and they were healed at once. Then she resumed: "Lord, would it not make you happy to find your wife again, your wife who suffered so much torment in order to remain chaste?"

"Of course, that is my dearest wish, because I love her as I love myself."

She then uncovered her face and said: "Look at me!" The emperor recognized her and embraced and kissed her while thanking God. He then had a large celebration organized, to which every noble of the kingdom was invited, and they made merry for seven full days. He then brought his wife back to his palace, where they ended their days in peace.

GESTA ROMANORUM, CHAP. 249

This story, which is originally a tale from India that was transmitted by means of an Arabic translation in the tenth century, enjoyed great popularity. In France, it first surfaced in the eleventh century as a miracle tale of the Virgin,[27] which can be found in sermons and exempla,[28] and it also appears in European fabliaux, Latin literature and the Gesta Romanorum,[29] *and in the work of Johannes Gobi (Scala coeli, no. 184, 242–43). It then turns up in the Middle English chivalric romance "Florence de Rome,"[30] which was written between 1228 and 1231. The story later circulated under two titles: "The Good Empress Who Loyally Kept Faith with Her Marriage,"[31] and "The Emperor of Rome Who Traveled Over the Sea."[32] This tale was translated into several European languages.[33]*

AaTh 712; TU 1898

   📖 BP 3, 517–31; EM, s.v. "Crescentia," Verleumdung"; Stefanović, "Die Crescentia-Florence-Sage"; Wallensköld, *Le conte de la femme chaste convoitée par son beau-frère.*

5. The Widow

A man died and was buried. His wife remained in mourning next to his grave both day and night.

Not far from there, a thief had been hung.[34] A knight who was a relative[35] cut him down from the gallows and buried his body. It was then proclaimed throughout the land that if the one responsible for this act were found, he would be hung from the same gallows. The knight was not sure how he would extricate himself from this predicament because many people knew that he regarded the robber as a relative.

One day he went to the cemetery and without any delay approached the noblewoman who was mourning her husband, spoke to her sweetly, and promised to bring her comfort. "I would be completely happy if you deigned to love me," he told her. She accepted his proposition.

"I took the thief down from the gallows and now find myself in a bad situation. If you are not able to help me, I shall have to go into exile," he said.

"Dig up my husband," the lady replied, "and hang him in the place of the other; no one will notice. Let us help the dead free the living from whom we expect comfort!"

MARIE DE FRANCE, "VIDUA,"
FABLES (TWELFTH CENTURY)[36]

The first appearance of this tale, known by the title of "The Matron of Ephesus," is found in the work of Petronius (Satyricon, 111–12) and the story became quite popular. It cropped up again in the exemplary literature[37] and spread throughout Europe. Marie de France bowdlerized the story to turn it into a fable, and La Fontaine gave us its proper version (Fables, XII, 27). In the seventeenth century, the story appears in the work of Saint-Évremont (1610–1703), and in 1870, Eugène Cousin turned it into a one-act comedy. In the "Histoire des sept sages" (The Story of the Seven Wise Men),[38] which is closer to the story by Petronius, the lady's behavior is much more horrible: the thief had been stabbed in the side with a sword and had two broken teeth. For the resemblance to be perfect, the wife stabbed her husband's body and broke two of his teeth with a stone!

AATH 1510; TU 5262

📖 Rastier, "La morale de l'histoire"; Ure, "The Widow of Ephesus."

6. Gregory's Incest

A king had a son and a daughter whom he loved tenderly. When they were little, they wanted to always sleep together. When they were around seven, they were inseparable in their games.

Their parents died, and the time came for the young man to ascend to the throne. He had shameful relations with his sister,[39] and when she realized that she was pregnant, she asked for cousel from a maidservant, who offered her aid. After the birth, they prepared a little skiff and placed the child inside[40] with expensive clothing and heaps of gold and silver. They then added two tablets with these words: "My father is my uncle, my mother is my aunt." They wished by this to make the child's royal origin known when the skiff came to shore and the newborn was rescued.

Some fishermen found him.[41] The abbot who owned the port where the skiff came to shore approached them. After seeing the richly clad child,[42] he read on the tablets: "The child must be given a royal education so that he may assume noble duties later." The abbot baptized the child and named him Gregory,[43] and then he entrusted him to a peasant woman. Later, the child went to school and made quick progress there. One day, though, he got into a fight with some of the peasants' sons, particularly the son of his foster mother. Gregory thought that this boy was his brother, but the other scolded him for being an illegitimate child. This shocked and saddened him so deeply that it took the abbot a long time to console him.

Once he had grown up, Gregory told the abbot: "Lord, when I pick up a stylus and a tablet, I always have the feeling that a lance would be more fitting in my hand." What more could be said? He urged the abbot to reveal the truth to him, for he had clearly seen that the peasant's son, the one who insulted him, did not look like him at all although he was the spitting image of his father. The abbot revealed the secret of his birth and the content of the tablets, which he had kept, and then saw to it he received an education on the arts of knighthood.[44] Gregory revealed such a noble nature that he became beloved by all.

It so happened that his father died[45] and his mother was harassed and besieged by a powerful lord.[46] News of this came to the young man's ears; he then gathered knights to train him to fight so he could defend the queen.[47] After learning as much as possible, he set off on his journey and entered the city to become her champion. He confronted the lady's adversary, transfixed him with his lance,[48] and thus brought an end to the hostilities. The noblemen of the land then assailed the queen with pleas:[49] "Marry this penniless knight!" Although she felt an aversion to this alliance, she eventually yielded. However, she had no suspicion that the one to whom she offered her hand was her son.

A maidservant saw that the knight often read tablets that made him weep before he hid them away again. At first she kept quiet about the matter, but one day she spoke to her mistress about her lord's tears and the tablets that she had gone looking for. The queen read them and sank into such despair that she tore at her clothes and pulled out her hair. The king was summoned when he returned from hunting. At the queen's request, everyone was told to leave the main hall, and she questioned her husband. She then confessed that she was his mother and revealed the entire story to him. On hearing this revelation, Gregory collapsed in tears, tore his clothes, gave away all his possessions, and left through a window with the intention of spending the rest of his life in atonement. The queen was consoled by those closest to her and from that point on led the life of a widow and penitent.

When Gregory came to the edge of the sea, a fisherman asked him: "What do you want?"

"I have decided to atone for my sin for the rest of my days." The fisherman showed him a boulder. "Can you shackle me to it?" asked the king. The fisherman did so and after shackling his legs tossed the key into the depths of the sea, saying: "When this key is found again, your atonement will be over."

During this time period, the pope died. Before electing his replacement, the cardinals invoked the Holy Ghost—this was customary and is still in force today—and a voice was heard that said: "Gregory the sinner will be pope." A search was started to find him, and this was how the papal nuncios found their way to the fisherman. When they told him for whom they were looking, he answered: "I chained a man to a rock, the one you can see over there, so that he could pay penance. Maybe he is the one for whom you are looking." Filled with joy, they wanted to go see him at once. "First break some bread with me!" the fisherman suggested, who then brought out some fish and wine. When he cut the fish open, he found the key[50] there, which he had tossed into the sea, and shouted: "His penance has been completed!" He showed the key to Gregory and unlocked his chains. When the papal nuncios revealed their mission, he replied: "God, may Thy will be done." He was brought to Rome where he was crowned pope.

Gregory was so indulgent toward sinners that the renown of his amazing compassions spread throughout the world. His mother the queen heard this and paid him a visit. He took her confession without realizing that he was her husband and her son. That was when he recognized her. He granted her a lodging not far from him and often visited to give her consolation. Both of them found grace in the expiation of their sin.

SOROR CONCIPIT A FRATRE ET PARIT . . .

(FIFTEENTH CENTURY)

This medieval version of the Greek myth of Oedipus, the Life of Pope Gregory the Great,[51] *written around 1190, enjoyed resounding success during the Middle Ages. It can be found in the* exempla, *in the* Saints' Lives, *in the* Passionael,[52] *and in the contemporary literature. Hartmann von Aue made a 4,006-verse-long adaptation[53] of it, which was translated into Latin by Arnold of Lübeck[54] between 1210 and 1213. This legend appears in Iceland (Gregorius saga biskups[55]), in England (twelve manuscripts), and so forth; we know of at least thirty-eight variations. In Italy, four poems, the last of them published in 1806, contain this story; there is also a version in a tale from Sicily.[56] The story was picked up by Thomas Mann in his novel* The Holy Sinner (Der Erwählte, 1951).[57]

The tradition split into two branches: in the older of these, which is represented by the Life of Pope Gregory, *the* Gesta Romanorum *(ed. Oesterley, chap. 170), and Hartmann von Aue, Gregory becomes pope. In the other branch, which is attested in the Low German* Plenarium,[58] *the Icelandic saga, and the popular book dating from 1732,[59] he becomes a bishop. There are significant differences in the details of the various versions. In the saga, the story takes place in Aquitaine, whereas in the* Plenarium *it is set in Italy. Gregory shows his tablets to the queen because he wishes to know his origin. She says nothing but refuses to sleep with him. After three months go by, he locks himself in a room with her, draws his sword, and demands to know the reason for her frigidity toward him. Another notable difference is that the fisherman does not know of any remote, solitary place and it is Gregory who tells him where to go. Once they get there, Gregory asks to be fed with whatever the dogs don't eat, but the fisherman often forgets and Gregory suffers from hunger. Depending on the text, the child's journey takes place on the sea or on a river (the Tiber) and lasts for three or six days. Gregory's period of penance lasts for sixteen or seventeen years. We should note that the Plenarium says that the mother put a bottle of milk within reach of the child's mouth when she placed him in the skiff. A final detail is that Gregory either beheads the oppressor of the queen or inspires them to reconcile.*

In the Gesta Romanorum, the story concludes at the moment when the mother and son recognize each other; they confess, take communion, and then die three days later.

François-Marie Luzel collected an amazing tale in Brittany from which we may note the following details: a hermit urges the brother and sister to sleep together to save the inhabitants of Guingamp who slandered them. Once he became pope, their son, named Cadou, took their confession without recognizing them and then punished them this way:

The next day when they returned, they were locked up completely naked in a small dark room with nine tomcats that had been given nothing to eat for four days. The tomcats tore out their eyes and ate the flesh off their bones, and then, while the brother and sister were still alive, they were cast into a blazing pyre where they were reduced to ashes. The ashes were collected in a white linen cloth and placed on the altar in the main church of Rome while the pope was holding a service there. At the moment Mass ended, two white doves flew down to the altar, picked up the linen cloth holding the ashes with their beaks, and carried it up to heaven.[60]

AaTh 933; TU 2368–75

📖 Allen, "The Relation of the German 'Gregorius auf dem Stein' to the Old French Poem 'La Vie de saint Grégoire'"; Elstein, "The Gregorius Legend"; EM, s.v. "Gregorius," "Inzest"; Herlem-Prey, *Le Gregorius et la Vie de Saint Grégoire.* Gilmore Allen, Clifford, "The Relation of the German Gregorius auf dem Stein to the old French poem *'La vie de saint Grégoire,'* in *Matzke Memorial Volume,* Stanford University Press (Leland Stanford Junior University Publications, University series, 1), 1911, 49–56.

CHAPTER VI

WISDOM, CUNNING, AND STUPIDITY

1. The Golden Apple

Once upon a time there was a king who had an only son whom he loved above all else. At great expense, he had had a golden apple[1] crafted. When it was ready, the king fell ill, summoned his son, and told him: "My dear child, I shall not survive this illness. I give you my blessing and after my death, travel the world over, taking the golden apple with you, and when you find the stupidest of all men,[2] give it to him for love of me." The prince promised that he would fulfill this vow. His father turned his face to the wall and died. After the funeral, the prince took the apple and left. He met many imbeciles, studied them closely, but did not give any of them the apple.

He reached a certain country and entered its capital. He saw the king riding through the city on horseback, accompanied by his court, and asked several inhabitants about local customs. "It is customary among us for the king to reign for only one year," they told him. "When that year ends, he must go into exile and die in disgrace."* Once he heard these words, the prince thought: "I have just found what I've been seeking for so long!"

He made his way to the monarch, knelt, greeted him, and said:

---

*In other words, alone and in misery.

"Good morning, Your Majesty! My father died and left you this apple." The sovereign took it and asked: "Dear friend, how is this possible? I've never seen your father the king and I have never done anything for him. Why would he leave me such a valuable object?"

"Your Majesty, my father did not leave this apple to you expressly; when he gave me his blessing, he charged me with giving it to the biggest idiot I could find. I have traveled through many countries, and it is certain that I have not found anyone crazier than you. I have therefore fulfilled my father's wishes by granting you this apple."

"Explain to me why it is me exactly whom you have found to be the most stupid?" the king asked him.

"Very well, sire, I will explain it to you," the prince replied. "In your country, it is customary for the sovereign to rule for only one year, then lose all honor and wealth, go into exile, and die in misery. By my faith, there is no one in the world as foolish as you: to rule for such a short time and then die so miserably."

"What you say is true. During my short reign, as long as I am in power, I am going to send immense quantities of wealth abroad so that I will be able to live on it until my death."

He put his words into action. At the end of the year, he lost his throne and left the country. He lived for a long time on his riches and ended his life in peace.

Gesta Romanorum, chap. 24

2. The True Friend

Once upon a time there was a king with a single son who was very dear to him. The king allowed him to go all over the world to make friends. The prince traveled for seven years and then came home. Filled with joy, his father welcomed him home and asked him how many friends he had made.

"Three," his son replied. "I love the first more than I love myself, the second as much as I love myself, and the third much less than that, and in truth, hardly at all.

"It would be good to put them to the test," his father said, "before you ever have to call on them in need. Kill a pig, wrap it in a sack, and when night is falling, go to the house of the first friend and tell him that you have killed a man by accident and that if the corpse is found at your house you will be condemned to die an ignominious death.[3] Beg him, in the name of your friendship, to help you in this dangerous situation."

The prince did as his father suggested, but his friend responded: "Because you have killed him, it is only right that you be punished. If the corpse was found at my place, I would be hung. However, because you are my friend, I will accompany you to the gallows and, after you have died, provide three or four ells of cloth to shroud your body."

After getting this response, the young man made his way to the house of his second friend, who rejected him like the first friend and added: "Do you think I am mad enough to take on such a risk? But because you are my friend, I will go with you to the gallows and comfort you to the best of my ability on the way there."

The prince then went to find the third friend and tested him this way: "I am ashamed to say that I have never done anything for you. I have just killed a man by accident . . ."

"I am going to help you without any reservation, take the blame upon myself, and climb the gallows in your place, if necessary."

This is how true friendship shows itself.

Gesta Romanorum, chap. 129[4]
AaTh 893; TU 2216

3. The Six Labors of Guy the Wise

A very long time ago, an emperor enacted a law: every man who wished to serve him had to accomplish the task he was ordered to fulfill. If he knocked three times at the palace door, then it was known he was looking for a job. A poor man named Guy was then living in the Roman Empire. When he heard about this law, he said to himself: "I don't have a penny, and I am of low birth; it would be better for me to try to find a position and earn some money rather than staying in poverty for the rest of my life." He went to the palace and knocked on the door three times, as prescribed. The porter opened it at once and let him in. Guy kneeled before the emperor, who asked him: "What do you wish, my good man?"

"A job, sire."

"What service can you do for me?"

"Sire, I have six tasks in mind: to concern myself day and night with the well-being of a prince, make his bed, prepare his meals, wash his feet; keep watch when all are sleeping; taste any drink and tell him its worth; organize a meal in honor of the host; make a smokeless fire that would warm those who stood next to it; and indicate a good route for pilgrims to the Holy Land so that they would return safe and sound."

"Those are all very useful things for people. Remain here and I shall test your capabilities to take care of me."[5]

"My lord, I am ready to satisfy your wishes."

Every night, Guy prepared the noble bed with great care; he washed the sheets and changed them every day. He slept fully armored in front of the bedroom door with a little dog capable of barking loudly to alert him if someone suddenly came in, or to wake him up if he fell asleep. Once a week, he washed the emperor's feet, and he served him with such intelligence that not a single flaw could be seen. The emperor sang his praises.

Once Guy had shown he could look after everything, the emperor made him seneschal at the end of a year. He worked all summer to put aside everything that would be necessary for the cold season and rested when winter arrived, thereby proving that he had spoken truthfully.

When the king saw how hard Guy had worked, he was overjoyed. He called his cupbearer and said to him: "Pour me a cup of vinegar, a cup of the best wine, and a cup of must, and have Guy taste them. This shall be his third task." The cupbearer did as he was commanded. After he tasted them, Guy said: "This was good, this is good, and this will be good," which meant that the vinegar had been good wine, and the wine was good, and the must would make good wine.

When the emperor realized that Guy had passed the test so intelligently,[6] he said to him: "Travel across my lands, go into my castles, and invite all my friends to a banquet because Christmas is coming; this shall be your fourth task."

"I am ready," answered Guy. He went everywhere and invited none of the emperor's friends but only his enemies.

On the day of the Nativity, the large royal hall was therefore full of enemies. When the emperor saw them, he was filled with fear and turned to Guy and asked: "Didn't you tell me you knew how to invite men to a banquet?"

"Yes, sire."

"I asked you to invite my friends, not my enemies."

"Permit me to respond. Every time you have had your friends come visit, they are given a friendly welcome, which is not the case for your enemies. I have therefore invited them so that a friendly glance and a good meal will make them your friends." This turned out as he said; before the banquet was over, they had all formed ties of friendship with the emperor.

"Dear Guy, praise to the Lord!" the emperor said, charmed. My enemies are now my friends. Now execute your fifth task and make us a fire without smoke."

"Sire, I am ready to do it!"

What did our Guy do? Over the summer, he had exposed the wood to the sun so that it had become so dry that it began burning quickly, producing a hot flame that had no smoke, which warmed the king and his friends.

"You now have to complete your one remaining task," the emperor told him. "If you succeed with wisdom, I will grant you honors and riches."

"Everybody wishing to go to the Holy Land must follow me to the edge of the sea," Guy said by way of reply.

At these words, a crowd of men, women, and children followed him to the shore; once they arrived there, he told them: "My dear friends, do you see everything in the sea that I see?"

"We don't know," was their response.

"There is a large boulder. Raise your eyes and look at it!"

"My lord, we have looked at it long enough," they told him, "but we don't know what you have in mind."

"On this boulder there is a bird that never leaves its nest, in which seven eggs are sitting that are its heart's delight. That is its nature. As long as the bird remains in the nest, the sea is peaceful, but if he leaves it, the ocean goes into such a rage that any who sail on it at that time will be dragged to the bottom."*

"How do we know when the bird is in the nest and when it has flown away?"

"There is only one reason that can force it to leave its nest. There is a second bird, its enemy, which waits day and night to soil the nest and break the eggs. When the owner of the nest sees that it has been ransacked and its eggs destroyed, it flies away immediately, filled with sorrow. Then the sea rises and a monstrous storm breaks out. You must under no circumstance brave the sea then."

"Lord, how do we prevent the intruder from doing this so that we may travel unscathed?"

"This bird hates nothing in this world so much as lamb's blood. If you sprinkle the inside and outside of the nest with this blood, the enemy bird will not dare come near so long as even just a drop remains. The sea will remain calm, and you will be able to reach the Holy Land safe and sound."

They followed this advice, and the pilgrimage could not have gone any better.

When the emperor saw that Guy had fulfilled his final task with great wisdom, he dubbed him a knight and made him a gift of great wealth.

Gesta Romanorum, chap. 17[7]

Motif H 500

📖 EM, s.v. "Scharfsinnproben."

---

*In the scholarly literature of the Middle Ages, it is the loon (*mergus*) that is connected to storms.

4. The Ogre and the Travelers

One day, twelve men had the misfortune of losing their way in a dark forest. They started walking at a doubled pace and finally, during the middle of the night, they caught sight of a fire. They went in that direction and found a house, where a pretty woman was waiting inside.

Once they entered, they heard from afar the thunderous noise of a giant[8] running toward them; great was their despair! "Oh woe," said the woman, "my husband is going to kill you! Climb into the cupboard beneath the stairs, I don't want anything to happen to you. I would love to save you, if I only knew how." And she made them climb in.

Racing into the house, the giant asked his wife where the men were. Not wishing to betray them, she said: "There is no one here."

"When someone is here, I know it at once,"* he replied.

He searched everywhere for them, high and low, and found them in the cupboard up high. "I must have one of you," he said, "and no haggling! Toss him to me or you are all going to die!" They did as he asked and threw the giant the weakest member of their company. This glutton who respected neither faith nor law soon devoured him.[9]

---

*Here is the ancestor of "that smells like fresh flesh."

In a rage, he told them: "Give me another one!" which they did. He gulped him down until there was nothing left. "You are all going to go!" the monster resumed. He roasted and feasted on them.

He had slain eleven without mercy. When he came to the last man, he ordered him to climb down from the cupboard.

"Never!" the last man responded.

"I am going to come get you myself and devour you."

"But I am going to defend myself," he shouted back with alacrity.

"Ah, it is too late now!" the insatiable glutton answered. When you were still with your eleven companions, you should have fought me and you might have saved your life. Now, you are at my mercy!"

DER STRICKER, DER TURSE (THIRTEENTH CENTURY)[10]

📖 EM, s.v. "Riese, Riesin," "Fressermärchen."

5. The Thieves and the Treasure

Once upon a time there was a knight who had two daughters and a son. He squandered all he had on tourneys and jousts. Emperor Octavian, who owned great wealth of gold and silver, was reigning at this time. He housed his treasure in a solid tower with thick doors that always had a knight guarding it.

When the son saw that his father was so poor that he was about to sell his inheritance, he told him: "Father, what shall we do when we no longer own anything?"

"I know a solution. The emperor has a tower filled with gold. One night we will try to make a hole in it so we can get in."

The idea pleased his son, and one night they put their plan into action and took as much treasure as they wished. The knight settled his debts as well as redeemed his possessions, but he resumed his careless lifestyle.

One day, the tower guard saw the hole in the wall. He became frightened, then placed a large cauldron filled with glue and pitch behind the hole. Whoever went through would fall into it and be trapped.

It was not long until the knight became poor again. He convinced his son to accompany him to the tower and help him take more of its wealth. One night they made their way there, where the father entered into the passage and fell into the cauldron. When he realized that he could not get out, he warned his son so that he would not fall into the trap. The latter was horrified that he was unable to help him. "I beg you to cut off my head," his father went on to say, "and to hide it so that no one knows who I am. My decapitated body will be found, and no one will be able to recognize me. Your honor and that of our family will be saved." The son steeled himself to obey, bolstered by the thought that he, too, would die if his father was identified. He drew his sword, cut off the head, which he tossed into a pond, and then returned home, where he told his sisters everything.

The guard inspected the tower and found the headless corpse. The emperor learned of this wonder and commanded him: "Tie the dead man to a horse's tail and have it dragged through the streets of the city and note well the house from which wailing and crying for him can be heard! Then hang all its inhabitants!"

When the horse passed before the house and the knight's daughters saw it, they burst out sobbing with loud, sorrowful cries. When he heard them, their brother inflicted a deep wound on his thigh that covered him in blood. The imperial servants entered the house and tried to arrest them. "My friends," the son told them, "do you see the wound I dealt myself when rushing to hear the order of the emperor and to see what was happening. It is because of this that my sisters were crying." He convinced them. They finished crossing through the city with the cadaver and hung it. It remained on the gallows for a long time because the son did not want to bury it and he left it to rot.

HISTORIA VON DEN SIEBEN WEISEN MEISTERN, V
(MID-FIFTEENTH CENTURY)[11]

This tale is quite old and its first trace can be found in the work of the Greek poet Eugammon of Cyrene (fifth century BCE) and later in that of Herodotus (Histories, II, 121: Rhampsinit). It seems to have been transmitted by way of the Dolopathos by Johannes de Alta Silva (ca. 1185) and the Romance of the Seven Sages. In 1378, Giovanni Fiorentino incorporated it into Il Pecorone (IX, 1).

AaTh 950; TU 1,996

📖 EM, s.v. "Rhampsinit," "Johannes de Alta Silva"; Gobi, *Scala coeli,* no. 520/5, 381–82; Johannes de Alta Silva, *Dolopathos,* vv. 2,857–3,038 (Gaza); Misrahi, ed., *Le Roman des sept sages;* Paris, "Le conte du trésor du roi Rhampsinite"; Prato, *La leggenda del Tesoro di Rampsinite nelle varie redazioni italiane e straniere;* Ser Giovanni Fiorentino, *Il Pecorone.*

6. Aristotle's Humiliation

Here are two version of the same legend, which, with a century span-ning between them, differ notably in the presentation of Aristotle and the woman: the first version is frankly misogynistic, while the second depicts the woman as the victim.

Aristotle the Hobby Horse

Alexander's teacher, Aristotle, told his student one day: "You should not share your wife's bed as often as you do, even if her beauty makes you love her above all else." Alexander grew distant from her, and, sad-dened by his chilly behavior, she pressed him with questions about his abrupt change of attitude. Once she became convinced that Aristotle was responsible, she grew concerned and gave the matter some thought. After a short time, she ended up finding a way to get her revenge against the wise man. So one day she took a stroll in the garden and looked up at the window of Aristotle's study with a smile on her face. Then with sweet words she began trying to soften him up. She removed her slip-pers and hiked up her dress, uncovering her legs. When she did this, she got him so excited that he begged her to satisfy his desire for her. "I simply believe you are trying to tempt me," she told him, "and to trick me, because I cannot bring myself to believe that a man of such wisdom would seek to find all his delight with me." As he quickly became persistent, she added: "I will believe that you love me with all your heart if, out of love for me, you do what I am going to ask you to do. Come join me tomorrow morning in the garden, while my husband is still sleeping, and get on all fours so that I may get up on your back." After the poor man, carried away by lust, accepted, she went to Alexander and said: "Come here tomorrow morning and you will see if you can trust your teacher, who wants you to keep me at a distance."

When the next day came and the queen was riding Aristotle as if he was a horse and the king found them there, he scolded his teacher sharply, and even threatened to kill him, causing his teacher to turn red and tremble. Once he recovered his senses, he said: "Now you see exactly what good advice I gave you because, if the trickery and wickedness of this woman has such power over me that she can provoke me into making a ridiculous spectacle of myself—me, a wise old man among the wise—how much more thoroughly she could deceive you,

seduce you, and catch you in her snares if my example had not served to put you on your guard."

Alexander forgot his wrath and thanked his teacher, who had responded with such intelligence.

JACQUES DE VITRY, *SERMONES FERIALES ET COMMUNES,* 15
(THIRTEENTH CENTURY)[12]
AATH 1501

☐ Schmitt, "Der gerittene Aristoteles."

Aristotle and Phyllis

Phillip, king of the Greeks, had his son, Alexander, raised by the great sage Aristotle; he gave them a large house surrounded by gardens with many servants. This education was interrupted when the young and hotheaded Alexander became passionately infatuated with the beautiful Phyllis, a companion of his mother. She responded to his passion with her own, and they would meet in the garden. When Aristotle discovered this idyll, he revealed it to the sovereign, who threatened to punish the young woman. She protested her innocence, which the queen confirmed, but the two lovers were put under a close watch and they were kept away from each other. Alexander attended his teacher's classes muttering, while the poor Phyllis contemplated ways to get her revenge. She put on a silk dress trimmed with ermine, placed a gold circlet that was studded with emeralds, hyacinths, sapphires, and carbuncles on her head, and went into the garden in the early morning, walking barefoot in the dew up to the bubbling fountain while gathering flowers and tying her dress above her knees. A woman on the prowl is irresistible, and no man has ever been too wise or too old to avoid being captured, much like a wild bird that is trapped with birdlime. No matter how shrewd one is, no one can escape female cunning. But let us get on with our story!

The old sage spotted her outside his window and was troubled by the young beauty who tossed him a handful of flowers and greeted him amiably. He shivered and began to sweat, and love caused him to become like a child again. He invited her to come in, and once she gently sat down next to him, he told her: "I am wise and just; I have traveled though many lands, and I have never met a young woman as beautiful as you. If you grant me your favors, I will give you twenty gold marks and I will open my chest so that you can take as much as you like."

"Master," she replied, "what do you expect from me?"

"I would like you to let me spend the night with you."

"Alas, how could I! I would never surrender my virginity so lightly."

Seeing how smitten he was with her and spotting a saddle, she told him: "If you put this saddle on your back, take my belt for your bridle, and carry me across the garden on your back, I will accept your proposition." The very wise Aristotle was not stronger than Adam, Samson, David, and Solomon: he allowed his desire to prevail and obeyed. The beautiful woman climbed onto the saddle holding a rose branch in her hand and launched into a love song while the old fogey trotted into the garden on all fours. Once she reached her goal, she joyfully leaped back to the ground, mocked him for regressing into a second childhood, and told him to go the devil.

From the top of the ramparts, the queen and her female companions had seen everything, and it was not long until the king and the entire court had gotten wind of this humiliation, the rumor of which spread beyond the castle. To escape his shame and the rude remarks, after a week, Aristotle took all his books and other belongings and secretly set sail for the island of Galicia, where he wrote a large tome on the ruses of beautiful and faithless women: there was no other solution but to keep your distance.

ARISTOTLES UND FILLIS (THIRTEENTH CENTURY)

These narratives are derived from an Indian tale of the Pañcatantra. To soothe his angry wife, King Nanda asked her what he should do and she told him: "If you let me put a bit in your mouth, and let me mount on your back and make you run, and if during this time you neigh like a horse, then I will be appeased." Taken up by Jacques de Vitry (died 1240), the bishop of Saint John of Acre, the tale became widespread. In France, it can be found again in the Lai d'Aristote, *written after 1240 by Henri d'Andely, who tells how the tutor of the young Alexander the Great tried to separate the young king from his lover Phyllis, who was causing him to neglect his political duties. While the philosopher was meditating in his chamber, she was dancing and singing, stripped bare, in the adjoining garden. Aristotle saw her and instantly he wanted her. She agreed on condition that he serve as her mount. The Philosopher, the "teacher of logic metaphysics, and ethics," brought low by desire, yielded to her and played the role of her courser.*

It appeared in Li Bastars de Bouillon *in the sixteenth century and enjoyed great success as vouched for by the religious buildings of the medieval West—sculptures, frescoes, capitals, church stalls, stained-glass windows—as well as objects and textile. There are more than ninety iconographic examples of this known; the Louvre Museum owns several. Several forms of this episode also exist in the Germanic and Latin countries, some of which are theatrical (Germany, Italy).*

AATH 1501; TU 328

📖 EM, s.v. "Aristoteles und Phyllis"; Johannes Gobi, *Scala coeli*, no. 306, 373; Morris, "The Aristotle of Fact and Legend"; *Pañcatantra* (trans. Lancereau), 296; Vincent of Beauvais, *Speculum historiale*, XXX, 23.

7. The Snow Child

A merchant had a wife whom he cherished above all else. She told him that she loved him, but this was a falsehood. One day, his business affairs compelled him to be absent for some time. He set sail and went into a foreign land, where he plied his trade for three years.

On his return, his wife gave him a friendly welcome, accompanied by a little child. The merchant asked who he was and she answered: "My lord, while I was pining for you, I went into the garden where I ate some snow and became pregnant.[13] I swear to you that this boy is yours."

"You may be speaking the truth," her husband responded. "We shall raise him."

For ten years, he never let her know that he had not been fooled. He saw to the boy's education, then readied a boat and set sail over the sea with the child. The waves carried them to a beautiful land where they met a merchant who bought the snow child for three hundred marks, and it was a bargain.

The husband returned home alone, and his wife asked him: "Where is our son?"

"The wind tossed our ship over a stormy sea," he answered. "He was drenched and transformed into water immediately. Didn't you tell me that he was born from the snow? If all goes well, he will return to the spring from which he was issued. Believe me, he will come back to you."

DES SNÉWES SUN (THIRTEENTH CENTURY)[14]

Most likely of Indian origin, this story was widespread in Europe, where it is first attested in a tenth-century Latin manuscript and turns up again three hundred years later in a French fable collection, The Child that was Returned to the Sun.[15] *Among the variants, we note that the child melts beneath the Egyptian sun. A Russian narrative tells how an elderly, sterile couple crafted a child from snow to whom God gave life (Motif D 435.1.1.). But one day he jumped over a Saint John's bonfire and was transformed into steam.[16] See appendix 1.*

AATH 1362

8. The Peasant and the Dwarf

One day a peasant captured a sprite for whom he had been lying in wait for a long time. The sprite gave him a gift of three wishes on the condition that he reveal nothing. Delighted and quite at ease, the villain went home and gave two of them to his wife.[17] He kept one by accident. Both went for a long time without making any wishes, but one day when they were eating the spine and bones of a lamb, the wife suddenly expressed her desire for the marrow. She then wished a hoopoe beak on her husband's face, and her wish immediately became true. Dumbstruck, the peasant desired to see it vanish so he could get his original face back. The man and his wife thereby lost their wishes without gaining any benefit.

MARIE DE FRANCE, "DE RUSTICO ET NANO,"

FABLES (TWELFTH CENTURY)[18]

There are many different forms of this tale known under the name "The Three Wishes." It is well attested in the Middle Ages, notably in "Saint Martin's Four Wishes"—in which a woman speaks a bawdy wish to give her husband a bit more vigor at certain moments—in Les Sohais *by Gautier le Leu, and in the work of La Fontaine (*Fables, VII, 5*). In general, it is a God or a saint who grants the wishes.*

AATH 750 A; TU 5326

📖 BP II, 210–29; CPF 3, 122–30; Grimm, KHM, no. 87; EM s.v. "Marie de France," "Wünsche: die drei W"; Gautier le Leu, *Les Sohais* (ed. Livingston); *Les Quatre Souhaits de Saint Martin* (ed. Noomen and Van den Boogaard).

9. The Three Knights

Once upon a time there was a nobleman of a certain age who married a young woman whom he loved above all else. She sang extraordinarily well; her unique voice made anyone who heard it fall in love. One day, in her summer home, she was singing sweet melodies while facing the street, as a knight whom the emperor valued most highly was passing by. He heard it and became inflamed with passion and entered her home. When he saw how beautiful she was, he said: "I will give you one hundred pieces of gold if you do as I wish." The money was tempting to the woman, who answered: "As you please. I will alert you when you come see me without risk. Bring me the money then." Full of joy, he took his leave.

The next day, another knight happened to pass by while she was singing. He, too, became infatuated with her immediately and offered her one hundred pieces of gold if she would yield to his desire. She accepted and added: "I will let you know when you can come." The same thing happened with a third knight, but none of them knew about the plans with the others.

Once assured that they would bring her the money, the woman told her husband: "My lord, I must share a secret with you. If you follow my advice, it will give us honor and riches. We are penniless and we need money." Her proposition pleased her husband, so she continued: "Three imperial knights came to see me one after the other; each promised me one hundred pieces of gold if I sleep with him. To obtain this money, I asked the first knight to come see me at nightfall, the second to present himself at ten o'clock, and the last one at midnight. Hide behind the door with your sword and kill them one after the other, and we shall be able to get their money without any dishonor for me."

"I am scared that this will turn out badly," her husband replied, "because we will not be able to hide these murders."

"I have gotten things started, and I will bring them to a good conclusion," she told him. "So have no fear."

Her husband gave her his consent.

The lady alerted each knight and arranged their separate rendezvous, and, when they showed up, her husband killed each of them. Once this was done and the money was recovered—three hundred pieces of gold!—he said to his wife: "My sweetheart, if the corpses are found in our house, we are dead, for the imperial court will launch an investigation."

"Things have gotten off to a good start; I am going to lead them to a happy ending," she said. "Fear nothing; you don't yet know what women are capable of."

The lady had a brother who was a night watchman for the city. When he passed in front of the house and cried "midnight," his sister engaged him from her doorstep. She invited him to come in, and then wined and dined him and outwitted him so well that he promised to reveal nothing.

"My dearest brother," she said, "a knight came looking for me tonight and tried to rape me in front of my husband. Quite justifiably, he lost his temper and struck this knight with all his might and killed him. I do not know anyone but you who can help us, because you are my brother."

"Have no fear! You did well to slay this wicked reprobate. Give me a sack; I shall throw him into the water from the first bridge I come to."

No sooner said than done. He returned to his sister's and asked for wine. She pretended to go fetch it but went to where the other two bodies were still lying. She then screamed: "The knight that you threw into the water has come back!" Her brother was stupefied but replied: "Put him into the sack, we will see if he can come back this time!" He carried it away and got rid of the body as before, returned, and asked for wine, and his sister staged the same routine. "He must be the devil!" he exclaimed. He carried the body away in a sack, tied a heavy stone around its neck, tossed it into the water,[19] then returned to his sister's house, where he amused himself before going back to walking the city streets.

On the next day and those that followed after it, questions about the disappearance of the three knights raced through the court and in the city, but the mystery remained impenetrable.

One day when the husband and his wife were quarreling, she insulted her spouse, who responded by hitting her. She yelled and screamed: "Wicked man. You are trying to murder me like you murdered the three knights!" Her words were overheard, the emperor got wind of them, and they were both arrested and interrogated. When the truth came out, each of them was bound to a horse's tail[20] and dragged to the gallows, where they were killed as was right by law.[21]

HISTORIA VON DEN SIEBEN WEISEN MEISTERN, XII
(MID-FIFTEENTH CENTURY)[22]

Included in The Romance of the Seven Sages (of Rome) *and of Eastern origin—from India and Persia—this story experienced great popularity in Europe and circulated independently in the fabliaux of the* Trois Boçus *by Durand de Douai,* D'Estormi *by Hues Piaucele, and* De Constant Duhamel. *In Germany, the tale "The Three Monks of Colmar" (fourteenth–fifteenth century)*[23] *is in the same vein. There are a large number of variants, which can be divided into two basic types of texts: in one, the husband kills the visitors; in the other, the wife locks them in chests or wardrobes in which they perish or only emerge in a wretched state. In* D'Estormi, *there is a fourth death, an innocent passerby who meets and surprises the husband's cousin. We can also find the plot of this story in* The Thousand and One Nights *transposed into an Eastern setting, and in the work of Straparola (*Piacevoli notti, *V, 3).*

AaTh 1537

📖 BP II, 10; *De Constant Duhamel*, in Barbazan, ed., *Fabliaux et contes des poëtes françois*, II, 204–52; *Die drei Mönche zu Kolmar*, in Niewöhner, ed., *Neues Gesamtabenteuer*, I, no. 30, 202–7; EM, s.v. "Leiche: die mehrmals getötete L"; Legrand d'Aussy, *Fabliaux ou contes, fables et romans du XIIe et du XIIIe siècle*, IV, 226: "De la dame qui attrapa un prêtre, un prévôt et un forestier"; *Les Mille et un Jours* (ed. Pétis de la Croix), nights 145–54; Piaucel, *D'Estormi* (ed. Noomen and Van den Boogaard); Pillet, *Das Fableau von den Trois bossus ménestrels und verwandte Erzählungen früher und später Zeit*; Suchier, *Der Schwank von der viermal getöteten Leiche*.

CHAPTER VII

HEROIC LEGENDS

1. The Archer and the King

A man named Toko was in the service of the king Harald Gormsson. When he got drunk during a festival, he bragged that he was so skilled with the bow that he could hit an apple placed on a stake with one shot, no matter how small it was. His enemies repeated what he said to the king, while at the same time altering his words, and the monarch commanded that Toko's beloved son stand in place of the stake and decided that if the archer did not hit the apple placed on the child's head with his first shot, he would pay for his imprudent pride with his life. Confident in his abilities, Toko accepted the test.

Once he got his son into position, he asked him to wait without budging and holding his head completely straight for the arrow whistling toward him. To make sure the child did not get scared, Toko asked him to turn his back toward him. He then took three arrows out of his quiver. The first shot struck the apple squarely.[1]

Harald asked Toko: "Why did you take three arrows from your quiver?"

"To avenge myself on you with the other two arrows if the first had not hit its mark," the archer replied.

By speaking so frankly, Toko compelled respect while at the same time showing the crime for which Harald would have made himself guilty.

One day, when Harald was walking through the forest, he squatted down to relieve his belly. Toko wounded him with an arrow and he died soon after.*

Saxo Grammaticus,
Gesta Danorum, X, 7–8 (1202–1216)[2]

Readers will easily recognize the oldest account of what would become the legend of William Tell in the second third of the fifteenth century with Melchior Russ's Cronika *and the* Chant de Tell *(Song of Tell). In the Saga of the Jomsvikings (Jómsvíkinga saga), our master archer's name is Palnatoki. Further along, we will find a similar legend inserted in the story of Velent (Wayland) the Smith.*

2. Velent the Smith

The giant Vadi, son of King Vilcinus and a water nymph, lived in Zealand and administered the properties left him by his father earlier. His son's name was Velent.[3] When Velent was nine years old, Vadi desired for him to learn a trade. Having heard that Mimir of Hunland was the best smith in all the land, he brought his son to him so that he could learn the art of the forge from him, and the lad spent three years with him before returning home.

Vadi had heard that two dwarfs lived in the mountain called Kallava.[4] They knew how to forge iron better than other dwarfs or men and knew how to make all kinds of objects, swords, helmets, and breastplates.[5] They even knew how to make whatever anyone could imagine as jewels in silver or gold. So the giant departed from home with his son and came to the Grönasund.† After waiting awhile in vain for a boat to bear them across the strait, he put his son on his shoulders and forded the channel although it was nine ells deep. He visited the dwarfs and told them: "I am accompanied by my son, whom I wish for you to engage as a servant for a year so he can learn your art; I will give you as much gold and silver as you want." The dwarfs agreed and asked for

---

*Saxo tones down an element of the saga that applies to someone else: the arrow enters the king's backside and comes out his mouth.

†This channel is located between the Danish islands of Møn and Falster.

a gold mark. They then set the day when, after a year had passed, he would return to fetch his son, and their bargain was concluded.

Apprenticeship with the Dwarfs

Velent remained with dwarfs, learned to forge, and showed such intelligence that he was soon able to imitate everything they did. They did not want him to leave when his father showed up on the appointed day to pick him.up, and they begged him to leave the boy for another dozen moons, preferring to give back the gold mark rather than part with him. They promised to teach him as many techniques as he had already learned, and Vadi agreed. Regretting that their purchase of Velent's service was so dear, they decided they would behead him if his father did not come on the day that had been set.[6]

Before going back, Vadi called his son and asked him to leave the mountain and to accompany him. He had a sword that he stuck in the thicket so deeply that no one could see it, and he told his son: "If I am not there on the day we have agreed—because there can always be a hindrance—and the dwarfs try to take your life, grab this sword and use it to valiantly and courageously defend yourself! That is better than letting yourself be cravenly murdered by two dwarfs. I would not like it said among our family that I raised you like a daughter. However, I cannot imagine how I would not be there on the appointed day." With these words, they parted. Before the dwarfs even realized it, Velent had become equally skilled. However, he served them faithfully, and they were quite satisfied with his work, even if they looked with envy upon how skilled he had become. They decided that he would never live to ply his skill, for they had his head as a pledge.

Death of Vadi the Giant

When the twelve months had almost passed, Vadi told himself it was time to go fetch his son. The road was long, and he did not want to miss the rendezvous. He traveled both night and day and arrived there three days early. The mountain was shut and he could not get in, so he lay down near the entrance to wait for it to open. He fell into a deep and long slumber. He was no small man, and as he rested he snored so loudly that it could be heard miles away. A heavy rain began to fall, and the earth shook. This triggered an avalanche that sent water, trees, stones, sand, and mounds of earth cascading over the sleeping giant, killing and burying him.

On the day that had been set, the dwarfs opened the mountain to see if Vadi was there. Velent went outside, but he could not find him anywhere. While looking for him, he came upon a cliff and realized that an earthquake had occurred. The thought occurred to him that it might have buried his father, and he realized that wishing for vengeance was pointless. He remembered the advice his father gave him before parting. So he cast his glance all around himself and saw the hilt of the sword sticking out of the ground. He jumped to where it was and dug it out. He spotted the dwarfs sitting atop a boulder on lookout and quickly made his way to them, keeping the sword hidden beneath his coat. He leaped on the one that was closest and struck him a fatal blow; he then cut down the second dwarf. He then went into the mountain and took all the dwarfs' tools as well as all their gold, silver, and jewels, which he loaded on his horse. He then set off for Denmark.

After marching at top speed for three days, he came to a wide river that he was unable to cross, and he lingered for a while in the forest bordering it. The sea was not far off. He looked for a strong tree on the riverbank and cut it down, then removed the branches and hollowed it out. He placed his tools and riches in the end of the trunk that was narrower, as it neared the top, and in the end closer to the roots he placed his provisions and drink before slipping into his skiff himself. He then sealed it hermetically so that nothing could happen to him. And this craft carried Velent, his riches, and his tools along the river until it sailed into the open sea. Eighteen days later, he came to land.

Velent at the Home of King Nidung

A king named Nidung ruled Jutland. His fishermen set sail on the sea with their net one day to catch fish for his table. They cast their net and pulled it back to land; it was so heavy that they had trouble pulling it, and they discovered that a large tree trunk had been caught in it. They inspected it and found to their surprise that it had been skillfully worked, and because it was so heavy and so well sealed, they suspected it held a treasure. They hastily sent a message to the king, telling him that he should come and see this trunk. After he examined it, he gave the order to his men to see what it held inside. His men began chopping at the trunk. When Velent realized what they intended to do, he yelled that there was someone inside. When they heard his voice, they thought Satan himself was inside the trunk and they ran off in terror. Velent then opened the tree, introduced himself to the king, and told him: "My lord, I am a man, not a troll. I urgently beg you to spare my life and my possessions." Nidung could clearly see that there was a man and not a monster there. He therefore granted him his protection. Velent then grabbed his tools and riches and hid them in the ground with his skiff, but one of the king's knights, a man named Regin, was spying on him.

Velent remained at King Nidung's court, enjoying the ruler's esteem. His task was to keep charge of the knives that the king used at the table. After twelve moons, he went to the shore to wash and sharpen the royal cutlery. The best knife fell from his hand into water that was so deep he had no hope of recovering it. He then went back the way he had come, thinking that this loss would anger the king.

There was a smith living in Nidung's realm named Amilias, who forged everything that could be crafted with iron. Velent went to his place, but he was not there. He set to work and forged a knife, then stuck a nail in it and placed it on the anvil—no one ever saw better craftsmanship—and he finished it before Amilias returned.

The Wager with Amilias

Velent rejoined the king, presenting himself at his table and serving him as usual, as if nothing had happened. The king grabbed the knife in front of him and cut a piece of bread. When he did this, he also cut a piece from the table, where the knife had gone too deep. The sharpness of the knife came as a surprise to him, and he asked: "Whoever could have made this knife?"

"Who, if not Amilias," Velent responded, "your smith who has forged all of your knives as well as all the other objects you requested of him."

Amilias heard this exchange and said: "My lord, I crafted this knife. No other smith could achieve all that you desire."

"I have never seen such fine iron come from your hands," replied the sovereign. "Whoever it was that forged this, it definitely was not you," and he cast a glance at Velent. "Did you make it?" he asked.

"It is possible that Amilias forged it as he said he did," Velent responded.

"If you do not tell me the truth, you will suffer the full weight of my wrath!"

"I definitely do not want that!" said Velent, who immediately explained how he had lost the knife and had crafted a new one to replace it.

"I did not recognize the work of Amilias in this," the king told him. "In all my life, I have never seen such an excellent knife."

The smith could not contain himself any longer.

"My lord, it is possible that Velent crafted this knife whose excellence you praise, but I refuse to let anyone say that his work surpasses mine and would like to put our skills to the test."

"My skill is mediocre," replied Velent, "but I would not hesitate to demonstrate what I have learned. Let's each forge something of our own and we shall see who triumphs."

"I accept the challenge!"

"I own very little, but if you like, we can wager something."

"If you don't have enough gold, wager your head—and I will wager mine! The one with the most skill shall lop off the other's head."

"Wager whatever you like, and forge whatever it is that you do best!"

"Craft a sword, as for me I will forge a hauberk, a great helmet, and shin guards. If the bite of your sword wounds me in the slightest, you can cut off my head. In the opposite case, you can be certain that I will take your life!"

That very day Amilias went to his smithy with all his companions and got down to work, while Velent attended to his normal duties.

The Theft of Velent's Tools

One day the king asked Velent how he was going to keep his part of the wager and when he was going to get down to work. "Whenever you wish," he replied. "I would like it, though, if you could have a smithy built for me where I might work." His wish was granted, and when the smithy was ready, he returned to the place where he had hidden his riches and tools. The skiff had been broken apart and all that it had contained was stolen. He went to see the king and told him everything. The sovereign took umbrage and promised to learn the identity of the thief and asked Velent if he would recognize him. "I would not have any problem doing so," replied Velent, "except that I do not know his name."

The king had an assembly called, which all were ordered to attend. Once they were all gathered together, Velent examined each man present, but this was in vain and he had to share his failure to spot the thief with the king, who became irate and said: "You are not as shrewd as I thought. You are mocking me and dishonoring me. All the inhabitants of my kingdom are present, and the thief must be among them. Only, you don't recognize him!" The king and his people then left the assembly.

A short time after this, Velent sculpted the statue of a man. It was so realistic it even had his hair. He placed it in a corner of the room that the king had to pass by when going to his chamber. When the king was about to leave the premises with his guard, Velent illuminated the statue with a candle. The king's gaze happened to fall on the statue, and he blurted out: "Hail and welcome, my good Regin! What are you doing here? When did you return? What happened to the mission on which I sent you to Sweden?"

"Lord," said Velent, "he will not answer you. I made this statue from memory. So that is the name of my thief."

"You would certainly not find him here, for he is on a mission," the king replied. "By my faith, you are inventive, handy, and skilled! If he stole your tools and belongings, I will make him give them back to you!"

Once Regin returned, Nidung summoned him and asked him if he had taken Velent's tools and other property. Regin did not try to deny it and claimed it was merely a joke. Velent got his belongings back and continued serving the king daily. Four new moons came and went this way.

Velent Forges the Sword Mimung

The king asked Velent if he wished to forge something to keep his wager.

"I will get started on it right away," replied Velent, "if that seems suitable to you."

"It seems to me," said Nidung, "that what's at stake is of importance to you. You are dealing with a skilled and wicked man. Get down to work!"

In seven days, Velent had forged a sword. On that seventh day, the king came to see him in person. The sword was ready and Nidung thought that he had never seen a sword as sharp and beautiful. Velent tested the weapon by letting a foot-thick flock of wool drift down the stream and touch blade, which sliced the flock in half.

"It is good," said the king. "I would like to own it."

"It is not really. I need to improve it," replied Velent.

He returned to the smithy, took a file and reduced the sword to shavings, and mixed these with feed. He then starved tame birds[7] for a period of three days and gave them the mixture to eat. He tossed their droppings into the furnace and with fire purified all the slag from the iron, which he then used to make a new sword. Nidung visited him and as soon as he laid eyes on the sword, he wanted it. "I have never been given or even seen anything more beautiful than this sword," he said. But Velent rebuffed him. "My lord, this sword is good, but it must be even better still." They went to the river, where this time Velent sliced a two-foot-thick flock of wool in half.

"Impossible to find a better sword, no matter how far one searched," said Nidung.

"I am going to improve it again," replied Velent, who returned to the smithy and filed down the sword and repeated the procedure as before.

After three weeks had passed, he was done. The sword was shiny, encrusted with gold, easy to wield, and had a beautiful grip. Nidung again visited Velent, looked at the sword, and at once stated that it was the sharpest and most beautiful sword he had ever seen. They went to the river, where this time Velent took a flock of wool three feet thick, tossed it into the current, and then thrust his sword into the water. The flock of wool floated into the blade, which cut through it easily.[8]

"No matter how hard you looked," said Nidung, "you could not find a sword this good anywhere."

"My lord, I am giving it to you, but first I have to make the scabbard and the ties." He returned to his smithy, where he got down to work and forged another sword that was alike in every way; no one would have been able to tell it apart from the original. He hid it beneath the bellows of the smithy and said: "Stay there, Mimung!* Who knows if I might not end up needing you."

Velent Wins the Wager and Becomes a Famous Smith

Once Velent had completed his work he continued to serve Nidung until the day of judgment arrived. Amilias then put on his armor in the early morning, went to the market square, and spent time with his sons. All who saw it said that never before had they seen such a beautiful breastplate. It was of double thickness everywhere and a masterpiece. Dressed in this fashion, he presented himself at the royal table. Nidung thought that this armor was the best in the world. This pleased Amilias no end, and he swaggered about in it. In the king's presence he put on his great helmet. It shone brilliantly and was of astonishing hardness and thickness. These pieces of armor pleased

---

*The oldest mention of this sword is found in the Old English poem "Waldere," where it is called "Mimming."

Nidung greatly. Once the meal was over and the tables cleared, Amilias left, went to an open space, and sat down in a seat that was standing there. The king, his guard, and Velent followed him. Amilias said he was ready to make good on the wager. Velent raced over to the smithy, grabbed Mimung, and came running back with his bare blade. He took up position behind Amilias's seat and asked his foe if he felt anything. The other responded: "Strike with all your strength and do as you must, if that will help you!" Velent pressed the sword so strongly against the great helmet that it sundered his foe's head, hauberk, and torso right down to his waist. Amilias died at once, and more than one person said: "The higher your pride takes you, the harder the fall." The king asked for the sword, which he wanted to carry away immediately, but Velent answered: "I must go fetch the scabbard, because I want to give you everything at one time." He reached the smithy, hid Mimung beneath the bellows,[9] grabbed the other sword, slid it into the scabbard, and brought it to the king. And time passed.

Velent, the illustrious smith whom the Varangians call Völund, was so famous in the northern half of the world that people paid homage to all excellent work by saying: "The one who made this has the skill of Völund." Velent enjoyed the favor of King Nidung, who honored him.

Velent Seeks the Victory Stone

One day when the king was dining, messengers arrived with the news that an immense army had invaded the kingdom and had already caused great damage. Nidung gathered his men, and five days later they ran into the enemy. One night, after his war tent had been set up, he remembered that he had forgotten to bring his victory stone. During this era, several monarchs owned a stone that had the property of bestowing victory on any person who carried it.[10] I don't know if this power came from the stone itself or from the confidence its bearer had in it. For Nidung, it was a huge misfortune that he had forgotten it. He therefore summoned his advisers and high officials. "I will give my daughter and half of my kingdom to the one who returns to me with this stone before the sun rises in the east tomorrow morning," he proclaimed. More than one man was tempted, but few dared to incur the risk, and night fell.

Seeing that no one was willing to undertake this journey, Nidung summoned Velent and said to him: "Velent, my dear friend, will you do it?"

"Since you wish it, my lord, it is my wish, too," replied Velent, "if you will keep your promise."

"I will keep the oath I've sworn," the king replied.

Velent left, spurring on his fine charger Skemming,* who was as fast as a bird in flight, in addition to being strong and splendid to look upon. So he left as evening fell and in twelve hours made the journey that had taken the king five days to travel. At midnight he was back at the castle. He took the stone, returned at breakneck speed, and found himself outside the royal tent before the break of day since he had driven his horse so relentlessly. At this same moment, seven knights mounted on brown horses emerged from the king's tent and rode to meet him. Their leader was the king's seneschal. They galloped up to Velent and greeted him amiably. The seneschal asked him: "Dear friend, do you have the victory stone?"

"It is true that I have it," responded Velent.

"Give it to me so that I may bring it to the king. In return I will give you as much gold and silver as you like."

"The path was not any longer for you than it was for me," Velent retorted. "You will not have an easy time taking the stone from me. It does not behoove the honor of a knight to make such a request."

"You are crazy to think," said the seneschal, "that a poor smith like you could obtain the princess, something that no man descended from the noblest families of the kingdom has managed to do. Death to the upstart, my companions! Take the victory stone from him along with his life."

They hurled themselves on him at once, but Velent brandished his fine sword, Mimung, and struck the seneschal's helmet with it, carving his head in two, whereupon he collapsed to the ground dead. The other six fled for their lives.

---

*German legends give him the same name: *Shemming.*

The Exile and Crippling of Velent

Velent presented himself to the king, gave him the victory stone, and received a warm welcome. He told him of his journey and said that he had slain the seneschal.

"Cursed be you!" shouted Nidung. "You have killed my most cherished vassal. Get out of my sight as quick as you can and may I never see you again. If you do not leave here at once, I will have you hung like a miserable thief!"

"So this is your reward," said Velent, "because you do not wish to keep your promise; few would find this cause for rejoicing," and, humiliated, he left.

The next day, Nidung confronted the Viking army and drove them from his land and returned home, basking in glory. For some time, no one knew what had become of Velent. The king remained in his kingdom.

Velent was furious. He had fallen in disgrace and been banished from the land. His thoughts were therefore fixed on his need for revenge, and in disguise he entered the king's castle one day and made his way to the kitchen, where he passed himself off as a head chef. He joined the other cooks roasting and boiling food as they did. When the plates were presented before the king and his daughter, the princess took her knife and stuck it into the piece placed in front of her. The handle of this knife had the ability to jingle when it found something wrong with the food.[11] The knife began to chime, and the daughter noted that there was treachery afoot with the food. The king became angry and started a search for the guilty party. Velent was found and hauled before the king. "Out of love for your art," said Nidung, "your life shall be spared although you committed this crime." The king then ordered that the two tendons of his feet be severed, followed by those of his knees and thighs, and then by the ligaments of his legs.[12] Crippled, Velent had to remain in the king's residence.[13] He said one last word to Nidung: "From this time on, I shall never be able to leave you for as long as I live, and even if I could, I wouldn't."

"By my faith, I shall show my thanks by giving you as much gold and silver as you desire," said Nidung. The king had a smithy built, where Velent worked for him morning to night. Nidung believed that he had handled the matter with intelligence and tact.

Velent's Revenge

King Nidung had four children, three sons and a daughter named Bödvild. The two youngest sons brought their bow to Velent's smithy one fine day to ask him to make them an arrow. "Although you are the king's sons," he told them, "I would not forge anything for you without your father's express permission, but if you still want something all the same, you must first grant me my wish." They asked him what it was, and he replied: "Come to the smithy, walking backward, as soon as there is a fresh snowfall." It did not matter to the boys if they walked forward or backward, so they agreed. It was winter, and that very night it snowed. The next morning, the princes made their way to the smithy before dawn. They had obeyed Velent's request. With no hesitation he locked the doors, killed the two boys, and threw their corpses into a deep pit beneath his bellows.[14]

The princes' disappearance was soon noticed, and Nidung assumed that they had gone into the forest to hunt game or fowl or to go fishing by the sea. When the time came to sit down to eat, the search for the princes was unsuccessful. Someone went to ask Velent if he had seen them. "They did come here," he said, "but they left again on the path back to the royal castle. They were carrying their bows and arrows. It is my opinion that they are in the forest." On their way back, the envoys saw the footsteps of the children going in that direction. This is why no one suspected the smith. For days on end, Nidung continued to send out searchers for his sons, but they were never found. He believed that wild animals had eaten them or else that they had drowned in the sea. Much speculation was made about their fate, but the truth was never discovered. It was in brooding on his humiliation that Velent had found the means to get his revenge.

Velent then took the corpses of the children, stripped the flesh from their bones, covered their skulls with gold and silver, and made them into two handsome goblets. He crafted beer steins from their shoulder blades and hipbones and set them in gold and silver. With their other bones he made knife handles, plates, and candle holders, intended to adorn the royal table. They were used when the king was hosting the great lords.

Bödvild was in the garden one day with her companions and broke her prettiest ring. She did not dare tell her parents about it, and, in her confusion, she asked the advice of her serving lady, who told her: "Velent would be able to repair this ring for you in no time." She thought that sounded like a good idea. The serving woman went to the smithy and said: "My young mistress sent me to you to ask you to repair her ring."

"I would not dare to work on it without the king's permission," he answered.

"The king would not be opposed to you granting the wishes of the princess," she replied. "You can do it out of love for her; she will be quite grateful, and the monarch shall reward you once he knows of it."

"Your assurances are of no interest to me. If the princess comes here herself in person, I will do as she desires," Velent replied.

The servant left and told Bödvild about it, and the princess answered: "If that impels him to forge it, I have no reason to oppose it, but he can expect nothing good of me if he refuses." She went to see the smith with her servant, entered the smithy, and begged him to repair her ring. He locked the door and lay down next to her.* He then repaired her ring, which was now even more beautiful than before.

---

*This means he raped her.

On Velent's Brother Egil and His Shot

At this same time, Velent was urging his brother, the young Egil, to enter the royal guard. Egil was exceedingly handsome and surpassed all other men on one point: he could shoot a bow better than anyone. The king gave him a warm welcome and wanted to verify for himself that his fame was well deserved. He ordered that Egil's three-year-old son be placed with an apple on top of his head. "Shoot and hit the apple!" he said. "You can only have one single arrow."* Egil took three, corrected the fletching on one, drew it back, and fired it,[15] hitting the apple dead center.[16] This master shot was long celebrated, and Egil's skill was a subject for praise in all the lands where he was nicknamed Ölrunar-Egil.[17]

The king then asked him: "Why did you take three arrows when you were only allowed one shot?"

"My lord," said Egil, "I will not lie. If I had hit my son with the first, the other two were intended for you."

The king did not become angry at this answer, but all the other men thought his response was quite bold.

Velent talking with Bödvild

Velent called his brother and asked him to arrange an audience with the princess. Velent and Nidung's daughter then met, and he told her: "I want no other woman but you."

---

*This is one of the oldest versions of the legend that later became connected to William Tell.

"I want no other husband but you," she replied.

"I am expecting you to give birth to a son. If it is impossible for me to tell him myself, tell him, when the time comes, that I have forged arms and armor for him and that I have hidden them where the water enters and the wind goes out."

This was the place where he cooled down his forge. They parted soon after this conversation.

Velent Makes a Garment from Feathers and Flies Away

One day Velent asked his brother to procure all kinds of feathers for him because he wanted to make a garment for flying. Egil went into the forest, where he killed many birds, and Velent used the birds' feathers to make his garment. It looked like the plumage of a griffin, a vulture, or of the bird called an ostrich. He then asked his brother to slip it on and fly to verify if it was good.

"How do I lift off, how do I fly, and how do I land?" Egil asked.

"You will lift off facing the wind and soar high into the air for a long time," Velent replied. "Then you will land with the wind."

Egil put on the feather garment and flew into the air like the nimblest of birds. When he wished to land, he lowered his head so sharply that he descended like an arrow.

"Tell me, brother, is the feather garment good?" the smith asked.

"If it was as easy to land as it is to fly," Egil replied, "I would now be in another country and you would never see me again."

"I am going to improve it."

With his brother's help, he put the garment on, rose into the air, and landed on a roof and said: "I lied when I told you to land with the wind because I was scared that you would keep my feather coat when you realized how good it was. All birds land against the wind and also fly against it. I am going to share my plan with you, Egil. I want to return to my home, but first I want to have a few words with the king. If my revelations irk him, he will demand that you shoot at me. Then aim your arrow below my left arm! I have tied a bladder there filled with the blood of Nidung's sons. Arrange it so you can shoot me without wounding me if our kinship carries any weight with you!"

Velent then alit on top of the highest tower of the castle. The king was just then on his way into his hall with his guard. When he saw the smith, he shouted: "Are you a bird now? You have made many wonders!"

"My lord," Velent replied, "henceforth I am a bird and a man at the same time. I am going to leave. Never again will I be in your power. Our first accord said that you would give me your daughter and half of your kingdom because it then seemed you were facing a great danger. But you exiled me and made me an outlaw because I defended myself and slew the one who was trying to kill me. You gave me a poor reward for my efforts. I did not forget anything, but I was dispossessed and powerless. You cut the tendons of my feet, and I killed your two sons. As evidence there are the two goblets that contain their skulls. I have put their bones in the best serving ware on your table. I have also slept with your daughter. I expect that I made her pregnant. So this puts an end to our quarrel." Thereupon, he rose into the air.

Nidung shouted: "Young Egil, kill Velent!"

"Impossible, he is my brother!"

"You shall die if you don't shoot!" the king responded. "Your life depends on it! You shall only be spared if you slay him."

Egil nocked an arrow and shot it beneath Velent's left arm. Blood poured down to the ground. The king and his retinue believed him to be mortally wounded, but the smith flew away to Zealand and settled in the farm that had belonged to his father, Vadi. Nidung succumbed to illness a short time later. His son Ortvin succeeded him. He was loved by all and treated his sister well.

Velent's Son

Bödvild gave birth to a son who was named Vidga.[18] Velent learned of it and sent a message to King Ortvin to sue for peace and reconcile with him. The monarch granted him a truce so they could meet. Velent left for Jutland, where he was given a good welcome. Ortvin gave him his sister to wed and invited him to stay as long as he liked. But the smith thought it better to return home with his wife and their three-year-old son. The king gave him gifts of great wealth and many splendid gems, and they parted as good friends. Velent went on to live several years, famous throughout the northern half of the earth for his skill and all his knowledge.

ÞIÐREKSSAGA AF BERN, CHAP. 57–7

(THIRTEENTH CENTURY)[19]

In the thirteenth century, Hákon Hákonarson (died 1264), king of Norway, gave the order to gather together all the Germanic legends, which ensured that we now have a monument of heroic legends, The Saga of Thidrek of Bern, *in which we find one version of the story of Wayland the Smith (here called Velent), which notably differs from the one passed down in a poem of the Poetic Edda (where he is called Völund), which does not mention the part concerning his apprenticeship in the craft of smithing. However, the saga does not include the story of Wayland and his brothers marrying swan maidens, but it does provide a number of details on the life of the smith.*

📕 Beckmann, *Wieland der Schmied in neuer Perspektive* (with a good bibliography); Maillefer, "Essai sur Völundr-Wieland"; Motz, *The Wise One of the Mountain;* Nedoma, *Die bildlichen und schriftlichen Denkmäler der Wielandsage.*

3. Valentine and Nameless

Once upon a time there was a very wise king of France whose name was Pepin.* He had a pretty sister, Phila, who was twenty-three years of age and had every virtue, as well as a twelve-year old daughter named Clarina, who was always merry. One day some messengers arrived from afar: they brought a request of marriage from Crisosmus, the sovereign ruler of Hungary,[20] who wished to wed Phila.[21] Pepin accepted and let him know that the marriage would be performed if he came to France.

The entire court of Crisosmus was overjoyed with this answer, but his mother was quite upset about it.[22] The bishop, Vrankart, told his ruler: "I shall not go with you. It would be better for you to remain here. It is Pepin's responsibility to travel, as is right and fitting." The

---

*Pepin the Hunchback (ca. 770–811), son of Charlemagne and his concubine Himiltrude.

king's mother told him the same thing. Furious, Crisosmus replied: "Whoever does not wish to join me, can stay here!" Dreading the royal wrath, Vrankart tried to soothe him with deceptive words: "My lord, what I said was in jest. I will follow you and your mother will obey you."

Crisosmus and his retinue made the journey to France in forty-two days, crossing through Austria and Swabia, and Pepin gave them a friendly and lavish welcome. The marriage took place, the couple stayed at the court for an entire year, and Phila became pregnant. Pepin asked an astrologer to tell him what the child's future would be. The next night, the adept read in the stars that Phila was expecting twins[23] who would have extraordinary strength and perform wonders. Vankart got wind of this and reported it to the king's mother, who immediately became enraged. Both of them turned their thoughts to finding a way of bringing these children misfortune. "Noble lady," said the bishop, "be present when she gives birth and bring a maidservant with you. Have her seize the children and drown them in a lake. You shall thereby be avenged and Phila dishonored."

When the time for Phila to give birth arrived,[24] they put this plan into action. The queen's serving woman, Philamine, was forced, much against her will, to abduct the newborn children. "If I forget my duty by killing these infants, I will be committing a crime, but if I do not obey my mistress's order, I will lose my life." She grabbed a strongbox, in which she placed one of the children. She then nailed it shut and made it watertight before tossing it into a lake.[25] She took the other child into the forest where she left it on the grass beneath a bush.

A she-wolf with cubs lived not far from there.[26] She carried the child[27] into her lair, where she treated him as one of her own and nursed him.[28]

In the meantime, Philamine had rejoined the queen and told her that the children were dead. Alone in her room, Phila wept and asked for her children.

In the morning, Crisosmus visited his wife, accompanied by his mother, and asked her: "Why are you alone?" His mother answered him: "No one was allowed to witness her giving birth."*

He then asked: "Phila, where are your children?"

"I don't know."

"She is like a lioness,"† the queen mother replied. "I would wager a thousand marks that she killed them, just so you know, my son."

Crisosmus went into a rage, much to his mother's great pleasure, and left the chamber. He found Pepin and accused Phila of murder.

Pepin responded in a menacing tone: "If this is true, then justice must be served!"

"I have heard it said that the princess was evil," said Vrankart. "She slew her children out of sheer malevolence."

The next day, the beautiful and valiant Clarina was walking outdoors accompanied by a servant. She spotted a chest floating in the lake, grabbed hold of it, and brought it to shore. In it she discovered a newborn whom she delightedly took into her arms and discreetly brought back to her room.[29] Her servant went to find food for the child and came back with some goat's milk that Clarina gave to the infant. She was sworn to keep their discovery a secret.[30] She saw a cross[31] between the child's shoulders and deduced from this that he was of noble birth. She was completely unaware of all Phila's misfortunes.

A short time later, the powerless Phila was brought before the court. "Stupid woman, why have you slain your children?" her brother demanded. "How could you be so wicked? You shall die at the stake!"

Vrankart then approached her: "Lady, confess and make your peace with God. Confess publicly and you soul shall benefit."

"Why do you claim that I am lost?" Phila replied, hurt and sad. "I know nothing about this. God will take my soul."

"She is guilty of this murder!" the bishop shouted. "She must pay!"[32]

Senseless from fear, Phila hurled herself on him, grabbing him by his hair and his beard and then biting off his nose,[33] adding: "Out

---

*The expressions of a taboo that can also be seen in the story of Melusine's mother.
†According to one tradition, the lioness ate her children at birth.

and out traitor! You know all about this murder that I have been accused of!"

A knight named Blandemer[34] who was present wrested Vrankart out of her clutches and then told the bishop: "If you were not a man of the cloth, I would challenge you to a duel because you know quite a bit about this crime." Pepin then shouted out in anger: "I think she is guilty; let her burn!"

Blandemer replied: "Very well, I will fight on her behalf if any of you have the courage to face me!"

"What kind of mess are you getting into?!" his father Baudouin blurted out.

"Father, when I was dubbed a knight, I promised to risk my life for every person who was unjustly thrown into distress."

This consideration aroused doubts in everyone there, even Crisosmus. Baudouin resumed: "My lords, here is what I suggest. To burn a queen would cover all of us with shame. Make her swear to go far from here with my son."[35]

Phila and Blandemer left the land by unknown paths and one evening came to the edge of a river. They had nothing to eat. A diabolical magician had erected a tent that the knight spotted; he went over to it with Phila, and they found an abundance of food there. At the moment the knight began eating, he made the sign of the cross while thanking God. In irritation the magician made the tent vanish at once. It had been his hope that the two would behave dishonorably together, but they were both too virtuous.

The next day, they resumed their journey and they caught sight of a black knight accompanied by a weeping maiden, whom he was striking in the face. He was getting his revenge on her for her refusal to satisfy his desires. Blandemer stepped between them, but the other knight mocked him: "My lord Sir Vagabond, you wish to fight, so be it! But if I am victorious, I will take your lady." After a hard fight, Blandemer killed him. The maiden told him that she was the daughter of the king of Arabia and that the black knight had abducted her against her will. Blandemar continued on his way with the two women.

Farther down the road they spotted a man lying next to it, who looked like a pilgrim. He had bread and wine and a sleeping potion like those possessed by swindlers.

"Do us the kindness of selling us something to eat," they asked him, "for we are starving."

"Sit down here next to me," said the treacherous rogue. "I shall share my provisions with you. Have you come across a black knight?"

"He will cause no more harm to anyone," Blandemer responded. "He is dead and lies out on the moor."

The rogue turned purple with rage because the dead man was his master—and now he planned to make them pay for their crime. He gave them the potion to drink, and, when all were sleeping, he threw Blandemer on his horse's back and led him to the castle, where he announced the death of the master of the house and had his captive incarcerated with the other prisoners.

When Blandemer woke up, he grew frightened and said to himself: "I am bewitched or else I am dreaming. Where are my arms and armor? I have never experienced anything so strange." When he saw that his legs were bound, he said: "How did I get here? I must still be sleeping, otherwise this would be a very poor joke."

"My friend," responded another captive, "you are quite awake. You have been cast into a dungeon through treachery, and you will remain here until you die."

But let us leave Blandemer and return to Phila and the maiden.

A leopard brushed by them as it went by. They woke up and began moving about, and the leopard withdrew away. Bemoaning the disappearance of Blandemer, they headed off with heavy hearts in a direction chosen at random. Unwittingly, they had picked the right road. It led them to a castle that the maiden recognized as the one belonging to her father. Once they entered, the recounted their adventures, then the maiden suggested to Phila: "Since you have lost Blandemer, stay here with me; we will never leave each other again." So the queen remained there for twelve years. But give me something to drink before I continue!

Clarina raised the child she had found in the lake until he reached the age of twelve. She had named him Valentine. He grew in wisdom, and as his other qualities were revealed by age, she fell in love with him. She told him of her love and kissed him.[36] "It does not seem fitting to wed a man who has yet to prove himself," he responded. "I am still a child; it is not reasonable to choose me."

There was a servant who lived at the castle who was named Gawain, an obnoxious reprobate, who had been present when Clarina found Valentine. He had his heart set on her and, blinded by his love, was filled with hopes. When he heard these words, he intervened: "Lady, it is shameful to kiss a foundling!" In a fury, Valentine charged at him like a wild boar. Gawain took flight, but Valentine pursued him until he caught up to him in the great hall where the king and his court were dining. There, with a single blow of his fist, he knocked the man's head from his body. All rose from the table in an uproar, and Pepin commanded: "Seize this murderer! How dare he commit a crime before my very eyes." He had no idea that Valentine was his nephew.

"He shall pay for this with his life!"

"My lord," the young man told him, "I was forced to kill him. If anyone comes near me, I will hit him."

Four men hurled themselves on him, and he slew them all with his bare hands. Forty others leaped upon him and captured him.

"My lord and father," said Clarina, "calm down, for the love of heaven! Know that this is the son of the king of

Portugal. He was entrusted to me so that he could be educated."*

"Let him remain here as a prisoner," Pepin decided.

A short time later, a messenger who had journeyed at full speed arrived from Spain. He entered the palace and said he had come to seek aid for his king because the Saracens were despoiling the land with fire and blood. Pepin left with twenty thousand warriors and reached Seville.[37] They met the Saracens in battle, but he lost so many men that he had to ask Clarina to send reinforcements. She had freed Valentine, who wished to take advantage of this opportunity to prove his worth. She equipped him, putting on him a coat of mail that had been made impenetrable by the blood of Christ. She dubbed him a knight,† girded a sword at his waist, and placed him at the head of three thousand knights. He then set out for Andalusia.

As soon as they arrived in front of Seville, Valentine and his army attacked the Saracens. Pepin and the king of Spain followed the battle from the crenellations and admired the deeds of the young knight, not knowing who he was. The gallant knight eventually captured Liamerin, the monarch of the pagans. He yielded him to Pepin's hands, asking that he be given good treatment.

"Brave knight," Pepin replied, "I shall reward you."

"I beg you to grant me one favor: restore me my freedom! It is me that you had tossed into the dungeon," said Valentine.

Pepin consented with good heart. Liamerin proposed they make peace: "If you release me, I shall go home with my troops and pay you damages for all the wrongs I have caused you." They reconciled, a large celebration was organized, and afterward Pepin returned to France with his men.

One morning at dawn, Pepin went hunting with twelve valiant knights. One of them brought his attention to a strange and unknown animal:[38] it was Valentine's brother, lacking all reason and knowing naught but instinct. Two of the knights set off in pursuit of the creature, and he stood his ground to defend himself, knocking the first

---

*This invention attests to Clarina's presence of mind.

†Valentine's status changes from student to knight.

knight from his saddle and killing him, then rending the other with his sharpened claws. He then charged Pepin and wounded him. The king took flight and reached the castle, where he informed Valentine what had happened. The young knight expressed his desire to see the beast. He armed himself and set off. When he found the animal, it leaped on him and unseated him from his horse. It tried to rip him to pieces, but his good coat of mail protected him. Seeing that Valentine was lying motionless on the ground, the animal turned around and left. When Valentine regained his senses, he reflected on what had just happened, grabbed a heavy branch, and rushed in pursuit of the creature. He struck the beast, which fell to its knees and put its hands together. Valentine then tied a belt around its neck. Pepin, who had come back in the meantime, was delighted that the beast had been captured.

On their return to the castle, Clarina heard the news and went to kiss Valentine, but the animal jumped on her and tore her garments. The knight struck the animal and let it know that it would need to change its behavior. The three of them then went into a room: "Lady, have no fear," Valentine told her, "it resembles a man. Give him something to drink to comfort him." She complied, and the beast thanked her by kneeling, a sign that it was beginning to learn reason. They gave him the name of Nameless. Valentine had him bathed and summoned a barber, but the wild man attacked him and the knight had to pick up a razor to personally shave off all the beast's hair.* He then discovered that Nameless had a cross between his shoulders. Once he was dressed, he looked like quite a handsome lad.†

Nameless learned how to stand, and his behavior improved every day; he soon learned how to understand the language of men. He accompanied Valentine everywhere. The knight commanded a blacksmith to forge Nameless a hefty cudgel,[39] which he gave to the creature to his great joy. Valentine decided to set off to find his parents and to bring Nameless

---

*The primary characteristic of wild men is their hairiness, which the miniatures in the manuscripts make abundantly clear.

†This marks Nameless's return to human status.

with him. It is impossible to describe the torment felt by Clarina when she heard this news. She wished to accompany him, but he was against it. She then took a vial and poured a potion that healed all wounds and gave it to him before they parted.

Two days later, Valentine and Nameless met a shepherd guarding his flock.

"Tell us, brave shepherd, where are we?" asked Valentine.

"If you walk ahead for another league, you will come to the castle of a nasty character, but you will first have to cross through a forest in which twenty-four cutthroats are hiding. Thanks to a sleeping potion, they have slain many folk. If you drink any of it, you shall die!"

Valentine and Nameless headed toward the castle, but a robber spotted them and warned his companions. Four of them armed themselves and rode to meet the two brothers. "Welcome, young lords! Have a cup of fine wine to drink," said one of them, holding a goblet out to Valentine, who took it and smashed it against the robber's skull while drawing his sword. Nameless charged at the other rabble and slew them. Their companions raced to the rescue. With four blows, Nameless slew eight of them, while Valentine slaughtered the rest. They resumed their journey[40] and came to the castle in which Blandemer was held captive.

"There are only two of them. What happened? How were they able to elude our companions?" the brigands asked one another. Four men armed and equipped themselves to take them captive, but the two brothers made short work of them. The men of the castle told each other: "Let us not delay in slaying them. We are holding prisoner a knight with the courage of a lion," one rogue said. "Offer him his freedom in exchange for their capture!" Everyone found this counsel to their liking. Blandemer was freed, and he accepted their offer. His arms and armor were returned to him, and, still a bit unsteady on his legs that had been bound for so long, he got into the saddle.

He rode to meet the two brothers, and combat was engaged.

"Damned traitor, you are going to die!" Valentine spat at him, once they had broken their lances.

"Valiant knight, I do not deserve that name," replied Blandemer, who told him the story of Phila. "My lord, listen to me and let us stop fighting. Give me your sword and have your servant give me his club; I am going to bring you with me as if you were my prisoners. Once we are through the gate, take back your weapons and I will help you slay these treacherous men."

The two brothers followed this advice, and, after they had entered, they slew the miscreants, freed all the prisoners, and set fire to the castle.[41]

Valentine then asked about Phila because the voice of blood was drawing him to her. "She is in Arabia," Blandemer told him. "If you wish to see her, you must go there." So they set off, and their journey proceeded with hardly a hindrance.

During this time, once he realized that Phila's loyalty to her husband was unshakeable, Gawain decided to bring about her ruin. So, while she was sleeping next to the king's daughter, he slit the girl's throat and left the bloodstained knife in Phila's hand.[42] He then went to awaken the king, telling him: "Lord, I had a dream about your daughter that has most alarmed me. That is why I am here. I believe she may be in danger." The monarch grew frightened and got up. He went to his daughter's room, where he found the maiden dead. "It was Phila who killed her out of jealousy!" Gawain shouted. "See, she is still holding the knife; she is guilty of this murder!" He roughly shook Phila awake.

"Get up! Your vile crime will earn you a death by fire."

"All-powerful lord, I know nothing of this crime!"

"Silence, traitor! You are holding the knife, the proof of your crime," replied Gawain, tying the weapon securely to Phila's hand before dragging her before the court. Everyone bemoaned the death of the princess, and Phila was condemned. She was then stripped* and led to the pyre.

Just then the two brothers arrived on the scene with Blandemer, who immediately recognized the queen and alerted Valentine. He immediately jumped to the ground, pushed his way forward, and asked: "For what reason are you executing this woman?"

"What do you want here?" Gawain asked him. "Why are you asking? She murdered our princess."

"No," Phila cried out, "that's not true! We were peacefully sleeping. When I woke up, I saw her lying next to me, dead. God alone knows what happened."

"Harken all," Gawain went on, "she will be burned alive for this murder!"

"Leave her in peace," Valentine ordered. "You shall not burn her before I have gotten the facts straight about this matter. I think that you know a lot more about it than this woman. I am going to be her champion. We shall fight because she is innocent."

Mad with rage, the king and his court summarily leaped into their saddles and set upon Blandemer and the two brothers, who exhibited such valor that a truce was quickly called for. Gawain took umbrage at this and said to his friends: "That man is too strong for me, and right is on his side because I killed the princess. What should I do?"

"It is better to fight than to have your head cut off," one of his kinsmen responded. "Fight! We will trick his companions and lock them in the tower. When you enter the enclosed field, we shall not be far away and we will come to your aid."

One of them then made his way to Valentine and courteously told him: "Lord, your companions should go up in that tower, for I am sure

---

*Which means stripped of her garments that indicate her rank, and clad in a shirt. This entire episode is missing from the French text.

they will not be able to refrain from coming to your aid if they see you are in trouble."

"Let it be so! Nameless and Blandemer, go there!" the knight ordered, and they obeyed.

Valentine faced Gawain in battle and defeated him easily. Immediately, the companions of the traitor charged at Valentine and unseated him from his horse. Driven into a fury at this sight, Nameless tore the bolts from the door, knocked it down with his club, and then rushed into the fray with Blandemer right behind him. All three performed such wonders that the king called a halt to the combat. Blandemer captured Gawain and threw him at the king's feet. The treacherous knave confessed to his crime. He was dragged throughout the city and cast into a boiling cauldron, where he perished,* and afterward his corpse was placed on the wheel that was reserved for the display of traitors. Everyone then returned to the city. The king asked Valentine to remain and offered Phila a throne. They refused—he because he was looking for his father, and she out of fear.

All four rode together across the moor until they came to a crossroads. "Choose one road," said Valentine, "and we shall take the other." Phila and he parted with heavy hearts because their voices of blood and the force of the elements† were making themselves heard. Blandemer and the princess took the road on the right, not knowing what dangers lay in wait for them.

The next day, they came to a castle where lived the ferocious giant Magros. He possessed not a single virtue and was terrifying and huge. He was bald on the front of his head, and his nose was an ell in length. His breath stank, his mouth was the size of a horse stall, and his ears were the size of pitchers. His eyes were black as pitch, his arms were long and thick, his hands were like paws, and the legs he stood upon were as solid as a wall.[43] He was a real devil. When he saw them, he came toward them, yelling: "What are you doing on my lands?" He grabbed them and

---

*The French text says a cauldron of boiling oil, although it is Bishop Vrankart who suffers this execution.

†An allusion to the configuration of the sky.

tossed Blandemer in a dungeon and told Phila: "Your place is with the other women because I love a lady and, at the same time, hate her for her pride. I would lavish her with gold and silver if she looked at me, but she ignores me. Because she owns a snakelet, I cannot use my strength, so I take my revenge on others—no one gets away from me." Phila was thus put with the other female prisoners in a marsh* in which they had to stand from morning to noon.[44] At that time the giant fed them and they were allowed to come out of the water. The incarcerated men were allowed to join them then and speak to them under the watchful eye of Magros. Several years passed by in this fashion. Phila became so stricken with grief that she could no longer eat. The giant noticed it.

"Lady, you love this young knight." He was thinking of Blandemer. "I don't condemn you for it; I know how it is. The one I love deprives me of all sense and reason."

"She is wrong," replied Phila. "She took your heart and her position is blamable."†

"Thank you for these kind words; for three days a week you will not have to go into the marsh."

Valentine and his brother took the road on the left, where great surprises awaited them. On entering a forest where the songs of many birds were echoing, they came upon a lady sitting beneath a tree. The knight approached her and asked: "Gentle lady, what are you doing here? Please satisfy my curiosity."

"Young gallant knight, do not come near me if you value your life. Near here lives a giant who will kill you; even if you offered him three thousand marks to spare your life, he would not do it. It has been nine years save a month that I have been beneath this tree, and the giant has slain more than one man. In thirty days, he shall take me as his wife. A prophecy, however, says that a mute, who is the son of a king and never nursed on human milk,‡ shall free me. The ring hanging here is intended for him.[45]

---

*Phila must suffer the water torture. In general, this more often concerns an icy spring.
†A curious observation, since a marriage like this would violate all the social codes of this era.
‡Description of Nameless.

"By my faith, we shall see about that!" Valentine answered intrepidly. "We shall wait for this monster. You shall never be his wife!"

Magros then loomed up.

"What are you doing here next to this lady?" he yelled. "You shall regret it!"

"He started it," said Valentine. "Let's fight!"

The giant wounded him, but Nameless struck him down and then strangled him. He gave his brother Clarina's potion to drink, healing him, and then he kissed the lady on the lips. She handed him the ring. "It is for you," she said. "If you wear it, you will be invisible and be able to discover the truth." She then turned toward Valentine: "My lord, I would like to wed your companion; I beg you to go find my father as quick as you can. He is a powerful duke of Carinthia.[46] I know that he will be upset about the death of Magros. If he attacks you, defend yourself."

The brothers left that place and a short time later saw an array of splendid tents in the distance. A lookout spied them and went to warn his lords: "Come and silently arm yourselves, for there are two men coming here with Rosemonde![47] I think that the giant is dead." Twenty-four knights readied themselves and charged at the brothers. Nameless slipped the ring onto his finger and made himself invisible, but not his cudgel, which caused their ruin. The duke approached with his retinue. "What a wonder this deadly club is!" he cried. "Rosemonde, make peace between us and your companions!" She obeyed; the duke housed them and granted his daughter's wish that a priest be summoned to unite her with Nameless.

After three weeks of festivities, Valentine said: "May God come to my aid! I have lost my companion and must pursue the quest for my parents alone."

"That is not at all true," his brother answered. "I shall accompany you."

"Don't take my husband!" Rosemonde cried in tears.

"If God wills it, I will bring him back to you safe and sound," Valentine promised her, and he rode off with Nameless.

While pursuing their journey, their path crossed that of a messenger from whom they demanded news. "If you wish to earn a great reward," he answered, "go to Hungary as quick as you can. The pagans are causing my sovereign great harm and ravaging his lands."

Without a moment's hesitation, the brothers went there and introduced themselves to King Crisosmus, who gave them a warm welcome although he had no idea that they were his sons. On the next day the battle took place, which he won thanks to the two brothers. Nameless performed such wonders with his club that all called it a miracle. Valentine captured the emperor of Kataria, and the Saracens fled.

On their return to the palace, all went in to dine and the king had Valentine and Nameless seated close to him. "This is an extraordinary thing!" the bishop Vrankart exclaimed. "Although there is no shortage of nobles here, I am astounded to see these two hardy fellows daring to sit where they are." On hearing these words, Nameless leaped in fury over the table and flung himself at the bishop, tearing a strip of skin from his back that was as wide as a hand. His victim was stunned and speechless but was raging inside, thinking of nothing but how to get his revenge.

When the hour came to go to sleep, he went to visit the captive emperor and said to him: "If you wish, I will help you flee and kill those who put you in this situation, for they have done me a great wrong."

"That would not be at all appropriate for me," the prisoner replied, fearing treachery. "I have been treated well, so I will not break my word, even if I must die."

"My lord, you speak rightly," responded the treacherous Vrankart. "I just wanted to see if you would be disloyal," and he withdrew, mad with rage because his ruse had been ineffective.

The next morning, all gathered to discuss the fate of the prisoner. They asked him for a ransom, and he offered a cask of red gold. Crisosmus accepted, freed him, and he returned to his own land. The two brothers then made their farewells to the monarch, who wanted them to stay, though it was in vain.

Four days later, a strange snakelet appeared in a meadow and spoke to them.[48] "My lord Valentine, I am going to tell you who your parents are. Follow me and pay attention; walk on the trail I leave."

"This is quite peculiar," the knight said. "This is no ordinary animal."

The reptile led them to the castle of a noble maiden; Rosilia was her name. The snake told her: "Valentine and Nameless are brothers; their father is the king of Hungary and their mother is named Phila. The giant Magros is holding her prisoner," and he told her the whole story. "Nameless has a band of skin that hinders his tongue; if it is cut as it should be, he will speak like everyone else. If you fall in love with Valentine, I shall die."[49]

The brothers then presented themselves before Rosilia, who immediately fell in love with the knight and her snakelet burst into two pieces, like an egg. "Young lord of high birth, I have lost my snakelet because of you, but I do not hold that against you at all. Swear you will marry me and I will reveal who your parents are." Valentine promised, and she told him that Nameless was his brother, Crisosmus was his father, and Phila was his mother. Filled with joy, the two brothers embraced, and then Valentine asked: "Do you know how to restore speech to my brother?"

"Yes, and I will take care of it," said the maiden, who then cut the strip of skin.

"Where is our mother?" they asked. "We wish to see her as soon as possible."

She is only two leagues from here. But do not rush off; follow my advice and with the help of God, you shall free her. Stay here tonight."

In the morning, Rosilia told them: "You are going to face a terrible giant who is so strong that no one in this land can defeat him because he wears a sparkling ring. He just needs to look at it for healing if he is wounded. Find it, and his strength will disappear! Next, you will find your mother in a marsh."

"God bless you!" said Valentine. "We are going to leave but we will return soon."

They avoided the main road and followed alongside a river until they spotted many pretty women in a marsh. Among them they saw their mother, whom they recognized at once. "Phila, noble queen, come to us, we are your children! Your pains and cares will soon be over because we are going to triumph."[50] These words filled Phila's heart

with joy as she went toward them. She replied: "My dear children, I dare not tarry near you because a giant is going to come and he will kill you."

"Have no fear! God will aid us!"

Magros joined them on the shore.

"Who asked you to pull that woman from the marsh?" he yelled at the two brothers. "You are going to pay for that!"

"En garde," Valentine replied. "Let's see how brave you truly are."

The giant lost his temper and attacked the knight, but Nameless lopped off his arm with his cudgel, the same arm whose hand wore the magical ring. His brother then cut off one of his legs, and together they finished off the monster. All the women cheered, and Phila said: "Run to the castle and free the loyal Blandemer, whom you know well, along with all the other prisoners!" The brothers did just this[51] and then went back to Rosilia's castle, where they were given a warm welcome.

The marriage of Rosilia and Valentine took place there shortly afterward. The brothers, accompanied by Phila and Blandemer, then returned to Hungary, where they introduced themselves to the king, whom they knew well. "Father, we would like to speak with you," said Valentine. Crisosmus brought them into a secluded room and Valentine told him the whole story. This is how the king reunited with Phila and they were not at all stingy with their kisses.

Nameless took care of the bishop Vrankart: he brought him before Crisosmus, bound hand and foot, and accused him of all the crimes I described to you earlier. Vrankart confessed and was drawn and quartered, then the four quarters of his corpse were displayed before the entire city, each piece on a wheel. Great rejoicing then broke out, after which everyone returned to France, where they were given a royal celebration by Pepin. Clarina welcomed Valentine and Rosilia with every honor and listened to their adventures. Blandemer married Clarina and ascended the throne of Spain. After the death of Pepin, Valentine ruled over France.

I have to say a few more words about Nameless and Rosamonde. After the husband left, she went in search of him, disguised as a minstrel,[52] after cutting off her hair and accompanied only by her maidservant. The former behaved as a man and the latter as a woman. They traveled through many lands, singing their own songs, and finally ended up in France, where they ran into Nameless. They saw him as they were headed toward the castle and he began teasing the maidservant. "Young lord, leave her be!" Rosemonde ordered. "Even if I am only a poor man, I look after the honor of my wife and none may scold her in my presence." Vexed, Nameless gave her a nasty look and replied: "You look like a woman—I will not fight against you. Tell me what arts you have mastered."

"We know how to sing, tell stories, and keep the nobility entertained; we have traveled many countries, from north to south and from east to west."

"Would you know a woman called Rosemonde the Beauty? She lived in Carinthia."

"Yes, I know of her and we have a song about her."

"Sing it to me; it would give me great pleasure!"

"Yes, but first we are hungry and thirsty!"

Nameless led them into the hall where meals were served and where the lords met. He found them a place to sit. "Hurry up and eat," he told them. "I am eager to hear your song!" But they took their time and left him chomping at the bit. At last they began singing about how Nameless met his beloved and their entire story, then Rosemonde revealed her identity. Nameless embraced her and began kissing her with great passion.

At the death of Crisosmus, Nameless succeeded him on the Hungarian throne. He lived in honor until the end of his life.

Now my story is done; pour me something to drink![53]

VAN NAMELOSS VNDE VALENTYN

Based on a now lost French source text, a thirteenth-century chivalric romance, an anonymous fourteenth-century author writing in Low German has provided us with the oldest existing version of the chapbook[54] known by the name of Valentin and Orson, *one of the folktales of the Middle Ages. It was printed in France for the first time in 1489 by Jacques Maillet in Lyon. The story was translated into English, German, Swedish, Dutch, and Italian. Thomas John Dibdin wrote a romantic melodrama based on this tale that was staged at Covent Garden in 1804 with a score by Jouve.*

With its open structure, the story lends itself to a variety of interpretations. The popular book version, which contains seventy-four chapters, includes the appearance of a dwarf magician named Pacolet, and the plot even takes us to India.

AATH 301; 502; 650 A

📖 Blom, "Valentin et Orson et la Bibliothèque bleue"; BP II, 285–97 ; Dickson, *Valentine and Orson;* EM, s.v. "Frau in Männerkleidung," "Valentin und Orson";

L'Histoire de Valentin et Orson tres preux, tres nobles, et tres vaillans cheualiers, fils de l'Empereur de Grece, & neueux du tres-vaillans, & tres-Chrestien roy de France, Pépin; Klemming, ed., *Namnlös och Valentin; Een schoone Historie Van de twee Gebroeders en vroome Ridders Valentyn en Oursson den Wilden-Man, Zoonen van Alexander keyser van Constantinopelen, ende Neven van Pipinus koning van Vrankryk; Een schoone en wonderlyke historie van Valentyn en Ourrsson, Twee edele vroome Ridders, Zoonen van den magtigen Keizer van Griekenland en Neeven van den Edelen Koning Pepyn, toen ter tyd koning van Frankryk* (other edition Amsterdam: De Groot, ca. 1670); Saintyves, "Les Jumeaux dans l'ethnographie et la mythologie"; Watson, *The hystory of the two valyaunte brethren Valentyne and Orson, sonnes vnto the Emperour of Grece.*

4. Henry the Lion

The valiant hero, the duke Henry, lived in his castle in Brunswick so happily with his noble wife that, in the opinion of his subjects, there was nothing more he could desire. However, he had a thirst for glory and adventure that pushed him to travel far. One day, he gathered round him the most courageous of his knights and counts, who were no less greedy than he for honors and glory. Equipped for a long voyage, he went to see his wife to bid her farewell. He broke his gold ring in two and gave one half to the poor weeping woman while telling her: "If I have not returned in seven years,[55] take another husband. May God and His saints protect you!"

He left with his elite troop. After several days' ride, they came to a wide river where a boat lay waiting, ready to set sail. Giving it little thought, the lords abandoned their horses and climbed on board. They sailed for many days and many nights over a vast sea without catching sight of any land. Repeated storms tore apart the sails, and they lost control of the ship.[56] The food ran out, and they began to starve. The duke prayed in vain, lifting his arms to heaven and pleading for divine mercy. Their misery and wails grew more intense by the hour and eventually the duke told them: "Lamenting will do you no good. Let each man here craft his token and mark it with his own blood.*

---

*The lots are sticks; the procedure is the same as drawing the short straw.

This token will determine the fate of the man chosen to be eaten. I will not exclude myself from this lottery!"[57] No one aboard refused, and they tossed their tokens into a hat. One of the boldest heroes pulled out his own token and remained undaunted, saying with words straight from his heart: "Dispose of me as you will, I give you the gift of my life. May God protect our duke and let fate designate each of us, one after the other, but spare him." This brave man was killed, dismembered, and eaten by his companions dying from hunger.

This sacrifice proved to be insufficient, and the lots had to be drawn repeatedly: no one refused to die, and all rejoiced that God continued to spare their lord. Finally, the only people left were the duke and one lone squire. Neither of them had any desire to draw lots, as each one was the sole consolation for the other. But hunger compelled the noble lord, after resisting for as long as he could, to tell his companion: "I would like for us to discuss our lots. Even if it falls on me, I will sacrifice myself."

"I would rather die than accept it!" his squire responded.

The duke was designated by lot, and he immediately commanded his companion to kill him, but in vain! The other could not bring himself to do it, despite his lord's insistence. "I would regret it my entire life if I owed it to the flesh of my noble lord," he cried out, and there matters rested.

As the duke would not give in on this point, the squire had an idea.[58] "I am going to sew you inside a cattle hide," he said, "and we will see what happens. Luck may smile upon you for you are young and strong." Henry accepted, and once he was sewn inside the hide, the squire prayed that divine clemency would not be long in coming. A monstrous griffin[59] swooped down on the duke, grasped him with its claws, and carried him off to its nest at the top of a tree.[60]

While he was being transported this way, our valiant hero kept up his courage and silently prayed for the flight to end well for him. After depositing its prey in its nest, the griffin went off again in search of more food. Henry took advantage of its absence to cut open the hide with his sword, but the griffin's chicks hurled themselves upon him with horrible cries. He brandished his weapon and decapitated the malevolent mob, with each stroke of his sword sending heads, claws, and wings flying. Once all were dead, he took their claws,[61] which can still be seen today hanging in the city of Brunswick, and used them to climb down the tree. Still feeling dazed at the sight of the gigantic monsters, he headed into the forest, where he fed himself on roots and berries until the moment when he heard the howls of wild animals. He went toward the sound and saw a lion fighting a dragon. The duke said to himself: "By my faith, the lion is known worldwide for its loyalty; I am going to help it against this vile reptile. Even if I am forced to lay down my life, I still hope I can defeat it with the help of God."

With this idea in mind and brandishing his sword, he leaped upon the monster, which attacked him, growling with its mouth wide open. The bold knight burst out laughing and urged the lion to defend itself. Encouraged, the animal planted his teeth and claws in the dragon's flesh while the duke struck its scale-covered hide with his sword, causing sparks to fly. The wounded beast began to howl in pain and rage. Henry finally managed to lop off its head with one blow, and the dragon died at once. The lion let out a joyous roar and when the duke, exhausted, stretched out on his shield, he casually lay down next to him. Henceforth, the lion remained by his side and hunted for him in the vast forest.[62]

They made their way to a wide river. There Henry built a raft from branches and climbed aboard with the lion.* The current carried them

---

*The following episode is very different in the Dutch song "Henry the Lion." The hero comes to the seaside; spies a boat; hails the sailor, who takes him aboard along with his lion; and brings him back to his country.

toward a mountain, where the waves carried them close to shore. They found themselves near a castle, came up alongside it, and the duke knocked at its door. The door opened, and he was asked where he came from, but he did not know what to say. The door warden left to alert the lord of the castle, who invited the visitor inside. Henry entered with his lion and discovered that the inhabitants of this place all had long beaks.[63] They questioned him, but he could not answer because he did not know their language. A woman was given the duty of asking him where he came from; Henry recounted his adventures, and he was served a meal. Because the woman was joking with the lord of Brunswick, the guests took umbrage and tried to kill him. However, the lion furiously leaped at them and laid them all low while Henry made his way into the forest with the woman.[64]

There he ran into Wodan's Army,[65] which is made up of evil spirits,[66] and was stricken with terror. One of them, which was monstrous and horrible, approached him. Henry conjured it at length and quite firmly: "Tell me how my son[67] and dear wife are doing!" he ordered it, and the spirit was forced to do as he asked. "I am going to tell you, and I shall offer you a pact,"[68] it responded. "I shall return you to your castle, but if I find you asleep there when I return with your lion, you will belong to me and my companions."

These words alarmed Henry, who directed a prayer to God: "Lord, advise me and help me so that I do not lose my life or lose my soul!" The God of charity responded and indicated to Henry that he should leave with the spirit. Henry thus concluded the pact.

The spirit brought him back to his own land and set him down in front of the castle, while reminding him: "If I find you asleep, you know what awaits you! I go now to fetch your lion," and he soared away, covering thousands of miles in little time. When he returned, the noble lord was asleep on the grass. The lion began to roar, which woke him up. "Brunswick, you tricked me!" cried the spirit as it cast the lion to the ground before disappearing.

The inhabitants of the city noticed him and raced over to see this amazing sight. Henry was completely covered in his beard and hair; he looked like a wild man or a pilgrim.[69] The news reached the castle that some peculiar visitors had arrived. The lady went out, saw Henry without recognizing him,[70] and said: "Have him come inside, but leave the animal to stay outdoors!"

"That will not do at all," the duke replied. "I would rather die. This lion has suffered the same torments as me. Believe me, Lady!"

"Let him come in, then!" she commanded her servants. Once inside, the lord with the long beard regarded his wife with joy, without wishing, however, to reveal his name until he knew what was likely to happen.

A number of lords then came in that had been invited to the wedding. They were loudly summoned to take a place at the table, where each was seated in accordance with their rank, but Henry and his lion were left in the courtyard. The guests were merry and their laughter could be heard everywhere. They had Henry and his lion come in; the lady's chamberlain ordered silence and spoke to Henry.

"Brother, tell us what the strange lands are like; it seems to me that you have traveled far. Have you not heard tale of a valorous duke?"

"If I were to tell you the truth," Henry replied, "you would not believe me. I have seen him but a short time ago, and he was in good health. He is going to return home soon. I know this, for I have been his companion. He gave me the task of greeting his daughter, his son,[71] and his wife if I should come before his castle."

All there asked him many questions about his adventures, but he responded: "Women have long hair and short memories; out of sight, out of mind." The lady offered him something to drink while looking at him closely. He dropped his half of the ring into the cup, where it gleamed like a diamond, and handed it back to her. She quickly grabbed it and found it was a perfect fit for the half a ring in her possession and cried out: "I have found my beloved husband and dear lord!"[72] She went up to him and said: "Forgive me for betraying you. I will perform whatever penance you ask of me."

"Hush, noble lady," her husband commanded, "do not be so hard on yourself! Let us say no more about it because your honor remains intact. But if I had returned any later,[73] who knows what would have happened."[74]

The man who had been on the verge of marrying the woman approached Henry and yielded to him.[75]

"Do to me what you will," he said.

"If I had been dead," replied the duke, "you would have been my successor. I have no quarrel with you that you aspired to higher honors. Remain by my side as the loyal vassal you have always been."

This was how Henry returned home with the help of God after traveling through many lands and going through many adventures. He lived another twenty-six years in happiness by the side of his wife, then came the day and hour for him to die. Never was such grief heard as that from the lion, who lay down on his grave and refused to leave until he died, too. A handsome bronze lion[76] was sculpted and placed in front of the castle so that all would remember the adventures of Henry and his lion in foreign lands.[77]

The Chap Book Version (variant)

One day the Evil One suddenly appeared and began mocking him: "I am going to share a piece of news with you that will come as a real surprise. While you have been drifting across the sea toward certain death, a foreign prince has come to Brunswick and taken possession of both your wife and your duchy. Their wedding will take place tomorrow, as the entire world knows."

The duke replied sadly:

"My absence has clearly been more than seven years and people must think I am dead. I will turn to divine will and let God do with me as he will."

"Fie! He is not the one who can save you; it is me. I will bring you back to your wife and your many friends within the hour, if you agree to be mine." Despite the devil's insistence, Henry would not yield an inch. "If I deny my faith, I will be damned for eternity," he replied. The devil then immediately came up with another suggestion: "I am going to set you down, safe and sound, in front of the city of Brunswick. You will wait for me there while I fetch your lion without any delay. If I find you sleeping when I return, your soul belongs to me! Decide now!" Henry, knowing the cunning and intention of the Evil One full well, took a long time to reflect on the matter but eventually agreed, impelled by the great love he had for his wife.

To fulfill the contract, the devil grabbed the noble lord and carried him through the sky before gently setting him down in front of Brunswick. "Keep your eyes open until I get back!" the devil snickered, as he immediately went back to fetch the lion. Henry felt like he was dead on his feet from fatigue, which is not at all surprising. Despite his prayers, he let sleep take hold. A short time later, the devil returned and his heart was gladdened at the sight of the dozing duke. When he saw the sleeping Henry, the lion thought he was dead and began to roar pathetically. Awakened by the familiar voice, the frightened duke leaped to his feet. Mad with rage, the devil hurled the animal next to his master so hard that his ribs cracked.

Accompanied by his lion, Henry entered the city and headed toward the stately castle from which the sounds of a large celebration were echoing. "What is going on?" he wondered and started to go inside to find out, but he was accosted by sergeants and heralds who prevented him from entering.

"What is going on here?" he asked them. "Has a foreign lord come to inspire such jubilation? Tell me, my fine fellows!"

"He's no longer a foreigner. This very day he is going to rule over this land and wed the lady of the castle, who, for seven full years, has been in mourning for her husband." The devil had told the truth! Henry cajoled the guard with his humble prayers and turned to one of the sergeants, who had made a good impression on him. "You look like a valiant man. Ask the princess to give you a cup of her wine as comfort for me. You shall not regret it."

The servant gave a long look at the stranger and his lion and raced to tell the princess of this strange request. Henry's audacity made her laugh, but she poured out a cup of her precious wine and ordered: "Tell him to drain it!" After he drank it, the duke threw into the empty cup his half of the gold ring on which his name was engraved and asked the servant to return it to his mistress.

While he was giving her back the cup, the servant asked: "Noble lady, deign to look at this ring. Did you lose it?" The duchess examined it closely. The longer she looked, the paler she grew. "It's my husband," she said to herself. She quickly rose and ran to her chamber. A short time later she asked her chamberlain: "Have you seen the stranger with his lion in front of the castle?"

"Yes, gentle lady. The lion is loyal to him, and he seems to be a gentleman that all regard with amazement." She looked at the ring again and said: "This comes from my beloved husband. May God grant me my dearest wish!" She did not want to wait anymore and ordered: "Have him come in so that I may personally ask him about the provenance of this ring! Know that my husband entrusted me with its other half while telling me: 'If I am not back in seven years, take another husband.'"

The duchess's counselors were particularly keen on getting to the bottom of this secret. They therefore interrogated the stranger, who laughed: "I am going to tell you everything. No one gave me this ring! I took it myself more than seven years ago." They stared long at him, trying to determine if he was mocking them, but the man seemed too serious for that. The duchess had the stranger brought inside. When she saw him, she swooned from joy. Oh, amazement! The duke carefully helped her back up. The lady held her white hand out to him, called him by name, and gave praise to God for bringing her husband home safe and sound. Everyone welcomed him home in unison, then they accorded him the honors due his rank. He was soon served a succulent meal—better than the fare he had on the raft!—and the lion had his fair share.

The fiancé learned of the duke's return and became despondent. Henry and his counselors deliberated on how to compensate the noble suitor. They agreed to offer him the hand of a Franconian maiden of high rank. She lived at the court and was a ravishing beauty. The prince heard them out and found no fault with their suggestion. He said: "If the duke agrees, and if she does not refuse me her hand, she will become my wife and I will take her back to my castle in the very near future." The counselors went immediately in search of the maiden, who first blushingly refused, then finally agreed. They brought word back of her consent to the prince, who said: "I can now return without dishonor. God willing this marriage be celebrated quickly!" he concluded. The wedding took place in great luxury. This was followed by knightly sport in which more than one lance was broken and more than one knight was knocked off his mount. Once the festivities drew to a close, the young couple, richly provided for, returned to the lands of the prince.

Duke Henry ruled for a long time with justice and generosity and never knew any illness. Only the weakness brought about by old age confined him to his bed. "My time to leave has come," he told his weeping wife. "May heaven protect you, my pious and faithful wife, and may he deign to keep watch over my land and my subjects!" These were his last words. He was buried in the castle of Brunswick with his sword at his side. The lion lay down on his tomb and remained there until he died. In memory of his loyalty, a tomb was also made for the beast and his effigy placed on a column that can still be seen today in the good city of Brunswick. As proof of this tale's veracity, the griffin's claws are hanging in the castle keep.

This story of a magical return home appeared circa 1200, a short time after the death of Henry the Lion (died 1195), who had a bronze statue of a lion erected in front of his Dankwarderode Castle in 1166, was banished from the empire for three years in 1180, and left on a crusade in 1192. The story of the grateful lion that has been inserted in the text is therefore etiological. Connected to a historical figure, the two tales form a legend that has been embellished with borrowings from Herzog Ernst, *an epic romance dating from around 1190. This is where the rescue by griffin and the encounter with the beaked men come from, but these episodes are no longer connected to the Magnet Mountain. There is a sixteenth-century Dutch song, with sixty-three strophes of four lines, that is quite similar to our legend but which contains some interesting variations.*

Tale type 974 *is found in a heavily Christianized form in the* Dialogue of the Miracles *(X, 2)*[78] *by the Cistercian monk Caesarius von Heisterbach, written between 1219 and 1223, and in the* Gesta Romanorum *(chap. 193, Osterley edition). In his* Weltchronik *(ca. 1270), Jansen Enikel tells how an angel brought Charlemagne from Hungary when his wife was being compelled to remarry. The "magical return* *home" enjoyed great success inEurope, especially in the Slavic regions, and a trace of it can be found in Boccaccio (*Decameron, X, 9*): a captive of Saladin, the merchant Torello is transported on a bed to Pavia, thanks to a necromancer's magic. See appendix 7.*

AaTh 974; 156 A; TU 1555; 1580

📖 Baumann, *Die Sage von Heinrich dem Löwen bei den Slaven;* BP, II, 318ff.; Caesarius von Heisterbach, *Dialogus miraculorum atque visionum,* II, 218–19; EM, s.v. "Heinkehr des Gatten," "Löwentreue,'" Herzog Ernst"; Grimm, *German Legends,* no. 523 (without the lion) and no. 526; *Historie-Liedeken van den Hertog van Bronswyk* (ed. Von der Hagen), of which there are only two printings; Splettstösser, *Der heimkehrende Gatte und sein Weib in der Weltliteratur.*

5. Saint Oswald and His Raven

Lords, if it pleases you to stop talking, I will tell you the story of the most remarkable man who ever lived. He was named Oswald;[79] he was king of England, and he lived in Salmiders. For vassals he had twelve kings, twenty-four dukes, thirty-six counts, nine bishops, and many knights and warriors. At the age of twenty-four he found himself an orphan without any life experience. He had always wished to serve God and asked Him for advice. "I would like to take a wife without sinning.[80] How do I do this? I am as innocent as a child. Tell me how!" Until he fell asleep, he was preoccupied with wondering about what would happen to his kingdom if he died without leaving an heir. He thought about where he might find a wife of his rank, but in vain.

His guardian angel advised him to travel overseas with a powerful army to find a queen among the pagans. He summoned his vassals, housed them for a twelve full days, and, giving them all the best of what he had on hand, he then made this speech to them: "Lords, hear me out! I have summoned you to get advice. This land has no queen; can you name one that would be worthy of me—Christian or pagan?" Everyone looked at each other in alarm. For three days they deliberated from morning to night, marshaling all their knowledge, and then said: "Alas, sire, we know of no one who is of your rank. There is no woman in your twelve kingdoms who is worthy of you." Having said their piece, they bid Oswald farewell and returned to their own lands.

A noble pilgrim named Warmunt then arrived at the court. He had traveled through seventy-two countries for love of God. The king received him a cordial welcome and gave him his best room to stay in. He then remained to speak with him alone.

"Warmunt, can you give me the name of a queen worthy of me?"

"I am going to try my very best. Beyond the sea, I know a princess named Pamige who has no equal in beauty. Her father, a warlike pagan, rules over Aron, the land that bears his name. Although she is a pagan, she secretly believes in God. If her father knew it, he would kill her. She would like to be baptized, but she has no one willing to help her."

"I must sail across the sea and help her, then," said Oswald. "However, I will need a messenger to learn if this is her true intention."

Warmunt regretted having mentioned this princess. "Without divine aid, you will not be able to win her." The pilgrim refused to be the king's messenger because Aron had beheaded all suitors for the hand of his daughter, whom he desired to wed himself on the death of his wife.[81]

"I am going to go there with my army and abduct Lady Pamige by force," Oswald replied.

"I strongly advise against it. His castle is very well defended; even if you had all the pagans and Christians in the world in your service, you could lay siege to it for thirty years without once catching a glimpse of the princess's face. Here is my counsel: a raven has grown up at your court; he will be your messenger. There is no man as intelligent as he. Over there he will be much more helpful to you than an entire army. God has bestowed him with the gift of speech."[82]

"That's incredible! I have raised that bird for eleven years, and I never once heard him speak."

"That is what you are now going to see. Send someone to fetch him, and if he doesn't speak, kill me!" But no one could bring them the raven that was perched on top of a tower.

"My lords, you who are listening to me, tell me, how can you bring the bird down from on high?"

God, through a miracle, made the raven drop down upon the king's table. "Welcome, Warmunt, noble pilgrim!" said the bird. Oswald asked his guest to forgive him for his disbelief. "You would never have heard me speak," the raven continued, "if God had not permitted me to speak. I will be your messenger,[83] and if I fail, you shall not see me again." Oswald thanked him with a kiss on his head and on his beak. "Listen," said the bird. "Summon a goldsmith to gild my feathers and craft me a gold crown. When I am among the pagans, instead of trying to capture or kill me, they will admire me. I will be given a warm welcome for they always judge by appearance. I will transmit your message to King Aron and recommend you to his daughter."

Oswald called for a goldsmith, whom his chamberlain went to fetch. He told him the king's orders and returned to the court with him. The master sent the bird to his home, and, four days later, the gilding and crown were ready. He took the raven on his hand and made his way to the court. "My lord," he said, "I have fulfilled your command. I deserve twelve gold marks." The chamberlain counted out that sum to him at once. The raven then urged the king to write his letter and seal it. His secretary wrote the letter. Oswald used a silver wire to tie a gold ring to his missive beneath the bird's wing and ordered him: "Tell the princess that after God, I love her best; she shall be my wife and be baptized. With her consent, I will come to fetch her with a large army." The raven soared off as fast as his wings could carry him.

He crossed the sea for ten days, without drinking or eating, and, because he was quite exhausted, he paused on a stone crag in the middle of the ocean. He saw a fish swimming nearby, swooped down, grabbed it, and then ate it. A mermaid,[84] who had been pursuing that fish for a long time, spotted the raven. She grabbed him by his claws and dragged him down to the bottom of the sea. There he found more mermaids, who gave him a worthy welcome. "Look, dear companions," said his abductor, "I think this is an angel sent from heaven." The others thought he was merely a wild animal. One of them challenged the bird to entertain them. "I am in the service of the great King Oswald," the bird responded. "On his court, it is customary for a minstrel to be first fed and given good drink before singing.[85] Bring me bread, cheese, wine, and a succulent roast! That puts artists in a good mood!"

After sating his hunger, he thought: "How can I escape these mermaids?" "Look," he told them while pointing into the watery depths, "the whole world is going to disappear!" They became so scared that they all scrambled to see what was happening. Pressed to fly away, the raven soared away from the table with the help of God. He perched on a rock and began crowing with joy, which the mermaids heard. "That cunning bird tricked us!" they lamented. His abductor was particularly sad about his escape: "It's too bad, he would have given me great joy. If I can catch him again, I will bring him back here to keep me company until the day I die."

"Stop whining!" the raven replied. I will never again go with you, for I must carry my lord's marriage request to the land of Aron."

After six days of flying, the noble raven reached his goal. Rejoicing, he circled above the castle while gazing at it intently. He then landed between two crenellations and began spying: he was looking for the princess. Her father was so infatuated with her that he kept her imprisoned in a chamber, and twenty-four maidens kept watch over her day and night. They had constructed a dais to protect the princess from the wind and sun when she went to dine. The raven saw this and said to himself: "She is heavily guarded. If I am discovered when I approach her, I will be in danger of death, and all my struggles will have been in vain. If I go to the king before he has eaten, he will kill me. I will therefore wait until he has dined; he will be more friendly as would be true of any man."

He landed on the table just as the last dish was being served, bowed before the monarch, the queen, the princess, and then the courtiers, and said: "May God bless your meal!" All in attendance were amazed to hear a bird talk and wondered who he belonged to. The king's fool, a real changeling,* exclaimed: "I can tell you about him. He has been sent here for the princess."

"Liar," the raven retorted. "It is the devil speaking through your mouth." Then, turning toward the court, he added: "I have come from a dark forest in hope that the king will give me bread and wine."

Aron had some brought to him at once.

"King, you will make no attempt on the life of one who is your guest?"

"Certainly not! Have no worry."

Relieved, the raven attacked his meal while reflecting on the way he could accomplish his mission with the pagan.

"Noble sovereign," he told him, "I will keep silence no longer about my message if you swear to give me safety and protection."

"You are quite a cunning bird," responded the suspicious king, "and I fear trickery, but I give you that promise in the name of Mahomet."

The bird was not at all satisfied, though, and demanded the protection of the queen. This he was granted, after which he told them: "King Oswald of England has sent me to ask for the hand of your daughter. You can grant him this request without a moment's hesitation, for he is powerful and rules over twelve kingdoms. When both of them are united, they will enjoy the protection of the Virgin." Aron flinched at this name and regretted that he had given his word. He ordered his men to take the bird prisoner. They locked all the doors and windows; the bird was captured, bound to a perch with straps, and the king swore he would be killed.

When the princess learned of the bird's capture, she threw a silk coat over her shoulders and went in search of her father. "Father, you are being unreasonable. If you break your word, your honor will be sullied from it. Everywhere people will say that you are disloyal and no honest

---

*In other words, a demon substituted for a human child at birth.

man will wish to spend time in your company because you are a traitor." In his fury, Aron dug in his heels. "I am going to hang him in front of the dark forest," he yelled. His daughter's pleas were of no avail.

"If you wish for me to marry a pagan, I will flee with a mountebank, and the shame will fall on you!" she shouted back.

"You have no gift for music or mime," the king replied, "and I have never yet seen you frolic."

"Don't be so sure. What I don't know today, I can learn tomorrow."

"You win, the raven shall live; if you want to take care of him, then take him!"

The princess thanked her father, took him into her bedroom, and gave him something to eat.

"Unfasten the letter and ring that are tied beneath my wing," the bird told her. "King Oswald sent them to you. He wishes to marry you. If you wish to embrace the Christian faith, he will come with a large army. Please let me now take my leave, for if your father's rage seizes hold of him once more, I will fear for my life."

She wanted to keep him close, so she hid and cared for him for nine full days before fastening a letter and a gold ring beneath his wing and sending him back to Oswald. "Tell him that I will be his wife and will be baptized. He should come with seventy-two ships and thousands of knights. The mast of his ship should be covered with precious stones that will light his way, and he should bring enough provisions and clothing for four years, as well as his golden stag, and he mustn't forget you."

The raven left but ran into a violent storm on the tenth day of his journey. He was buffeted by the wind three times, and the ring fell into the sea. The bird flew on until he came to a cliff where a hermit had been living for thirty-two years. "I know well who you are," the hermit told the bird, "you serve King Oswald of England. Tell me about your mishaps!" The raven complied. "Stay brave and put yourself in God's hands," the hermit concluded, who then prayed to heaven for the return of the ring. His wish was granted immediately. A fish brought it to the shore.[86] The hermit tied it back to the letter beneath the raven's wing and wished him a pleasant journey.

Six days later, the bird perched on a tower of Oswald's castle and began to crow. Four servants heard him and alerted the king, who was dining. He wrapped himself in his sable robe and ran to find him. He spread his robe over the ground,* and the raven landed on it. Oswald then brought him into his chamber, where no one could see or hear them.

"Give me news of the princess at once!" he said, which irked the raven.

"Not so fast," the bird responded, "I am almost dead from hunger and exhaustion. Let me be given something to eat first. Come back tomorrow when I will be in better shape to speak with you."

In the morning the raven spread his wings and said: "Untie the bond, and take the letter and the ring the princess has sent you! She wishes to marry you and to be baptized."

Oswald read the missive and ordered his people to outfit the ships. By Saint George's day, all was ready. He ordered seventy-two thousand gold crosses from his goldsmiths, then summoned his vassals to court. All made haste to attend, followed by their warriors. Oswald announced his intention to cross the sea to wed a pagan princess and, at the same time, convert her country to Christianity. He commanded them to follow him. "Those who die during the course of this voyage shall go to heaven. You will be richly rewarded," the king told them, to general acclaim. He then handed out gold crosses to each of them. "They will allow us to identify each other," he added, and they attached them to their mail coats.†

An eighteen-year-old stag‡ lived at court, whose antlers had many tines. He was the admiration of all, and no one gave any further thought to the raven, whom Oswald forgot about as he had so much to do getting ready.

They finally set sail and arrived in the country of Aron one year and twelve weeks later. The castle, which shone in the sun as if it were

---

*The mark of deference is ordinarily reserved for a sovereign.

†The bridal quest is combined with a crusade. Oswald fights the pagans of England and not those of the Middle East.

‡This stag is connected to Oswald, part of whose name, *Os-,* means "fawn." It plays a role in the story later.

made of gold, had twelve red marble towers, and soldiers kept watch from them day and night.

Oswald asked for counsel: "How can we make our way to the castle without being seen by the pagans?"

"I can see a meadow surrounded by two mountains over there near the coast," said an old servant. "That is where we can set up camp in complete safety."

They landed alongside the spot and set up their tents.

"Bring the raven," Oswald told his chamberlain, who grew quite alarmed at his king's request.

"I have not seen him; I thought he was with you."

His absence troubled and terrified all the Christians present. "Get a grip on yourselves," the king exclaimed. "Behave like men and start praying now!"

God heard their prayers. An angel flew to England and found the raven, whom he informed of Oswald's dismay. "Listen to me," the bird retorted, "I fulfilled my mission and warned him that his undertaking would be in vain if he left without me. But he brought a stag! If he doesn't send it to the princess, he will suffer the consequences, but I will not be responsible." The angel tried to convince him to assist the king, but the raven replied: "Impossible! Since he left, the kitchens no longer provide me food and I have to fight the dogs for the scraps under the tables; my feathers are all a mess and I can no longer fly or give aid to my lord." Yet the angel forced him to fly. He agreed to let him land if he did not manage to fly farther than three spear-lengths, but the bird did much better than that, and he compelled him to rejoin Oswald.

He alit on the mast and let out a loud caw, his exhaustion now completely forgotten. A sailor announced the good news to the king, who rewarded him with a knighthood* and asked him to bring the raven. Oswald took him on his wrist and gave him his message for the princess.

"Tell her that I am at her service and she must tell me how I can get her out of the castle. I am ready to go to war for her."

---

*A manifestation of Oswald's generosity when overcome by joy. It is surprising to see a sailor dubbed a knight for bearing good news.

"I will take care of it and bring you back her answer."

The raven found the princess just at the moment she was leaning over the crenellations.

"Where is your master?" she asked.

"Lady, he is with his army, between the two mountains. I must ask you how he can get you out of the castle."

"Go back and tell him that even if the entire world was at his command, he would not be able to conquer it. Tell him to take a ship with one hundred men. During the night they shall discreetly erect a tent in front of the castle and tell any who ask that they are skilled goldsmiths traveling from land to land. My father and his men will give your master a proper welcome, then I shall find a way to sneak around them."

The raven returned to Oswald, who told him: "That will be very difficult! I have no tools, and where am I going to find a dozen goldsmiths?" Twelve of his men overheard his words and responded: "We are former goldsmiths who have been knighted. However, we have brought our tools with us to earn a living if we are impoverished by the hazards of war. We will gladly help you."

One hundred men and the goldsmiths set sail with the king. Overnight they erected a small tent, and the goldsmiths went to work, making a good deal of noise with their tongs and hammers.

A watchman heard them and ran to Aron's chamber, crying: "Strangers are in front of the castle and seeking to take over the country."

"No one would dare!" the king replied. "They are foreign messengers, Christians who have come for my daughter. Wake everyone up! We must capture them!"

The guard obeyed. Everyone quickly equipped themselves. The princess saw this happening and, throwing on a silk coat, raced to her father's room. "I want to tell you who these strangers are," she told him. "They are skilled goldsmiths who have come because of the great renown of your country. Treat them well! We need new rings and bracelets, and you need a new gold crown." She convinced her father and his men to put down their weapons.

She urged her father: "Go and give them a worthy welcome!" The king commanded everyone to put on their feast-day clothes and then, followed by five hundred knights, he left the castle and made his way to the Christians. Oswald came to greet him.

"Welcome, Christians!" Aron said. "Your coming brings me great joy. Were you sent here as messengers?"

"No one sent us," Oswald replied. "We are goldsmiths. We were told that you were marrying your daughter. We came in hopes of making our fortune. If you have no need of our services, tell us, and we shall leave."

"Masters, have no worries! I shall bring you help and food for a year's time," and he put his promise in writing. They remained there for one year and twelve weeks without catching a glimpse of any women, something that alarmed them.

One night at dawn, after Oswald had spent a restless night, he dreamed of a way that he could get the princess out of the castle. When he woke, he told his people: "Make me golden claws that I can attach to the hooves of my stag and two hollow gold antlers that he can wear on his head. He must also have a gold caparison that hangs down to the ground. Once he has been fitted out like this, I will lead him to the moat at dawn. Once the king sees him, he will want to hunt him with his men, and the gate will have no one watching it."

Eight days later, Oswald put his plan into motion. A watchman went to alert Aron. "I saw a golden stag! Go hunting for him and your renown shall be all the greater!" The king ordered, under pain of death, all those who could carry at least a club to take part in tracking the animal down. Young and old, nobleman and vassal all armed themselves and leaped into their saddles. The horns rang out, the gates were opened, and the dogs were set loose. All set off! The door warden closed the gate behind the hunting party so that the princess would remain heavily guarded.

The stag fled in the direction of the dark forest on the mountainside. This mountain was so high that no living being, except for birds, could cross it. The stag scattered the pagans and led them astray in the woods.

Let's leave them to their hunting and now speak of the princess!

She was on the ramparts with her mother and twenty-four serving maids. She turned toward one of them and whispered: "Dear friend, put on my crown and my robe and take my place. I have a headache and I want to recover in my room. When I feel better, I will return." She raced to her chamber, where three other maidens disguised as lads—as they had planned—were waiting for her. They charged the gate, swords in hand, but found that, alas, it was sealed shut with heavy bolts. They then tried another tactic; climbing up to the ramparts, they looked to see if it would be possible to jump, but because the walls were too high, they returned to the gate. The princess asked the Virgin Mary for her help. The bolts burst open as if a furious wind had shaken the doors.[87] The young women jumped through, and the gate closed behind them more solidly than before.

Without any hesitation they made their way to Oswald's tent, on top of which was perched the raven. He told the king: "I see four maidens heading this way; one of them is the princess. Go meet then and give them a proper welcome!" Oswald came out and recognized the princess by the gold ribbon she wore in her hair. They lovingly embraced each other, then returned to the tent, followed by the three young lasses. "Get up!" he shouted at his vassals. "We are leaving, I have the princess!" They raced to the ship. The entire army decamped and set sail. The sailors hoisted their anchors and began rowing; once they reached the open sea, they let out a loud victory cry. Let us now leave them to their sailing, with their fate in God's hands!

We now return to the conversation King Aron is having with his wife. This is how she welcomed him on his return: "Welcome! How was your hunt? Did you find the stag?"

"No, but that doesn't matter. The goldsmiths can craft another one for me."

The queen started laughing.

"A waste of time! Our daughter and three of her serving maids have left with them, and they are already a long ways off."

"Why did I allow that raven to keep his life?" Aron exploded, wild with rage. "It is Oswald who took my daughter, but he will not escape from me!"

He brought an enchanted gold horn to his lips and began to blow.[88] It echoed throughout the entire world. The lords heard it and knew that their master needed them. They equipped themselves and made their way to the court, where they learned of the abduction of the princess. They raced to their ships and cast off in pursuit of Oswald.

This was a Monday morning. Things would have turned out badly if Oswald did not have the raven, who alerted him to the arrival of the pagan ships. The princess shook with fear. "If my father catches us, in his wrath he will drown us all." Oswald reassured her: "No Christian can die if it is not by divine will; everyone dies at his own time." He then fell to his knees and begged God and promised Him to grant the prayers of all those asking something in his name, even if it were his own head. God sent a storm that pushed the fleet three and a half thousand leagues away and enveloped the pagans in a fog so they lost their way. Then the sun returned.

The Christians had made landfall in the meantime and disembarked to rest, but their pursuers were soon there. Seeing them, Oswald told his people: "We must defend ourselves to the death! I tell you this: anyone who perishes from the blows of the pagans shall gain eternal life,"* and all swore an oath to follow him.

Oswald grabbed the standard, and a brutal battle broke out:

---

*A cliché of heroic literature featuring a battle against pagans.

thirty thousand pagans were slaughtered, and King Aron was captured and presented to Oswald, who greeted him ironically.

"Hello, father-in-law! I am happy to see you; you should have yourself baptized!"

"Don't you dare mock me!" replied Aron in wrath. "I do not believe in your God."

"Don't insult him! I have defeated you and my God has the power to bring men back to life."

"If he does that, then I can be baptized!"

Oswald asked God to grant his prayer and immediately all the dead men got back up as if waking up from a deep sleep.

"Aron, do you see the power of my God? You should now believe in Him, and you shall receive the kingdom of heaven."

"I cannot obey your God. I prefer to believe in mine, and even if I had seven heads, I would have them all cut off before I would convert; the pagans would jeer at me. Can't you see that all my men have come back to life? They can therefore resume the battle!"

But the resurrected warriors refused.

"Lord, we shall not help you in any way; we would be doomed to burn in hell. We no longer believe in Mahomet, who gave us no help, but in Jesus Christ, who can help us."

"King Oswald, I am in your power," said King Aron. "I will allow myself to be baptized, but the sea is salty and bottomless. If I fall in, your army cannot save me. You say that your God performs miracles. Do you see that cliff? If he can make a spring gush forth there, I will have myself baptized."

Oswald went to the cliff, took his sword in his right hand with its tip pointing toward the ground, kneeled, lifted his eyes to heaven, and began to pray. A supernatural force pulled the sword from his hand and struck the rock face with it. A block of stones that even a thousand chariots would not have been able to budge fell from the cliff and a fountain gushed forth.* "Have yourself baptized, or I will behead you," Oswald told Aron. He acquiesced and took the name of Zentinus.

---

*Oswald acts like Moses in the desert.

Oswald then baptized the four maidens and, over the next four days, the entire army of pagans. There then remained seventy-two yet to be baptized, who jumped into the water,* drank three gulps of it, and exclaimed: "We have conquered death! Will we not live for eternity?"

"Be aware that you will all die within the next year," replied Oswald, who returned to England on the Pentecost, where his homecoming was celebrated for seven days.

Then he invited the poor to visit his court, and they came by the thousands. Among them was Our Lord,[89] who wanted to verify that Oswald was prepared to pay the price for His assistance. After the meal, he stepped forward and said: "Give me a gift, king!"

"Most gladly!" Oswald replied, but his chamberlains stepped in.

"Sire, this pilgrim has eaten enough today to last him for an entire year!"

"But I have ten children and a wife," the pilgrim replied. "They were not able to come with me!"

Oswald ordered that he be given twelve loaves of bread and twelve gold sovereigns, to the great anger of his chamberlains. "Don't let us ever see you again!" they hissed. Jesus distributed the bread to the poor then returned to the king sitting at the table with his people, but the courtiers and squires pushed him around. Oswald got up, took the pilgrim by the hand, made him take a seat, and said: "I am going to give you something to eat and drink." He was brought every kind of food, and then he demanded the chalice while saying: "Its place is not on this table but on an altar," after which he asked for the gold and silver embroidered tablecloth, and the king gave them to him.

The courtiers grew wild with rage at the sight of the pilgrim demanding and receiving so many things. They tried to stab him with their knives, but Oswald leaped from the table, boxed the ears of one squire, then punched another in the mouth. He knocked a third courtier out cold and dragged the other away by his hair. In wrath, he told them: "What does it matter what he asks me for! This does not belong to you. When I was in fear for my life during the storm, I made a vow

---

*An ancient form of baptism by immersion.

to grant every request made in the name of the Lord," and he forbid them from attacking the pilgrim. "Relent with your anger," the pilgrim then told them. "If you stab me, you shall regret it."

Then he fearlessly approached Oswald.

"Noble prince," he said, "I am going to ask one more thing of you. Give me all your lands, your scepter, and your crown! A king must keep his promises. God will repay them. I am now going to demand the greatest of sacrifices: give me your wife. What use are kingdoms to me without a queen?"

"I will give her to you if she consents," Oswald replied, frightened and distressed as he watched his wife acquiesce.

"Give me your clothing, pilgrim," the king said.[90] "I am going to leave to start begging through the mountains and valleys." He took his leave of everyone there and started to depart, but the pilgrim hailed him.

"King Oswald, wait a moment!"

"What do you want now?" the king asked.

"Don't you want to know who I am? I am the living God; I have tested you and you have kept all your promises. I will give you back your belongings, but you must remain chaste and never touch your wife.[91] Here is how you will repress your desire. Have a tub of water placed in front of your bed; when you and your wife feel a desire to couple, jump into the water!* The kingdom of heaven will be your reward."

Until their death, Oswald and his wife lived a chaste life, then the kingdom of heaven welcomed them.

This is where my story ends.

SAINT OSWALD[92]

The hagiographic legend Saint Oswald uz Enngellant, *written circa 1170, has only come down to us in fifteenth-century manuscripts that are in different forms and increasingly Christianized. The text is based on a story of a quest for a bride whose religious recuperation involves a number of inconsistencies, for example: Oswald must leave in search of*

---

*A unique mention in medieval literature of this method of cooling one's ardor.

a wife, for the implied reason of assuring the continuation of his line, but once he has married her, he is forbidden from coupling with her carnally. As for the raven, who plays such an important role, he suddenly vanishes. . . .

📖 Curschmann, *Der Münchener Oswald und die deutsche spielmännische Epik;* Geissler, *Brautwerbung in der Weltliteratur;* Miller, "Brautwerbung und Heiligkeit"; Rank, *Das Inzest-Motiv in Dichtung und Sage;* Zingerle, *Die Oswaldlegende und ihre Beziehung zur deutschen Mythologie.*

SURVIVAL AND TRANSFORMATION OF THE NARRATIVES

1. The Snow Child

Once upon a time, in a certain place, there was a young merchant who went away on a journey. When he returned after being gone for several years, he knocked at the gate to his yard, with his heart overflowing with joy, and his wife came to embrace him while holding a one-year-old child.

"Where did this child come from," her husband asked her curtly, "seeing that I have been absent for such a long time?" His wife answered without batting an eye: "One day I was standing at the window while it was snowing. Some snowflakes flew into my mouth and I became pregnant right away, until I gave birth to this child while thinking about my dear husband."

The man seemed to believe this story. When the lad grew old enough to read and write, although his wife begged him to leave the child behind, he brought him with him far away so that he could discover the world early in life and at the same time learn the merchant trade. Eventually, the husband came back home, without her son.

"What happened to my child?" his wife asked in alarm. "I told you to keep a close watch over him." Her husband replied without batting an eye: "Something truly amazing happened with this strange child of the snowflakes. While we were crossing over a sunny mountain, he melted in my arms!"

AUGUST VON PLATTEN, *DER ROMANTISCHE OEDYPUS*, ACT 2

(*GESAMMELTE WERKE*, IV, 125FF.)

2. Crescentia: The Young Girl in the Chest (Albania)

This variant of Crescentia makes it possible to see how strong the Christian influence is in the medieval text. Here, there is not a single miracle.

Once upon a time there was an old woman who had a son named Constantine. When he was grown, she told him: "My child, we are poor. You have reached the age to find a job that will permit us to live, for I cannot feed you anymore." The young man, who could clearly see just how destitute they were, replied: "Mother, I don't feel any desire to work, but we shall write to my godfather, who is a merchant in Smyrna, and ask him to welcome me so that I can earn a living and support you." His godfather responded that he would be happy to have him there. His mother made him some new clothes, and he set off for Smyrna. His godfather welcomed him with open arms and gave him a position in his store. Because he was a bachelor, he gave him money so he could shop and cook.

One day when Constantine was sitting by the doorway to the store, he saw a porter carrying a chest and shouting: "I am selling this chest! Whoever buys it will regret it, and whoever doesn't buy it will also regret it!" Hearing these words, the young man thought: "What is he saying? What could be in that chest? I am going to buy it." Then he asked the porter: "How much do you want for it?"

"Five hundred piasters," the other man replied. Having saved what he needed little by little over time, Constantine bought the chest and, unknown to his godfather, placed it in a corner of the house.

The next day was Sunday, and the young men left to do the shopping. Then he went to church while thinking: "After Mass, I will go home to make the meal." When he got back to the house, he found the meal already prepared as if a master chef had taken care of it. "Hold on, my godfather must have come by and prepared this meal while I was away." When this latter came home, they sat down to eat and his god-father relished his meal so greatly that he told his godson: "Son, I would wager that the king himself has not eaten as well today. Here you have become the best chef in the city." Constantine told himself: "Godfather cooked the meal himself and wants me to understand that it is my job." He blushed and did not reply.

Another time, Constantine bought some fish and set it down before going to the store, planning to come back and cook it at noon. When his shift was over, he came back and found the fish cooked as he had never cooked it before. "Ah, Godfather did this work in my place." The merchant returned home for lunch and took such delight in the meal that he could not find words strong enough to praise his godson.

Thinking that his godfather was pretending not to know any-thing, Constantine decided that he would stay on the lookout. The following day he returned to the house after shopping, but instead of going to the store, he hid inside a wardrobe. He saw a young woman coming out of the chest he had bought; she was so beautiful that her beauty lit up the entire room. She put on an apron and got to work. Enchanted, Constantine came out of his hiding place, fell at her feet, and asked: "Are you an angel or mortal?"

"I am a woman," she replied, "have no fear! When I came to this country, I saw you and fell in love because you are so handsome! I am the daughter of the king of Egypt and one day, when I was spending the summer in Smyrna, I saw you. From that moment I have been in love with you. When I was back with my father, he decided it was time I got married, but I, knowing that he would never agree to giv-ing you my hand, told him: 'I refuse to get married.' He became red with rage and commanded one of his servants to lock me in a chest and sell it in secret, far from Egypt. I told that man that I would give him a great deal of money if he brought me to Smyrna so that you could buy me. We shall see what my father does, for I am his only child."

Learning that she was a princess, Constantine again fell at her feet, but she stood him back up, kissed him, and they got married secretly without telling anyone. The next day, the young man went to find the captain of a boat and told him: "I am going to give you a chest; take care of it as if it were the apple of your eye and transport it to my mother." The sailor consented and delivered it to the woman along with a letter in which was written: "My wife is inside." The mother welcomed her charitably and grew to love her.

One day, a Jewish merchant entered the old woman's home and, seeing the beautiful young woman, wanted to make her his.* Another time, while she was standing on the steps to the house, he tried to show her merchandise he was selling, but she went back inside. Day after day, the Jewish merchant passed by the house hoping for a glimpse of her but had no success. He sent people to speak to her on his behalf, but she refused to listen to them. Finally, the Jewish merchant wrote a letter in a fury to Constantine, saying that his wife was welcoming all the young men into the house unbeknown to his mother and that she was worthless. The young man became so angry that he left Smyrna to return home. When his wife saw him coming from the window, she raced to meet him and kiss him. The door opened, and Constantine was so angry that he did not take the time to question his wife to learn if the Jew had told him the truth. He grabbed her and threw her into a wide river nearby, then went to his mother and asked her about his wife. She told him everything the Jewish merchant had tried to win his wife, and how she had turned him away. Constantine was within a hair's breadth of killing himself! He returned to the river and sent men to see if she was drowned, but no trace of her was found. Then, like a madman, he went into the mountains.

Let us return to the young woman. When she fell into the river, fishermen had just cast their nets. They pulled her from the water half dead and wrapped her in a cloak. A Turk passing by just then asked them if they had any fish. "The only thing we have caught is this woman," they replied. At the sight of the young woman, he became possessed with

---

*The Jew has taken the place of Dietrich, the son of Narcissus.

love for her, and he bought her for fifteen thousand piasters. When she regained consciousness, she saw a Turk* near her and then remembered what had happened. "What do you want with me?" she asked him. "If you take me, there is a risk that someone stronger than you will abduct me. Here is what we are going to do: give me your clothes so I can dress as a man; no one will see through this subterfuge." The Turk acquiesced. She therefore took his clothes and slid behind some bushes to change. The Turk's horse was tied there. She climbed astride it and fled. Thinking she was taking a long time, the Turk went in search of her, but she had vanished. He was therefore forced to continue his route alone and on foot.

The fugitive continued to ride for hours, over mountains and through valleys, until night fell, when she entered Egypt without knowing it and came into the city where her father ruled. Because the city gates were closed, and it was snowing and raining, she huddled next to them. The king had just died, and, because he left no heirs, the ministers gathered to send messengers in search of his daughter, in accordance with the late monarch's last wishes. They had looked high and low for her for several days without success, but as the land needed a sovereign, they declared: "As the late king left no child, we shall place on the throne the first person we find at the city gates at the end of this wicked night full of ice and snow."

The next morning, the young woman, dressed as a man and half dead from the cold, saw the gates open and the ministers come out. When they saw what they took for a handsome young man, they bowed low and brought her back to the palace to be crowned. She was so wise that she ruled with fortune on her side, and all her subjects, not knowing that she was a woman, loved her as if she was the Good Lord. In her honor, her people hung her portrait by all the fountains in the land so that anyone coming to draw water could contemplate it. "If any of these people lets out a sigh at the sight of my portrait, bring him to the palace and keep him there for as long as I tell you to," she secretly ordered her men.

---

*This Turk corresponds to the duke that rescued Crescentia.

One day, the Jewish merchant who had written the letter to her husband passed by there, and when his eyes fell upon the portrait, he sighed. The royal servants brought him to the palace immediately. On another day, it was the turn of the fishermen to pass by and sigh upon seeing the portrait, and thus they, too, were taken to the palace. A short time later, it was the turn of the Turk, who found himself a prisoner like the Jew and the fishermen. Lastly, her husband walked past a fountain and saw her portrait. "How much it looks like her!" he sighed. "What a misfortune that I lost her!" He broke down in tears and began wailing and was at once taken to the palace.

When the young woman saw that they had caught everyone she wanted, she summoned her ministers as witnesses when she pronounced her sentence on them. They grouped themselves around the one who was enthroned as their king. She sent for the prisoners to be brought in and ordered them not to respond unless she interrogated them directly.

"Jew," she said, "why did you sigh when you saw that portrait by the fountain? Don't lie or I shall have you beheaded immediately."

"What can I say, your majesty? I recognized the features of a certain woman on it," and he began to tell the whole truth, how he had written the letter because the young woman refused to marry him. When he fell silent, she told him: "Good, you have told the truth. Sit down on the other side." When the woman's husband heard this story, he leaped to his feet to strangle the man, but her royal highness ordered him: "Stay where you are and don't move, otherwise you'll get burned!"

The sovereign then addressed the fishermen. "And you, what are the reasons for your sighs?"

"Alas," they said, "we pulled this woman from the water and then we sold her to a Turk."

"And you, Turk," said the king, "why did you sigh?"

"I was the one who bought her," he replied. "But she fled and left me in only my shirt and without a horse."

All the ministers turned then to look at the king, but she made a sign telling them not to react. Then she spoke to her husband. "Why did you sigh?"

"Alas, poor me," he replied with tears streaming down his face, "I was her husband and I lost her."

"No," retorted the king, "you did not lose her. Wait for me!" She left to change her clothes, slipping on a dress that her husband would recognize, and returned. When they saw her, everybody's eyes widened—the ministers recognized the late king's daughter; her husband and the others, the young woman.

Her husband was the first to throw himself at her feet, begging forgiveness. She stood him back up, kissed him, and placed him beside her. She gave money to the fishermen and returned to the Turk his property. Her ministers refusing to hang him, she gave the Jewish merchant a pardon but ordered him to leave the kingdom within twenty-four hours. Then she had a proclamation made announcing the return of the king's daughter, and great celebrations with every possible luxury ensued. Constantine became king, and, if they are still alive, they are still eating and drinking.

MEYER, "ALBANISCHE MÄRCHEN," 127–34

3. Death and His Messengers

Riding a white steed, Death came one day looking for a rich and greedy old man. The man was caught completely by surprise and, dumbfounded, he yelled: "I am still too young to have to accompany you! I was a long way from thinking of you, and I would really like to know why you are surprising me like this without any warning."

"I am a great lord and I have no need to announce myself, all doors are open to me."

"Do you have servants in your domain?"

"In abundance! And I believe you have often met them—I send them every day."

"I have never seen any yet, but since there are so many of them, I would very much like to meet them. Can't you send me one from time to time? Perhaps one a year, so I can get to know them?"

The old man did not want to die; that was the meaning of his words.

"Since you are crazy enough to wish to know them, I am going to give you the pleasure of sending them in the very near future," Death replied.

"Send me all of them! However, I ask you to refrain from knocking at my door until I have seen all of them."

"Agreed, I hope they will entertain you."

A short time later, the old man suffered terribly from an abscess, and this ordeal outraged him. Then he caught cold and was stricken with pneumonia; next, he had a fever and was horribly hot. When he was cured, he fell flat on his face, breaking a leg and an arm. Later, he lost an eye and his hearing. His tongue grew heavy, and he could hardly swallow a thing. One consolation remained in the midst of all these sufferings: Death's servants had not yet introduced themselves, and this was a cause for great rejoicing as he thought the Grim Reaper had forgotten about him.

But one day the Grim Reaper returned, scythe in hand, mounted on his white steed, wrapped in a black robe studded with pale eyes. The old man cried out: "You have not sent me your servants, yet. What do you want?"

"I have come to fetch you."

"But we made a bargain! You were not to return before I had met your messengers! I haven't seen a single one!"

"How is that? Didn't you have an ulcer, a fever, pneumonia?"

"Yes, but . . ."

"Didn't you have a broken foot and a broken arm? Weren't you afflicted by many vexing illnesses?"

"Yes, but . . ."

"So how can you say you have not seen or welcomed my servants?"

"Yes, but I didn't know . . ."

"These ills were the messengers that should have warned you of your imminent decease. Now, I am taking you!"

"Alas, alas, my lord! Let . . ."

Death gave him a slight tap with his scythe, and the old man expired.

ILG, *MALTESISCHE MÄRCHEN UND SCHWÄNKE,* I,
NO. 54, PP. 192–93

4. Gregorius

1. Simon the Foundling (Serbia)

The story of Gregory can be found in a Serbian folk song composed of fourteen stanzas of unequal length. This is a summarized version.

A monk found a lead chest [*sic*] in the Danube and carried it back to his monastery, thinking that it contained money. Instead he found a seven-day-old baby inside with a copy of the Gospels next to him. He had him baptized with the name of Simon and fed him on honey and sugar. At the age of one, Simon had the size of a three-year-old; at three years of age he looked like a seven-year-old. When he was twelve, he looked twenty.[1]

During athletic games, he was superior to all his companions, who treated him as a foundling. Upset, Simon retreated to his cell; the abbot went to see him there and questioned him. Simon asked him who he was and decided he wished to leave when he learned that they knew nothing about his birth. The abbot gave him a gift consisting of a nice suit of clothes and a white horse.

Simon wandered for five years in search of his origins, then decided to return to the monastery. He passed through Buda (Hungary), where the queen of that land saw him and sent a serving maid to fetch him. When he joined her, she gave him drink and, once evening fell, she told him: "Stay close to me, unknown knight. You are worthy of the love of a princess and the kiss of a queen." Simon gave her a kiss. The next day, ashamed of his action, he tried to leave and the queen prevented him. He ignored her and fled. However, because he forgot his Gospels, he returned and found the queen in tears reading them. She then revealed that she was his mother.

Simon returned to the monastery and made a full confession to the abbot, who locked him in a dungeon full of snakes and scorpions, where the water rose to his knees. The churchman then tossed the key into the Danube while saying: "When it comes out of the water, Simon will have atoned for his sin and God will have forgiven him."

Nine years later, a fisherman caught a fish and found the key inside it. He showed it to the abbot, who then freed Simon. "But look! The dungeon is empty of water, snakes, and scorpions; it is bathed in sunlight; and Simon, Gospels in hand, is sitting on a gold chair."

📖 Karadžić, *Volkslieder der Serben,* I, 139–46.

2. Johannes, the Coptic Gregorius

No doubt by means of the Gesta Romanorum, *the story of Gregory made its way to the Copts while undergoing, of course, a number of transformations. I have summarized it as follows.*

Once he became king, Johannes raped his sister when he returned drunk from a celebration. When he learned that she was pregnant, he stole away from the palace and went to a monastery. After nine months, she gave birth to a boy in secret. She immediately had a cradle made along with three tablets, one of gold, one of silver, and the third of ivory. The following words were carved on this third tablet: "The father of this child is his uncle and his mother is his aunt." The child and the tablets were placed in the cradle along with a piece of paper, upon which was written: "The gold tablet will belong to the child when he is grown and the one in silver will go to the person who raised him." The cradle was then launched into the river that flowed through there.

On the feast day of Saint James Intercisus,* a fisherman pulled the cradle onto the bank, not far from a monastery dedicated to this saint. The abbot kept the gold and ivory tablets and gave the fisherman the silver tablet for raising the child. One day when he was grown, during a quarrel Johannes learned from the children of his foster father that he was not their brother. The fisherman took him to the abbot, who gave him back the two tablets.

Reading the ivory tablet deeply upset Johannes. He sold the gold tablet and with the money bought a horse, weapons, and armor, and he left. He came to the city where his mother ruled, captured the king who was besieging the city, and married the queen. On noticing how he would come out of his private chambers pale and his eyes red from weeping, the queen mentioned it to her companions. One of them spied

---

Intercisus (cut to pieces) describes a martyr who was mutilated.

on Johannes and saw that he took out an ivory tablet, studied it, and then placed it near a window. She brought it to the queen, who fainted as soon as she recognized it. Johannes was summoned, and, when he learned that he was her son, he fled and eventually made his way to the edge of the sea. There he met a fisherman. He ordered him to change clothes with him[2] and to buy an iron chain that he bound around his feet. He then threw the key into the waves. He had himself taken to an island where he spent many years alone, living on plants and exposed to the heat and cold.

One day, the envoys of a king—which one, we do not say—who were seeking a new patriarch came to the fisherman's house by chance and asked him for some fish for their meal. In the first fish, the fisherman's wife found a key that her husband recognized as the one King Johannes had thrown into the sea. On hearing the story their host was telling his wife, the envoys asked to be taken to the island that next day, from which they retrieved the penitent. They presented him to the king, who had him crowned as patriarch by twelve bishops.

The mother of the new patriarch was still alive but gravely ill and engulfed in mourning and repentance. When she heard of his holiness, she made her way to his seat and begged him for succor. He recognized her and identified himself, once his prayer had healed her. God forgave them and through them performed miracles and granted them a peaceful death.

Köhler, "Eine koptische Variante der Legende von
Gregorius auf dem Stein"

3. The Husband of His Mother (Spain)

El marido de su madre, a three-act play by Juan de Matos Fragoso (seventeenth century), provides an example of how a story can move into literature while undergoing—when all is said and done—very little distortion. It is adapted to its new land and to the morality of the day. The incest between the mother and son is avoided. Here is a summary.

Prince Carlos of Antioch had carnal relations with his sister Rosaura and was forced to leave the country. She gave birth to a boy, whom she put in a chest that she then placed in a river that ran through her park. A peasant named Enrique saw it, pulled it to land, took out the child, and raised it.

Once, when Gregorio had grown up, Enrique sent him to the city to buy books, but he came back with a dagger. In a fury, the peasant revealed that he was a foundling, and he gave him a tablet explaining that he was the child of incest.

During that time, Rosaura had rejected the marriage proposal of the Duke of Tyro, who declared war on her.[3] Gregorio joined his mother's army, and it was not long before he was leading it. He defeated the duke, and, at the request of her people, Rosaura reconciled with him.

A short time before, Carlos, who was still passionately in love with his sister, came to Antioch in disguise under the name of Gerardo and claimed he had served in the army of Godefroy (de Bouillon). Rosaura noticed his resemblance to her brother and had her suspicions. So on their wedding day, she told Gregorio that she had taken a vow to not consummate her marriage until she had news of Carlos. Something she hoped to have in the very near future.

That same night a lady of the court freed the duke of Tyro, who sought to kill Gregorio, but Carlos sounded the alarm. When Gregorio came out of his room half-dressed, Rosaura saw the tablet hanging around his neck and learned of his origins. She did not inform him that she was his mother and told him that she could not be the wife of a foundling.

Gregorio left Antioch in secret to become a hermit in the deserts of Syria, where he acquired a great reputation for holiness. Not knowing that he was his adopted son, Enrique paid him a visit to confide in him a secret for the kingdom. Then Rosaura showed up with her retinue, among which was also Carlos/Gerardo, and some clerical emissaries who, having heard a voice from heaven, wanted to name Gregorio patriarch of Syria.

Enrique discovered that Carlos was not the natural brother of Rosaura but had been adopted secretly by the king of Antioch, who wanted a male heir. When he learned this, Carlos identified himself to Rosaura, who told him she was ready to marry him, but Gregorio objected that she was already married to him. Rosaura explains that

Gregorio is her son and the son of Carlos. The play ends with the appearance of an angel who gives Gregorio the patriarch's staff.

Another Spanish author, Juan de Timoneda (died 1583), recast the story in El patrañuelo, *a collection of novellas published in Valencia in 1567 (reprinted in Valencia as* Albatros hispanofíla, *1987). The fifth* patraña *is inspired by the* Gesta Romanorum, *and there is no incest between the mother and the son.*

📖 Matos Fragoso, *El marido de su madre.*

4. Paul of Caesarea (Bulgaria, seventeenth century)

In the city of Caesarea, a certain king named Anthon had a son and a daughter. On the death of their parents, the children ruled jointly over the country. A monarch requested the sister in marriage along with half of their kingdom. The brother and sister consulted each other and asked: "What should we do? If we accept, the kingdom will be carved up."

The brother and sister conceived a son. "It would not be decent to raise this fruit of incest," they told each other. They made a chest and placed the child inside with a letter that said: "This child was born of a brother and sister," so the person who found it would know what he was, and then they cast the chest into the sea. The brother died, and the sister remained as the sole sovereign.

The wind carried the chest to the land of Herod, where a monk named Hermolaus found it. He hid the letter, raised the child, whom he named Paul, and taught him. Paul showed himself to be quite courageous. He inherited the country. His mother learned that a young king was ruling in this place and, not knowing that he was her son, sent him a missive with a request of marriage. Their wedding was performed, and they became king and queen of Caesarea.

One day, Paul went to see Hermolaus to ask for his blessing.

"Paul, my son," said the monk, "if you knew who you are, you would know it is not fitting for you to be alive in this century, and even less so to rule."

"Why isn't it suitable? I am wise, courageous, educated, and know good and evil."

Hermolaus gave him his parent's letter with these words: "Read this and learn the secret of your birth!" Paul grabbed it without reading it, gave it to a squire, mounted his horse, and returned to Caesarea. He then remembered the letter, went to a remote location, and, when he discovered its contents, began grieving and beating his chest. "Woe is me, I am damned! The earth is going to swallow me up alive. And I who wished to rule!" From this day on, he avoided his mother, who was surprised by his cool attitude. Every evening, Paul locked himself in his room and wept; the queen summoned a valet and asked him what anxieties were afflicting the king.

"He weeps while reading a letter that Hermolaus gave him," he replied.

"I shall try to learn what's in it," she said. After reading it, she shrieked: "Oh, woe is me! Not only did I sin with my brother, but in my blindness, with my son as well." She told Paul the truth. From that moment on, the queen wore only sackcloth and each day ate only five mouthfuls of bread covered with ashes.

Paul went to see John Chrystostom to tell him the whole story. Learning of this infamy, John had an attack of weakness, his hair stood on his head, his heart clenched, and he said: "Brother, where can a sin like this be truly confessed and forgiven?" Paul raised his voice and shouted: "O great Chrystostom, grant me death!" John knew of a small islet in the sea on which stood a marble pillar. He tied Paul to that column, bound his hands and feet in chains, and locked him there with iron keys that he tossed into the waves.

Paul asked him: "When will you come see me again, great teacher?"

"When those keys come back out of the water is when I shall come to see you again," and he returned to his patriarchate.

Twelve years passed, and on the day of the Assumption of Mary, John was brought some freshly caught fish. He was amazed to find in one of them the keys, which he did not recognize immediately. During the night, he remembered Paul, and in the morning he said to the brothers: "Christ is alive, my soul is alive!* Let us go yonder and exam-

---

*A phrase from Eastern Orthodox religion.

ine the pillar." Once they got there, he tried the keys. They worked, and he opened it and saw Paul shining like the sun, with balm flowing from his face. "How happy I am!" Paul said. "Rejoice, my good teacher!" Blessed by John, he gave testimony of his veneration and commended his soul to the hands of God. As for his mother, she found salvation through her sincere penance.

📖 Köhler, "Zur Legende von Gregorius auf dem Stein," 288–90.

5. Henry the Lion

1. Fidelity and Redemption

After being sent into exile, Duke Henry the Lion went to the Holy Land in search of redemption. One day when he was fighting a pasha and about to cut him to pieces, the latter begged for mercy, which Henry granted to him. As thanks, the pasha gave him a lion, who was very loyal and followed him everywhere. One day someone came up to him to say: "Hurry back home, for your wife will not be able to resist much longer—she is going to get remarried!" Henry did not want to believe this and, lowering his eyes, saw that this individual had the hooves of a horse.

"You are the devil and you are trying to pull the wool over my eyes!" he exclaimed.

"Yes, that's me. I don't wish to deceive you, but to come to your aid, because you are a valiant man and you have aroused my pity," the devil replied. Unnerved, the duke agreed to let the devil bring him back home. When he grabbed Henry to carry him, the lion pressed against him and gripped his legs with all his strength. Henry did not want to abandon the loyal beast, and the devil finished by promising to transport the animal, too, on the following day.

This was how he returned to Brunswick, to the spot indicated, before the duchess's remarriage was celebrated. When she saw him, she cried out in joy: "My husband has returned!" Both of them lived happily for many long years.

When the duke was buried in the cathedral, the lion wished to follow him, but the doors were closed to keep him out, and the animal stuck his claws deep into the casements in his attempt to rejoin his master. Force had to be used to take him away. The lion died a short time later. In memory of his fidelity, a bronze effigy was made of the lion, which was placed in front of the castle. It can still be seen today, just as the mark of its claws can be found on the cathedral doors.

KUHN AND SCHWARTZ, *NORDDEUTSCHE SAGEN,*
MÄRCHEN UND GEBRÄUCHE, NO. 174

2. The Wonderful Rescue

Here is how the legend of Henry the Lion was changed into a folktale in nineteenth-century Austria, mainly by eliminating all of the elements specific to time and place, and by stripping the hero of his name.

One upon a very long time, there was a king who ruled over a vast kingdom. One day, he made preparations to go on a hunting expedition.* Because he was going to have to cross the sea to reach the territory where he planned to hunt and there would be numerous dangers facing him there, he told his wife before he left: "I could perish during the course of my wanderings or I could remain away for a long time. We therefore need something to serve as a sign of recognition. Slip this ring onto your finger; it is similar to the one I am wearing. This will be our sign.[4] If I am not back at the end of ten years, you will be assured that I am dead, and then you can choose a new husband."

After a pleasant voyage lasting several days, he reached his objective and disembarked with twenty of his loyal men and twenty horses. Their hunting was fruitful, but one day they became lost. They entered a forest whose magnetic trees† pulled them into the depths of the woods. There were no game animals of any kind in this woodland, so they were therefore condemned to suffer from hunger and forced to kill and eat their horses to avoid death; only the king's horse was spared.

Nineteen men perished of exhaustion, and the king remained alone

---

*This expedition replaces the crusade of the original text.
†This detail shows that the Magnet Mountain formed part of the legend during the Middle Ages.

with the sole survivor. They worked together, looking for an exit from the forest. The sovereign's companion knew that a monstrous bird with twelve heads* haunted these woods, so he came up with an ingenious plan. It would be necessary to slay the one remaining horse and sew its hide around the king. The king could only keep his sword and his knife, and his faithful servant would kill himself after he had sewn the king inside the hide.

In the beginning, the king would hear none of this plan, but after many long discussions, he admitted that the plan was a worthy one and it was put into operation. Sealed inside the hide, the monarch was placed at the top of a mountain that stood in the heart of the forest, after which his companion killed himself.

For many long hours, the king remained in this very uncomfortable situation until the bird came and picked him up as if he weighed no more than a feather and had no idea of the noble burden it was carrying! Its flight lasted for several hours before it came to rest at the top of an extremely old oak tree where he had its nest and its young, all provided with twelve heads! He abandoned his prey in the nest and went off again.

As soon as the king realized that the bird was gone, he pulled out his knife and split open the horsehide. He then emerged and slew the ignoble flock outside. He climbed down the tree and quickly found a place to hide nearby—which was a good thing, for the bird was already coming back. The howls it emitted at the sight of its dead offspring were indescribable. The bellowing of an ox is nothing by comparison! It beat the air with its wings with such violence it could be heard several hours' walk away. This racket attracted a lion. In a fury, the bird hurled itself on the animal, thinking it was the murderer of its fledglings.† The noble beast would have been done for if the king had not raced to its aid, and the two of them still had their hands full confronting the monstrous winged creature, for each of its heads would grow back immediately. It was only after much relentless effort that they managed to vanquish it.

---

*An amplification of the monstrous nature of the bird.
†The bird replaces the dragon of the medieval legend.

"Am I now going to have to face this lion?" the king wondered. But to his surprise, the king of beasts came to lie down at his feet and began to lick his hands. They traveled together for a number of days, with the lion bringing game back to the monarch every day, until they eventually came to the bank of a river filled with boiling water. The king wanted to build a raft so as to sail down it. First he built a small hut for protection from the rain, and then he cut down trees with the help of his sword and stuck them together with resin. While he worked, the lion would go hunting in the forest, and he brought back so much food that there was even some left for their voyage.

Once his raft was finished, the king was ready to set out. He planned to leave the lion behind at this time, as he still did not trust him entirely. He jumped onto the raft and was already pushing away from the bank when the lion returned from hunting, with its prey in its jaws. When he saw him, the lion was taken aback, but barely hesitated and with a singular leap, jumped toward the raft. Only its front paws landed on it and the rest of its body plunged into the burning water and it began to get scalded. The hair fell off all the places where the lion was burned and since that day, the hide of lions is smooth in this spot.[5] After many efforts, the animal managed to pull itself onto the raft and gave the king a look that sent a shiver racing up his spine. However, the lion was a magnanimous creature and did him no harm, and the ship sailed on! If food began to run out, the lion would go hunting.

They sailed for days and days, crossing through many uninhabited lands. After many months, they found themselves in front of an inn, which they entered. In the main room they found only the innkeeper, who was astounded by the king's strange garments because he was only wrapped in an animal hide; but the king's companion surprised him even more! The visitor asked the name of the place in which they found themselves, and it proved to be fairly close to his castle, but the time span he had given his wife was almost expired.

A sword[6] that moved of its own accord was hanging on the wall of the common room and the king was keen to own it. As he had no money with which to buy it, he swapped his own for it when the innkeeper was away. He brandished it, left the inn, and jumped back on the raft with the lion. They wished to sail away but were prevented from doing so by the aquatic plants and the morass of branches that blocked the river. The king hung his new sword on the prow of his craft and it made short work of the obstacles, and they pulled away free. They still had to sail for some time, and when they pulled up to the bank close to the castle, it was the eve before the ten years ran out.

During this time, the queen had lived in a state of constant tension because the ship that had taken the king and his men far away had returned with news of her husband's disappearance. The noblemen and other dignitaries of the kingdom pressed her to remarry, to which she always responded: "I will choose a new husband if the king has not returned at the end of ten years and not before!" Not wishing to be governed by a woman, the nobles threatened her until she gave them her consent to remarry. The ceremony was scheduled to take place at the end of the ten years. Accompanied by the nobles, the suitor had just come to go to the church when the marriage was interrupted by the king's return. The fiancé and his friends rebelled and tried to kill him, but the monarch unsheathed his sword, which caused such a massacre that none of the noblemen remained alive.* The king went on to live a long, happy life with his wife, and the lion remained as his loyal companion. At the sovereign's death, the lion refused to eat and let himself wither away and die on his grave.

VERNALEKEN, *KINDER- UND HAUSMÄRCHEN IN
DEN ALPENLÄNDERN*, NO. 25

---

*This is strongly reminiscent of the return of Ulysses.

ORIGINAL LANGUAGES OF THE TALES AND LEGENDS

Animal Tales

1. The Bat: Middle French
2. The Grateful Lion: Latin
3. The She-Wolf: Latin
4. The Brave Serpent: Latin
5. The Field Mouse: Middle French
6. The Rescusitated Horse: Latin

Oddities and Wonders

1. The Bell of Justice: Middle High German
2. The Dead Guest: Latin
3. Alexander and the King of the Dwarfs: English
4. The Venemous Maiden: Middle French; Latin
5. King Gontran's Dream: Latin
6. The Water of Youth: Latin
7. The Dolphin Knights: Latin
8. Albert the Leper: Latin
9. The Ship in the Air: Latin

10. Hippocrate's Daughter: Middle High German
11. The Carpenter and Mercury: Middle French
12. The Skull: Latin
13. The Messengers of Death: Middle High German

Deviltry, Spells, and Magic

1. The List of Sins on the Cowhide: Latin
2. A Visit to Hell: Latin
3. The Knight Devoted to the Virgin Mary and the Devil: Middle High German
4. The Diabolical Pope: Middle High German
5. Gerbert and Meridiana: Latin
6. Love Spell: Middle High German
7. The Shoemaker and the Malefic Head: Latin
8. Virgil the Enchanter: Middle High German
9. The Talking Statue: Latin

The Supernatural Spouse

1. Seyfried von Ardemont: Middle High German
2. Liombruno: Medieval Italian
3. Frederick of Swabia: Middle High German
4. Aeneas, the Swan Knight: Latin
5. Helias, the Swan Knight: Middle High German

Licit and Illicit Love

1. Hero and Leander: Middle High German
2. Zellandine, or the Sleeping Beauty: Middle French
3. Crescentia I: Middle High German
4. Crescentia II: Latin
5. The Widow: Middle French
6. Gregory's Incest: Latin

Wisdom, Cunning, and Stupidity

1. The Golden Apple: Latin
2. The True Friend: Latin
3. The Six Labors of Guy the Wise: Latin
4. The Ogre and the Travelers: Middle High German
5. The Thieves and the Treasure: Middle High German
6. Aristotle's Humiliation: Latin; Middle High German
7. The Snow Child: Middle High German
8. The Peasant and the Dwarf: Middle French
9. The Three Knights: Middle High German

Heroic Legends

1. The Archer and the King: Latin
2. Wayland the Smith: Norse
3. Valentine and Nameless: Middle High German
4. Henry the Lion: Middle High German
5. Saint Oswald and His Raven: Middle High German

INDEX OF FOLKTALE TYPE

The examples in this concordance follow the international classification system developed by Antti Aarne and Stith Thompson, as presented in their reference work *The Types of the Folktale: A Classification and a Bibliography*. The columns to the left give the number and name of the tale type, while the column on the right lists the stories in this collection that feature it, cited by chapter (Roman numeral) and section number (Arabic numeral).

Story Type

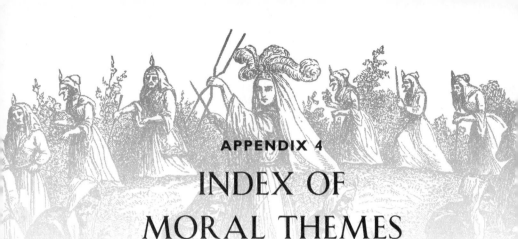

INDEX OF
MORAL THEMES

The entries in this index are based on F. C. Tubach's *Index Exemplorum: A Handbook of Medieval Religious Tales,* which shows the incorporation of popular beliefs into religious texts, homilies, and sermons. This handbook contains 5,400 examples collected from the most popular medieval tales.

The columns to the left below give the number and name of the exemplum type, while the column on the right lists the stories in this collection that feature it, cited by chapter (Roman numeral) and section number (Arabic numeral).

Exemplum Type

APPENDIX 5

INDEX OF MOTIFS

This index is based on American folklorist Stith Thompson's *Motif-Index of Folk Literature,* a six-volume catalog. A "motif" is a term used by folklorists to describe individual details within a tale. A motif may refer to a character, action, setting, or object. The examples of motifs found in Thompson's catalog, and included in this appendix, are organized by a motif number and a descriptor, defined as follows:

- The **motif number** is a letter and a series of numbers that are a shorthand way of referring to specific details found in folktales.
- The **descriptor** is a short verbal explanation of what each motif is about.
- The column on the right indicates the tale(s) in this collection featuring the motif—identifed by chapter (Roman numeral) and section number (Arabic numeral).

A 165.2.3:	Angels as God's messengers	IV, 4
B 31:	Giant bird	IV, 1
B 42:	Griffin	VII, 4
B 81:	Mermaid	VII, 5
B 151.1:	Beast determines road to be taken	IV, 3
B 211.2.4:	Speaking wolf	I, 3

K 1837: Disguise of woman in man's clothes — VII, 3

K 1840: Deception by substitution — IV, 7

K 1923.1: Nurse exchanges children — IV, 4; IV, 5

K 2110.1: Calumniated wife — V, 3

K 2112: Woman slandered as adulteress (prostitute) — V, 3

K 2322: The three hunchback brothers drowned — V, 1

M 21: Man sells soul to devil — III, 4

M 201.1.2: Pact with devil signed in blood — III, 4

M 369.7.1: Prophecy: birth of twins — VII, 3

N 6.1: Luck in gambling from compact with devil — III, 4

N 211.1: Lost ring found in fish — VI, 5; V, 6

N 513.2: Sword hidden under water — VII, 2

N 511.4: Treasure found in snake hole — I, 4

N 531: Treasure discovered through dream — II, 5

N 681: Husband (lover) arrives home just as wife (mistress) is to marry another — VII, 4

N 774: Adventures from pursuing enchanted animal — IV, 3

N 815: Fairy as helper — III, 5

P 453: Shoemaker — III, 7

Q 3.1: Woodsman and the gold axe — II, 11

Q 211: Murder of children punished — V, 3

Q 413.4: Hanging as punishment for murder — VI, 10

Q 416: Punishment: drawing asunder by horses — VI, 10

NOTES

Introduction.
Religion, Romance, and Fable

1. Cf. Zink and Ravier, *Réception et Identification du conte au moyen Âge;* Berlioz, Brémond, and Vellay-Valentin, eds., *Formes médiévales du conte merveilleux;* Piniès, ed., *Le Conte de tradition orale dans le bassin méditerranéen;* Walter, *Canicule, essai de mythologie sur Yvain de Chrétien de Troyes,* 73ff.; Berlioz, "Un petit chaperon rouge médiéval? La petite fille épargnée par les loups dans la *Fecunda ratis* d'Egbert de Liège (début du XIe siècle)."
2. Cf. Brémont, Le Goff, and Schmitt, eds. *L'"Exemplum,"* 40; Berlioz and Polo de Beaulieu, *Les Exempla médiévaux.*
3. Cf. Madden, *The Old English Versions of the* Gesta romanorum. See also Marsan, *Itinéraire espagnol du conte médiéval (VIIIe–XVe siècle).*
4. For the principal discussions on this subject, cf. Petzoldt, ed., *Vergleichende Sagenforschung.*
5. Cf. Lecouteux, *Dictionary of Ancient Magic Words and Spells.*
6. Cf. Sprandel, "Die *Gesta Romanorum* als Quelle der spätmittelalterlichen mentalitätsgeschichte."
7. Bechstein, *Le livre des contes.*
8. Cf. Micha, ed. and trans., *Lais féeriques des XIIe et XIIIe siècles.*
9. Cf. Lecouteux, *Mondes parallèles.*

Chapter I. Animal Tales

1. Marie de France, *Die Fabeln,* no. 23.
2. Motif B 381: Thorn removed from lion's paw.

3. Oesterley, ed., *Gesta Romanorum.*

4. Motif B 211.2.4: Speaking wolf.

5. Motif D 113.1.1: Werewolf.

6. Dimrock, ed. *Giraldi cambrensis opera*, vol. V.

7. *De hominibus qui se vertunt in lupos,* in Wright and Halliwell, eds., *Reliquiae antiquae,* II, 105.

8. Name borrowed from the Bible (1 Esdras 1:46) and borne by a king of Judah.

9. Motif J 1701: Stupid wife.

10. Cf. Numbers 24:17–18; Revelation 2:14.

11. Motif B 211.6.1: Speaking snake.

12. Motif N 511.4: Treasure found in snake hole.

13. Oesterley, ed. *Gesta Romanorum.*

14. Marie de France, *Die Fabeln,* no. 73.

15. Cf. Bechstein, *Le Livre des contes.*

16. For more on the festivities connected to this date, cf. Walter, *La mémoire du temps,* 424ff.

17. For more on this complex of legends, cf. Lecouteux, *Witches, Werewolves, and Fairies,* 76–77.

Chapter II. Oddities and Wonders

1. His seneschal in other, later versions.

2. Von der Hagen, ed. *Gesamtabenteuer,* II, 617–34.

3. This would be Fastrada († 794), Charlemagne's fourth wife.

4. Motif C 13: The offended skull.

5. Motif D 2012: Moments thought to be years. In the version from Croatia, when the man returns from sharing a meal with the dead man, he no longer recognizes his farm, and his house has vanished; he therefore returns to his host for eternity.

6. The popular Italian book dates from 1906 and is titled *Leonzio ovvero La terribile vendetta di un morto.* Leonzio invites the skull to dance at a party; it does not return his invitation but comes and kills him.

7. Hersart de la Villemarqué, ed., *Barzaz Breiz,* no. XXXVI, 262; the event is dated February 27, 1490.

8. In "Alexander und Antiloie," the dwarf demands payment from Alexander for the game he has killed, then offers him his friendship and has him visit

his kingdom. He is four-and-one-half spans tall. In the version by Ulrich von Etzenbach, Alexander explains himself; the visit to the dwarf kingdom is described more briefly and ends with Alexander finding accommodation in the home of Antilois, who is the size of a two-year-old child.

9. Depending on the text, the dwarf's name is Anteloye, Antilôis, Antiloie, Antelan.

10. This motif (D 812.12: Magic object received from dwarf), which remains unused in the rest of the story, is likely the remnant of an older version.

11. In the rhyming *Weltchronik* by Heinz Sentlinger, the dwarf plays tricks on the men of Alexander's court to expose the wicked and envious among them. Cf. Zingerle, "Anteloye und Alexander," 221.

12. Gaster, "The Old Hebrew Romance of Alexander," 505–6.

13. Thomasset, ed., *Dialogue de Placides et Timéo,* 109–12. See also Thomasset, *Une vision du monde au XIIIe siècle,* 73–108.

14. Motif N 531: Treasure discovered through dream.

15. Waitz, ed., *Pauli Historia Langobardorum.*

16. Cf. Weiske, *Gesta Romanorum.*

17. *La Scala coeli de Johannes Gobi* (ed. Polo de Beaulieu), 399–400.

18. Motif D 100: Transformation: man to animal.

19. Cf. Job 42:12–13. Job's patience has become proverbial through the intermediary of Saint Augustine, cf. *De patientia,* chap. 11–12.

20. Motif F 955: Miraculous cure for leprosy; D 2161.1.1: Magic cure of leprosy.

21. Although it is not explicitly stated, Henry must bathe in blood, a variant of motif D 1500.1.7.3.4: Bath in blood of king as remedy.

22. Klapper, ed. *Erzählungen des Mittelalters,* 233–34.

23. Hartmann von Aue, *Der arme Heinrich* (ed. Paul).

24. Motif D 735: Disenchantment by kiss.

25. John Mandeville, *Reysen und wanderschafften durch das Gelobte Land* (trans. Otto von Diemeringen; fifteenth century), chap. 9.

26. Motif Q 3.1: Woodsman and the gold ax.

27. Macho, *Ésope,* ed. P. Ruelle, in *Recueil général des isopets,* vol. 3., §2020.

28. This is comparable to motif F 866.4: Cup made of skulls.

29. Oesterley, ed., *Gesta Romanorum.*

30. AaTh 332 (Godfather death).

31. Motifs Z 111.6: Death's messengers; J 1051: Death's three messengers.

32. Hugo von Trimberg, *Der Renner* (ed. Ehrismann), 277ff.

Chapter III. Deviltry, Spells, and Magic

1. In Johannes Gobi's book, he has the shape of an ape and the story takes place in Toledo.
2. Motif G 303.24: The devil in church.
3. Edited in Barack, "Bruchstücke mittelhochdeutscher Gedichte in der Universitäts- und Landesbibliothek zu Straßburg," 189–90.
4. TU 5027.
5. Caesarius von Heisterbach, *Dialogus miraculorum* (ed. Strange).
6. Motif D 435.1.1: Statue comes to life; D 1610.21.1: Image of the Virgin Mary speaks.
7. Motif E 754.1.2: Condemned soul saved by Virgin Mary.
8. Von der Hagen, ed. *Gesamtabenteuer*, III, no. 83.
9. Motifs M 21: Man sells soul to devil; M 201.1. 2: Pact with devil signed in blood.
10. Motif N 6.1: Luck in gambling from compact with devil.
11. In the version of William of Newburgh, it is simply said: "Having lost his reason due to pain, he asked that he be cut up into little pieces" (*Gesta rerum anglorum*, § 172).
12. *Des teuvels bâbest,* in Von der Hagen, ed., *Gesamtabenteuer,* II, no. 94. Shorter version: Martin of Opava (thirteenth century), *Chronicon pontificum et imperatorum,* fol. 216 r°–v°.
13. Motif F 393: Fairy visits among mortals.
14. Motif N 815: Fairy as helper.
15. Cf. motif T 111: Marriage of mortal and supernatural being.
16. The Latin *illudere* refers to the deceits of the devil, who plays with human beings and takes advantage of their senses.
17. Cf. motif C 900: Punishment for breaking tabu.
18. Walter Map, *De Nugis Curialium* (ed. James; rev. Brooke and Mynors).
19. For more on the motif of necrophilia, cf. the first version of the tale "Snow White" by the Brothers Grimm.
20. Variant of the motif D 1355.2: Magic love-philtre. This stone could be the agate from a swallow (from the Latin *chelidonia*); cf. Motif B 722.1: Magic love-working stone in swallow's head.
21. Jansen Enikel, *Weltchronik,* fol. 271–73.
22. Motif P 453: Shoemaker.
23. Motif T 466: Necrophilism: sexual intercourse with dead human body.

24. Motif D 2061.2.1: Death-giving glance.

25. Motif D 581: Petrification by glance.

26. Motifs D 2177.1: Demon enclosed in bottle; R 181: Demon enclosed in bottle released. Cf. AaTh 331.

27. Motif K 1211: Vergil in the basket.

28. Motif D 2158.2: Magic extinguishing of fires.

29. Motif D 1268: Magic statue.

30. *Der zauberer Virgilius,* extract in Von der Hagen, ed., *Gesamtabenteuer,* II, 509–27.

31. Motif D 1268: Magic statue; D 1620: Magic automata; D 1620.1.7: Speaking statue of man.

32. Oesterley, ed., *Gesta Romanorum.*

Chapter IV. The Supernatural Spouse

1. This is how I've summarized the first part of the story, which is constructed from the customary stereotypes of the Arthurian romance.

2. Cf. Lecouteux, "L'arrière-plan des sites aventureux dans le roman médiéval" and "Les marches de l'au-delà."

3. We should not be misled by this word, for the Middle High German *kröte* is one of the names for a dragon; cf. Lecouteux, "Der Drache."

4. This is a variant of the motif of the Proud Kiss (the courageous kiss)—motif D 735: Disenchantment by kiss—which can be seen in the earlier tales of Irish mythology. It consists of kissing a monster or a hideous witch on the mouth, thereby proving that the individual is equal to undertaking the quest in question, which leads to sovereignty. In France, Renaut de Beaujeu uses it (cf. Walter, *le Bel inconnu de Renaut de Beaujeu,* 267ff.). In Germanic regions it first appeared in the *Lanzelet* of Ulric von Zatzickhoven, at the end of the twelfth century, in ll. 7,817–8,040. It can also be seen in *Orlando innamorato* (II, 25, str. 25–38) by Matteo Maria Boiardo (1440–1494); *Tirant lo Blanch* by Joanot Martorell (1410–1465); and Felix Fabri (ca. 1439–1502) in the *Evagatorium in Terrae sanctae Arabiae et Egyptii* (ed. Hassler); III, 267–68. See also Frank, *Der Schlangenkuß,* and Smith, "Snake-maiden Transformation narratives in Hagiography and Folklore."

5. Cf. "Hippocrates's Daughter," in the present volume, which indicates that the deliverance is followed by death.

6. Motif E 732: Soul in form of bird.

7. Seyfried and Waldin have reached the border of the otherworld, represented by this obstacle; cf. Lecouteux, "Aspects mythiques de la montagne au Moyen Âge."

8. Variant of the motif of the animal guide.

9. Motifs C 901.1.5: Tabu imposed by fairy; C 400: Tabu: speaking.

10. We find the exact same motif in the *Lai de Lanval* by Marie de France, in which the fairy reveals herself to save the hero and then leaves. He pursues her and vanishes in her kingdom.

11. This shows that the taboo is consubstantial with its otherworldly nature; cf. Lecouteux, *Mélusine et le Chevalier au cygne.*

12. Motif B 31: Giant bird and variant de B 551.2: Aquatic bird carries man across water. The motif comes from the legend of Alexander the Great. Circa 1170, Benjamin of Tudela notes that the fishermen of the China Sea, in order to escape drowning, have the custom of sewing themselves inside animal hides that griffins carry away. This lifesaving method occurs again mainly in *Herzog Ernst,* a romance of adventure written circa 1190, in the story of *Heinrich von der Löwe* (circa 1471–1474) by Michael Wyssenherre. The griffin corresponds to the giant Roc that carries Sinbad away in *Thousand and One Nights.*

13. *Seyfrid von Ardemont* (ed. Thoelen) in Füetrer, *Das Buch der Abenteuer,* II, 67–168.

14. Motif S 211: Child sold (promised) to devil.

15. Motif d 2121: Magic journey.

16. Motif F 302: Fairy mistress.

17. Motif D 1456.2: Magic ring provides money.

18. Motif D 1470.1.15: Magic wishing ring.

19. Motif H 335: Tasks assigned suitors. Bride as prize for accomplishment.

20. A variant of motif C 932: Loss of wife for breaking tabu.

21. Motif D 1361.14: Magic cap renders invisible.

22. Motif D 1521.1: Seven-league boots.

23. Cf. motif F 757.2: Wind continually blows from cave.

24. The hermit is the Christianized form of the Master of the Winds, who can be encountered, for example, in *Apollonius von Tyrland* (ca. 1300) by Heinrich von Neustadt.

25. Cf. Motif F 132: Otherworld on lofty mountain.

26. A variant of motif H 94.3: Identification by ring dropped in pitcher of wine.

27. Motif T 111: Marriage of mortal and supernatural being.

28. *La Historia del Liombruno.* From the fifteenth to the nineteenth century, the text was republished twenty times.

29. *Cantari leggendari i, fiore di leggende, cantari antichi.* See the fine study by Predelli, *Alle origini del Bel Gherardino,* and the one by Walter, *le Bel inconnu de Renaut de Beaujeu.*

30. Cf. Motif B 151.1: Animal determines road to be taken; N 774: Adventures from pursuing enchanted animal (hind, boar, bird); Krappe, "Guiding Animals"; Pschmadt, *Die Sage von der verfolgten Hinde.*

31. Motif close to H 1239.2.

32. S 31: Cruel stepmother.

33. Motif D 1711: Magician.

34. Motif D 2161.3.1: Blindness magically cured; D 1505. Magic object cures blindness; D 1505.17: Magic stone restores sight.

35. Motifs D 117.2: Transformation to hare; D 661: Transformation as punishment.

36. Motif D 621.1: Animal by day; man by night.

37. A variant of H 1472: Test: sleeping by princess three nights without looking at her or disturbing her.

38. Motif D 701: Gradual disenchantment; D 753: Disenchantment by accomplishment of tasks.

39. This is the most complex Melusinian taboo of medieval literature, an expansion of motif H 1472.

40. Motif C 300: Looking tabu.

41. Motifs C 900: Punishment for breaking tabu; Q 451.7.0.1: Loss of one eye as punishment.

42. Motif D 150: Transformation to bird.

43. Motifs D 721.2: Disenchantment by hiding skin (covering); D 361.1: Swan Maiden.

44. Cf. motif F 771.6: Phantom house: disappears at dawn.

45. This detail indicates that we are dealing with a medieval variant of the story of *Cupid and Psyche* by Apuleius.

46. Motif D 1382.11: Magic ring protects against fire.

47. Motif D 1383.3: Magic ring protects against poison. There is no need for three rings: one ring alone could possess all these functions!

48. Motifs C 932: Loss of wife (husband) for breaking tabu; F 302.6: Fairy mistress leaves man when he breaks tabu.

49. Cf. AaTh 400: The Man on a Quest for His Lost Wife.

50. This is the same that occurs in *Lohengrin*.

51. In Germanic texts, royal authority over dwarfs is often held by a woman. The oldest manuscript of this romance does not include the story of Jerome and Frederick; it was therefore inserted into the original story.

52. Motif F 759.2: Hollow mountain.

53. Cf. D 1552.11: Magic stone opens treasure mountain. Variant of the lock-picking plant.

54. The dwarfs of courtly romances are identical to humans in all particulars; cf. Lecouteux, *The Hidden History of Elves and Dwarfs*.

55. Motif B 211.2.6: Speaking hare. The entrance of the adjuvant—a fairy given a logical explanation—into the story.

56. This is a variant of the theme of the Proud Kiss, motif D 735: Disenchantment by kiss.

57. The mapping out of a sacred site; cf. Gallais, *La Fée à la fontaine et à l'arbre*.

58. D1361: Magic object renders invisible, motif D 965: Magic plant.

59. D 350: Transformation: bird to person.

60. Cf. AaTh 40: The Princess Transformed into Deer. Pragnet's story closely resembles that of Angelburg and reveals the content of the original tale.

61. Motif T 56.3: Wooing bathing nymphs by stealing their clothes.

62. Jeroparg tries his new appearance out on Flanea: if she does not recognize him, no one will.

63. Motif D 90: Transformation: man to different man.

64. Motif d 1271: Magic fire. This is likely Greek fire and borrowed from *Wigalois,* the thirteenth-century romance by Wirnt von Grafenberg; cf. Wirnt von Grafenberg, *Wigalois*, 295ff.

65. Jellineck, ed., *Friedrich von Schwaben*.

66. Motif T 586.3: Multiple birth as result of relations with several men.

67. Motif Z 71.5.1: Seven brothers and one sister.

68. Motif S 31: Cruel stepmother.

69. *In arte magica nimis edocta.*

70. Motif K 1923.1: Nurse exchanges children.

71. Motif D 536.1: Transformation to swans by taking chains off neck.

72. Motif A 165.2.3: Angels as God's messengers.

73. Depending on the version of the story, he is still named Helias, and, in the Germanic tradition, Lohengrin. Wolfram von Eschenbach (ca. 1170–1220) was the first to tell this story and make Lohengrin the son of Parzival.

74. Motif H 215: Magic manifestation at execution proves innocence.

75. Motif D 1101.1: Magic shield.

76. The Latin text expands on the questions that Aeneas asks as he is armed head to foot; he asks what each piece of armor is, etc.

77. Motif D 361: Transformation: swan to person.

78. In Reiffenberg, ed., *Le Chevalier au Cygne et Godefroid de Bouillon*, I, 181–205. After a lacuna in the manuscript, the story recounts the battle of Aeneas against a certain Aygoland, and then the swan returns and carries him away.

79. A fairy, as the following text implicitly reveals, but one whose nature has been rationalized. She is a Swan Woman, motif D 361.1: Swan maiden.

80. Motif T 586.3: Multiple birth as result of relations with several men.

81. Motif S 31: Cruel stepmother.

82. Motif K 1840: Deception by substitution.

83. Motif Z 71.5.1: Seven brothers and one sister. Cf. EM, s.v. "Mehrlingsgeburten."

84. Motif K 1923.1: Nurse exchanges children.

85. Motif D 536.1: Transformation to swans by taking chains off neck.

86. Variant of AaTh 451.

87. Motif D 361: Transformation: swan to person.

88. A curious assertion: in correct terminology, "Nothing happens to its wearer."

89. The beginning of the legend of Lohengrin as recorded by Wolfram von Eschenbach, Konrad von Würzburg, and the anonymous *Lohengrin*. Cf. appendices.

90. In the anonymous *Lohengrin* (first half of the fourteenth century), the lady's name is Elsany of Brabant.

91. The various versions of the tale never justify this taboo.

92. Grimm, *Deutsche Sagen* [1891], no. 540; *Deutsche Sagen* (ed. Rölleke), no. 534.

Chapter V. Licit and Illicit Love

1. Motif T 83: Lover drowned as he swims to see his mistress.

2. Von der Hagen, ed., *Gesamtabenteuer*, I, no. xv, pp. 317–30. The story is followed by an epilogue of seventy-five verses with musings on fidelity and excessive love, and the author establishes a connection between Hero and Leander and his lady and himself.

3. Motif D 1364.17: Spindle causes magic sleep.

4. This motif later gave birth to that of the enchanted castle (D 6).

5. Zephyr is a sprite who can assume the shape of a horse. Cf. Ferlampin-Acher, *Fées, Bestes et Luitons,* 239 ff.; and Ferlampin-Archer, "Le Cheval dans *Perceforest.*"

6. Motif T 475.2: Hero lies by princess in magic sleep and begets child.

7. Motif F 312: Fairy presides at child's birth.

8. For more on this custom, cf. Lecouteux, "Romanisch-germanische Kulturberührungen am Beispiel des Mahls der Feen."

9. In Perrault's version, there are seven fairies plus an eighth, the wicked one; in the Brothers Grimm version there are twelve plus a thirteenth, the evil one.

10. Motif F 316: Fairy lays curse on child.

11. Motif F 361.1.1: Fairy takes revenge for not being invited to feast.

12. Motif F 316.1: Fairy's curse partially overcome by another fairy's amendment.

13. *Le Roman de Perceforest,* vol. III [1531], chap. XLVI, fol. CXXVII–CXXVIII; and chap. LV, fol. CLV. Roussineau, ed. *Perceforest: Troisème partie,* III, 209–12. Cf. Ferlampin-Acher, "Fées et déesses dans *Perceforest.*"

14. Roussineau, "Tradition littéraire et culture populaire dans l'histoire de troïlus et de zellandine (*Perceforest,* troisième partie), version arthurienne du conte de *la Belle au bois dormant.*"

15. *Pentamerone,* V, 5, tranlated into French in Deulin, *Les Contes de ma Mère l'Oye avant Perrault,* 150ff.

16. In the chivalric romance *Florence de Rome,* the two brothers are named Esmere and Milon.

17. Motifs K 2110.1: Calumniated wife; K 2112: Woman slandered as adulteress (prostitute).

18. Motif K 2112: Woman slandered as adulteress (prostitute). The *Miracle* says this: After being slandered, she was to be beheaded in the forest but her executioners wanted to first take advantage of her. Hearing the prayers of the empress, the Virgin sent a savior that killed them and rescued the poor woman.

19. Cf. motif Q 551.6: Magic sickness as punishment.

20. Motif K 910: Murder by strategy.

21. In the *Miracle,* Saint Peter is replaced by the Virgin Mary, who gives the lady a healing herb.

22. Motif W 11.5.9.1: Calumniated woman intercedes for accusers.

23. Schröder, ed., *Kaiserchronik,* ll. 11,367–12,828.

24. Motif Q 451.2: Laming as punishment.

25. Motif Q 451.7.0.2: Miraculous blindness as punishment.

26. We realize that he has been punished for the murder, cf. motif Q 211: Murder of children punished.

27. *De pudicitia et tolerantia cujusdam imperatricis;* cf. Wallensköld, *Le Conte de la femme chaste convoitée par son beau-frère,* 32–60 and 116–20; Stefanović, "Die Crescentia-Florence-Sage," 470–80.

28. Cf., for example, Klapper, ed., *Erzählungen des Mittelalters,* no. 28: "De imperatrice et leprosis."

29. *Gesta Romanorum* (ed. Dick), chap. 150 *(De fratre imperatoris, qui concupivit imperatricem et suspendit eam vivam);* Vincent of Beauvais, *Speculum historiale* VII, 90–92 (Florentia).

30. Wallensköld, ed. *Le Conte de la femme chaste convoitée par son beau-frère.*

31. Legrand d'Aussy, *Fabliaux ou contes, fables et romans du XIIe et du XIIIe siècle,* 125–29.

32. Legrand d'Aussy, *Fabliaux ou contes, fables et romans,* V, 164–69.

33. For example in Dutch: *Florentina de getrouwe* (Magdeburg: Koch, 1500).

34. *Histoire des sept sages:* there are three hanged men. In Petronius, we are not told the number of those crucified.

35. *Romance of the Seven Sages:* Gerard, the knight who must keep guard, lingers in the lady's company, and when he returns, one of the condemned has disappeared. In Petronius, the father and the mother take down the hanged man.

36. Marie de France, *Die Fabeln,* no. 25.

37. Cf., for example, Crane, ed. *The exempla or Illustrative Stories from the Sermones vulgares of Jacques de Vitry,* no. 232.

38. Misrahi, ed. *Le Roman des sept sages,* ll. 3,685–930.

39. Motif T 415: Brother-sister incest.

40. Motifs S 141: Exposure in boat; S 312.1: Child of incest exposed.

41. Motif R 131.14: Sailor rescues abandoned child.

42. *Gesta Romanorum:* when he sees the valuable linens, the abbot guesses that the baby is of noble stock *(de nobili sanguine).*

43. The title of the collection prompts an error: *De albano: Soror concipit a fratre et parit et post contractauit matrimonium. Hystoria rara sed graciosa.*

44. *Gesta Romanorum:* it is Gregory who demands this, but the abbot is reluctant because he views him as his successor.

45. *Gesta Romanorum:* he traveled to the Holy Land to atone for his sin.

46. *Gesta Romanorum:* the duke of Burgundy asks for her hand in marriage and

when she refuses, he invades and destroys her lands before besieging her city.

47. *Gesta Romanorum:* Gregory leaves the abbot and sets sail for Palestine, but contrary winds drive him toward the queen's city. Here some texts insert an episode in which Gregory provides military service to the king of Naples.

48. *Gesta Romanorum:* Gregory beheads the duke and presents the queen with his head while trumpets blare and cymbals clash.

49. *Gesta Romanorum:* it is the seneschal who offers this advice.

50. Motif N 211.1: Lost ring found in fish. A variant on the legend of Polycrates's ring.

51. Luzarche, ed., Vie *du pape Grégoire le Grand;* Sol, ed., *La Vie du pape saint Grégoire, Huit versions françaises médiévales de la légende du Bon Pécheur.*

52. *Passional,* fol. CCLI.

53. Hartmann von Aue, *Gregorius.*

54. Schilling, *Arnold von Lübeck.*

55. Thorleifsson, *Reykjahólabók.*

56. Gonzenbach, *Sizilianische märchen,* 134.

57. On the connections between this romance and that of Hartmann von Aue, cf. Mertens, *Gregorius eremita.*

58. *Plenarium, Evangelien unde Epistolen;* the text is titled "Gregorius de grote sunder."

59. Martin von Cochem, *Außerlesenes gar anmuthiges und sehr nutzliches History-Buch,* 291–305. Used by Simrock in *Die deutschen Volksbücher,* XII, 85–113.

60. Luzel, *Légendes chrétienne de la Basse-Bretagne,* II, 19–29, here at 29.

Chapter VI.
Wisdom, Cunning, and Stupidity

1. Motif F 813.1.1: Golden apple.

2. Variant of motif H 1312.1: Quest for three persons as stupid as his wife.

3. Motif H 1558.1: Test of friendship.

4. Oesterley, ed., *Gesta Romanorum.*

5. Motif H 500: Test of cleverness or ability.

6. Motif H 961: Tasks performed by cleverness.

7. Oesterley, ed., *Gesta Romanorum;* Dick, ed., *Die* Gesta Romanorum; see Weiske's excellent two-volume study, *Gesta Romanorum,* with a considerable bibliography.

8. Motif F 531: Giant. The author uses the word *turse* that corresponds to the Norse *þurs* and designates a race of giants. Cf. Lecouteux, *Encyclopedia of Norse and Germanic Folklore, Mythology, and Magic,* s.v. "thurse."

9. Motif G 11.2: Cannibal giant.

10. Mettke, ed., *Fabeln und mären von dem Stricker.*

11. Steinmetz, ed., *Historia von den sieben weisen Meistern,* 17–19.

12. Frenken, ed., *Die Exempla des Jacob von Vitry,* 105–6. Stephen of Bourbon was inspired by this.

13. Motif J 1532.1: The Snow-Child. (Modus Leibinc.) A sailor's wife bears a son in his absence and says that it came from eating snow. Later the husband makes away with the boy who, he says, melted in the sun.

14. Von der Hagen, ed., *Gesamtabenteuer,* II, 379–85. Cf. Röhricht, *Erzählungen des späten Mittelalters,* text nos. 204–21, pp. 294–99.

15. Montaiglon, *Recueil général et complet des fabliaux des XIIIe et XIVe siècles,* I, 162–67.

16. Cf. Wenzig, "Slavische Sagen."

17. Motif J 2075: The transferred wish.

18. Marie de France, *Die Fabeln,* no. 57.

19. Motif K 2322: The three hunchback brothers drowned.

20. Motif Q 416: Punishment: drawing asunder by horses.

21. Motif Q 413.4: Hanging as punishment for murder.

22. Steinmetz, ed *Historia von den sieben weisen Meistern,* 43–47.

23. The author has the pseudonym of *Niemand* (No one).

Chapter VII. Heroic Legends

1. Form taken by the motif F 661.4.1: Archer shoots eggs through middle.

2. Saxo Grammaticus, *Gesta Danorum* (ed. Olrik and Raeder).

3. For more on the legend, cf. Maillefer, "Essai sur Völundr-Wieland."

4. Motif F 451.4.1.1: Dwarfs live in caves. The Swedish *Chronicle of Didrik* (chap. 56) calls this Mount Kallafa or Balve, and other texts Ballova; it is located in northern Germany.

5. Motifs F 451.3.4.2: Dwarfs as smiths; F 451.3.16: Dwarfs are artful.

6. Motif F 451.5.2: Malevolent dwarf.

7. "Geese" in *Chronicle of Didrik,* chap. 64.

8. Motifs F 833: Extraordinary sword; F 611.3.3.1: Hero tests sword by cutting steer in two; F 833.5.1: Sword cuts cloth, etc., as well as steel and stone.

9. A variant of motif N 513.2: Sword hidden under water.

10. Motif D 931: Magic stone. Several stones were supposed to provide victory during the Middle Ages: the rooster stone, the thunder stone, and the memmonius are the ones most often mentioned in the lapidaries.

11. Motif D 1317.0.1: Magic object detects poison.

12. Motif S 160: Mutilations.

13. The poem *Deor,* written in Old English between the sixth and seventh centuries, attests to the spread of the legend and says: "Wayland knew exile; the valiant warrior suffered great torment and grief, desire, and winter's cold were his companions. An excellent man, he often knew pain after Nithad had him bound and his tendons severed" (ed. Holthausen, *Beowulf nebst den kleineren Denkmälern der Heldensage*).

14. This scene is depicted on the Auzon chest; cf. Nedoma, *Die bildlichen und schriftlichen Denkmäler der Wielandsage*.

15. For more, see "The "Archer and the King" in this collection.

16. Form taken by the motif F 661.4.1: Archer shoots eggs through middle.

17. The Egil of Ölrun, Ölrun being the name of the swan maiden he took as his wife.

18. According to one German tradition, Wayland had two sons: Wittich (Vidga, Witege) and Wittichowe (Vidigoia).

19. Jónsson, ed *Þiðrekssaga af Bern; The Saga of Thidrek of Bern* (trans. Haymes); *La Saga de Théodoric de Vérone* (trans. Lecouteux).

20. In the French texts, Alexander, king of Constantinople.

21. Bellisant in the French texts.

22. This figure does not appear in the French text. My reference is the *Histoire de Valentin et Orson* (pub. Girardon, no date, in-4°), which includes seventy-four chapters. The popular Dutch book *(Historie van Valentyne en Oursson)* follows this text faithfully but divides it into seventy-two chapters.

23. Motif M 369.7.1: Prophecy: birth of twins. Cf. also T 685 (twins) and 587: Birth of twins. Cf. Saintyves, "Les Jumeaux dans l'ethnographie et la mythologie." This passage is not in the French text.

24. French text: exiled after a slanderous denunciation by the traitor, Bellisant gives birth in the Orleans Forest. Philamine does not appear in the text.

25. Motif S 314: Twins exposed.

26. French text: a female bear. The child was therefore named Orson [*ours* is "bear" in French —*Trans.*]. Motif B 535: Animal nurse. Animal nourishes abandoned child.

27. Motifs R 13.0.1: Children carried off by animals; B 535.0.9: She-wolf as nurse for child.

28. Motif B 535: Animal nourishes abandoned child.

29. French text: it is Pepin who rescues Valentin without knowing that he is his nephew.

30. There is no servant in the French text.

31. French text: an absent detail.

32. Variant of motif S 322.4.2: Evil stepmother orders stepdaughter to be killed.

33. Motif Q 451.5: Nose cut off as punishment. None of this appears in the French text.

34. Blandimain in the French text.

35. The function of this form of banishments is to trigger the plot; this is the first function of Vladimir Propp (*Morphologie du conte*, 46–47).

36. French text: Clarina is named Eglantine; Pepin entrusts Valentin to her and she falls in love with him.

37. French text: the pagans are besieging Rome and the pope asks for aid.

38. French text: following complaints (Ourson attacks the merchants and rapes their wives), Pepin decide to capture or kill him.

39. A huge club that is the prerogative of courtly giants like Rainouart in the geste of Guillaume d'Orange (William of Orange).

40. French texts: two of Pepin's sons make the request of their relative Grigard to capture the brothers.

41. French text: Grigard comes to Pepin's court, where he must face Orson in a duel; he is defeated, confesses his crime, and is hung.

42. The same scene is found in "Crescentia."

43. One of the most classic descriptions, cf. C. Lecouteux, "Un phénomène d'enlaidissement dans la littérature médiévale."

44. Motif R 51: Mistreatment of prisoners.

45. French text: this entire episode remotely corresponds to the meeting of the Green Knight, the brother of the giant Ferragus, and includes a magical shield in addition to the ring that will serve as an identification sign.

46. French text: Duke of Aquitaine. Valentin and Orson go to his aid.

47. French text: Fezonne.

48. Motif B 211.6.1: Speaking snake. French text: there is a bronze head that the sister of Ferragus, Esclarmonde (Rosilia here), owns. Valentin and Orson learn who their parents are when they are at her home.

49. This odd detail reflects the notion of an individual's animal *alter ego;* cf. Lecouteux, *Witches, Werewolves, Fairies.* French text: the bronze head no longer speaks.

50. Motif R 111.1: Princess (maiden) rescued from captor.

51. Motif R 110: Rescue of captive.

52. Motif K 1837: Disguise of woman in man's clothes. AaTh 514; 880; 881; 884.

53. These last two verses are in Latin: *Explycyt hoc totum / Infunde da mychy potum.* I have used the edition of Geeraedts, ed., *Die Stockholmer Handschrift Cod. Holm. Vu 73,* 119–81.

54. Then by Pierre Rigaud in 1605, in Paris between 1504 and 1511 by Jean Trepperel, in Troyes in 1698 by Jacques Oudot, then in 1723, and reworked in May 1777 for the Bibliothèque universelle des romans (pp. 60–215).

55. In the work of Johannes Gobi, who uses the same story without connecting it to the Duke of Brunswick, the time alloted is five years, but his absence lasts for ten years and the hero has gone to India (*Scala coeli,* chap. 850).

56. The author borrows this episode and those that follow from *Herzog Ernst,* a courtly romance written circa 1190, in which the storm leaves the travelers at the foot of the Magnet Mountain but adds the drawing of lots for their fates. *Liedeken* stanza 13 indicates that the ship is trapped in the Coagulated Sea (Leverzee) and indicates the presence of magnet stones (verse 14). Cf. EM, s.v. "Magnetberg," AaTh 322*.

57. Only the German medieval text includes the drawing of lots. Connected to the Magnet Mountain, this motif is present in "The First Voyage d'Abul'fauaris," cf. Pétis de La Croix, *Les Mille et un Jours,* 226–28. It appears again in the fourteenth century in *Bérinus* (ed. Bossuat).

58. *Liedeken,* the Dutch song, differs on this point: it is Henry that has the idea of having himself sewn in an ox hide because he has seen the griffins coming to the ship every day in search of food.

59. Motif B 42: Griffin.

60. Variant of motif B 542.2.1. Transportation to fairyland on griffin's back.

61. *Liedeken* does not include this detail.

62. Variant of AaTh 156 (the lion of Androcles).

63. The Czech chapbook (sixteenth century) follows the story faithfully, cf. Lecouteux, "*Herzog Ernst* v. 2164ff."

64. Marbach, *Volksbücher,* vol. 52, 3–16.

65. In other words, the Mesnie Hellequin, the Wild Hunt; cf. Lecouteux,

Phantom Armies of the Night; Ueltschi, *La Mesnie Hellequin en conte et en rime.*

66. In *Liedeken* stanza 36, the spirit is Satan in person, who spontaneously says: "Your wife should be getting remarried tomorrow."

67. Only Michael Wyssenherre mentions a son.

68. *Liedeken* stanza 40, the devil says: "What will you give me if I carry you while you are sleeping to Brunswick?" and Henry answers: "I will not give you my soul" (stanza 41).

69. *Liedeken* stanza 50: "a beggar" *(bedelaere).*

70. *Liedeken* stanza 51–52: Henry finds himself a spot on the path his wife takes to go to church.

71. There has been no mention of this until now. Is it the trace of an older version?

72. Motif H 94.5: Identification through broken ring.

73. *Liedeken* stanza 54: Henry has been absent or ten years.

74. Motif N 681: Husband (lover) arrives home just as wife (mistress) is to marry another man.

75. *Liedeken* stanza 59: the suitor flees with his friends.

76. *Liedeken* stanza 63: the duchess has a stone lion sculpted that is placed next to Henry's tomb.

77. Michael Wyssenherre, *Eyn buoch von dem edelen herrn von Bruneczwigk als er uber mer fuore* (verses 1471–74), fol. 91 v°–104 v°.

78. *De Winando qui infra unam horam ab Jerusalem translatus est in dioecesim Leodiensem.*

79. Oswald of Northumbria (604–642), a saint whose feast day is August 5. In Carinthia and in Styria, he is a protector of livestock.

80. Motif H 1381.3.1.1: Quest for bride for king.

81. Motif T 410: Incest.

82. Motif B 211.3.6: Speaking raven.

83. Motif H 1381.3.1.1: Quest for bride for king.

84. Motif B 81: Mermaid.

85. This demand punctuates the text and refers to the position of the minstrel.

86. Variant of the legend de the ring of Polycrates, motif N 211.1: Lost ring found in fish.

87. A cliché of hagiographic legends (motif D 1557.1: Door (lock) magically opens for saint). In folktales and legends, it is a stone or an herb that forces locks, cf. motif D 1557.2: Magic herb causes door to open.

88. Cf. motif D 1421.5.1: Magic horn summons army for rescue.

89. Motif K 1811: Gods (saints) in disguise visit mortals.

90. Cf. EM, s.v. "Kleidertausch."

91. The historical Oswald had a son, Æthelwald of Deira, but it isn't certain that this is the offspring of his union with the daughter of Cynegils of Wessex (verses 611–43).

92. Baesecke, ed., *Der Münchener Oswald;* Baesecke, ed., *Der Wiener Oswald.*

Appendix 1.
Survival and Transformation of the Narratives

1. Motif T615: Supernatural growth.

2. Cf. EM, s.v. "Kleidertausch."

3. Motif T 104: Rejected suitor wages war.

4. It will be noted that this motif doesn't play any role in the story; it is a remnant from an earlier version.

5. An etiological legend inserted here.

6. A new motif whose trace has not been found before.

BIBLIOGRAPHY

Afanasyev, Alexander. *Narodnye russkie legendy.* Moscow: N. Shchepkin i K. Soldatenkov, 1859.

Agobard de Lyon. *Agobardi Lugdunensis Opera Omnia.* Edited by L. Van Acker. Turnhout: Brepols, 1981.

Albert-Lorca, Marlène. *L'Ordre des Choses: Les récits d'origine des animaux et des plantes en Europe.* Paris: CTHS, 1991.

Alexander und Antiloye. Edited by Moriz Haupt. *Altdeutsche Blätter,* vol. I, edited by Moriz Haupt and Heinrich Hoffmann. Leipzig: Brockhaus, 1836. Pp. 250–66.

Allen, Clifford Gilmore. "The Relation of the German 'Gregorius auf dem Stein' to the Old French Poem 'La Vie de saint Grégoire.'" In *Matzke Memorial Volume.* Stanford: Stanford University Press, 1911. Pp. 49–56.

Amelineau, Émile. *Contes et Romans de l'Égypte ancienne,* vol. 1. Paris: Leroux, 1888.

Antti, Aarne. *The Types of the Folktale: A Classification and a Bibliography.* Translated and enlarged by Stith Thompson. Second revision. Helsinki: Suomalainen Tiedeakatemia, 1964.

Baasch, Karen. *Die Crescentia-Legende in der deutschen Dichtung des Mittelalters.* Stuttgart: Metzler, 1968.

Bacon, Roger. *Secretum secretorum, cum glossis et notulis.* Edited by Robert Steele. Oxford: Clarendon, 1920.

Baesecke, Georg, ed. *Der Münchener Oswald: Text und Abhandlung.* Breslau: Olms, 1907.

———, ed. *Der Wiener Oswald.* Heidelberg: Winter, 1912.

Barack, Karl August. "Bruchstücke mittelhochdeutscher Gedichte in der Universitäts-und Landesbibliothek zu Straßburg." *Germania* 25 (1880): 161–91.

Barbazan, Étienne, ed. *Fabliaux et contes des poëtes françois des XII, XIII, XIV & XVes siècles tirés des meilleurs auteurs.* 3 vols. Paris and Amsterdam: Vincent/Arkestée et Merkus, 1756.

Baum, Paul Franklin. "The Young Man Betrothed to a Statue." *PMLA* 34 (1919), 523–79.

Baumann, Winfried. *Die Sage von Heinrich dem Löwen bei den Slaven.* Munich: Sanger, 1975.

Bechstein, Ludwig. *Deutsches Märchenbuch.* Leipzig: Wigand, 1845.

———. *Neues Deutsches Märchenbuch.* Leipzig: Einhorn, 1856.

———. *Le Livre des contes.* Introduced, translated, and annotated by Corinne and Claude Lecouteux. Paris: Corti, 2010.

Beckmann, Gustav Adolf. *Wieland der Schmied in neuer Perspektive.* Frankfurt: Lang, 2004.

Berlioz, Jacques. "Virgile dans la littérature des *exempla* (XIIIe–XVe siècle)." In *Lectures médiévales de Virgile.* Rome: École française de Rome, 1985. Pp. 65–120.

———. "Un petit chaperon rouge médiéval? La petite fille épargnée par les loups dans la *Fecunda ratis* d'Egbert de Liège (début du XIe siècle)." *Merveilles et contes* 2 (1991): 246–62.

Berlioz, Jacques, and Claude Brémond. Edited by C. Vellay-Valentin. *Formes médiévales du conte merveilleux.* Paris: Stock, 1989.

Berlioz, Jacques, and Marianne Polo de Beaulieu. *Les Exempla médiévaux: Introduction à la recherche suivie des tables critiques de l'*Index exemplorum *de F. C. Tubach.* Carcassonne: GARAE/Hesiode, 1992.

Blangez, Gérard, ed. *Ci nous dit: Recueil d'exempla moraux.* 2 vols. Paris: Société des anciens textes français, 1979–1986.

Blom, Helwi. "Valentin et Orson et la Bibliothèque bleue." In *L'épopée romane au Moyen Âge et aux temps modernes,* vol. II. Edited by Salvatore Luongo. Naples: Fridericiana Editrice Universitaria, 2001. Pp. 611–25.

Bolte, Johannes, and Georg Polivka. *Anmerkungen zu den Kinder- und Hausmärchen.* 5 vols. Leipzig: Dieterich/Welcher, 1913–1918.

Bossuat, Robert, ed. *Bérinus: Roman en prose du XIVe siècle.* 2 vols. Paris: Société des anciens textes français, 1931–1933.

Brémond, Claude, Jacques Le Goff, and Jean-Claude Schmitt. *L'"Exemplum."* Turnhout: Brepols, 1982.

Caesarius von Heisterbach. *Dialogus miraculorum.* Edited by J. Strange. 2 vols. Cologne, Bonn, and Brussels: Heberle, 1851.

Cantari leggendari i, fiore di leggende, cantari antichi. Edited by Ezio Levi. Bari: Laterza, 1914.

Carozzi, Claude. *Le Voyage de l'âme dans l'au-delà d'après la littérature latine (Ve–XIIIe siècle).* Rome: École française de Rome, 1994.

Cifuentes, Don Julio Vicuña. *Romances Populares y Vulgares.* Santiago de Chile: Barcelona, 1912.

Comparetti, Domenico. *Virgil im Mittelalter.* Translated into German by Hans Dütschke. Leipzig: Teubner, 1875.

———. *Virgilio nel medio evo.* Edited by Giorgio Pasquali. Florence: La Nuova Italia, 1937.

Crane, Thomas Frederick, ed. *The* exempla *or Illustrative Stories from the* sermones vulgares *of Jacques de Vitry.* London: Folk-Lore Society, 1890.

Creytens, Raymond. "Le Manuel de conversation de Philippe de Ferrare O.P. († 1350?)." *Archivum Fratrum Praedicatorum* 16 (1946): 107–35.

Curschmann, Michael. *Der Münchener Oswald und die deutsche spielmännische Epik: Mit einem Exkurs zur Kultgeschichte und Dichtungstradition.* Munich: Beck, 1964.

Delarue, Paul, and Marie-Louise Ténèze. *Le Conte populaire français.* 4 vols. Paris: Maisonneuve et Larose, 2002.

Delbouille, Maurice. *Le* Lai d'Aristote, *publié d'après tous les manuscrits.* Paris: Bibliothèque de la Faculté de Philosophie et Lettres de l'Université de Liège, 1951.

Deulin, Charles. *Les contes de ma Mère l'Oye avant Perrault.* Paris: Dentu, 1878.

Dick, Wilhelm, ed. *Die* Gesta Romanorum: *Nach der Innsbrucker Handschrift vom Jahre 1342 und vier Münchener Handschriften.* Erlangen and Leipzig: Deichert, 1890.

Dickson, Arthur. *Valentine and Orson: A Study in Late Medieval Romance.* New York: Columbia University Press, 1929.

Di Maio, Mariella. *Le Cœur mangé: Histoire d'un thème littéraire du Moyen Âge au XIXe siècle.* Translated into French by Anne Bouffard. Paris: P.U.P.S., 2005.

Dimrock, James F., ed. *Giraldi cambrensis opera,* vol. V. London: Longman & Co., 1898.

Dinzelbacher, Peter. *Vision und Visionsliteratur im Mittelalter.* Stuttgart: Hiersemann, 1981.

Dits en quatrains d'alexandrins monorimes de Jehan de Saint-Quentin. Edited by B. Munk Olsen. Paris: Société des anciens textes français, 1978.

Duchesne, L., ed. *Liber pontificalis.* 3 vols. Paris: Thorin, 1886–1957.

Elstein, Yoav. "The Gregorius Legend: Its Christian Versions and Its Metamorphosis in the Hassidic Tale." *Fabula* 27 (1986): 195–215.

Enzyklopädie des Märchens. Edited by Kurt Ranke, et al. 11 vols. Berlin and New York: De Gruyter, 1979–2006.

Felix Fabri. *Evagatorium in Terræ Sanctæ, Arabiæ et Egypti peregrinationem.* 3 vols. Edited by Konrad Dieterich Hassler. Stuttgart: Literarischer Verein, 1843–49.

Ferlampin-Acher, Christine. "Le cheval dans *Perceforest:* Réalisme, merveilleux et burlesque." *Le Cheval dans le monde médiéval, Senefiance* 32 (1992): 209–36.

———. "Fées et déesses dans *Perceforest.*" In *Fées, Dieux et Déesses au moyen Âge, Bien dire et bien aprandre.* Lille: Centre Études médiévales, 1995. Pp. 53–72.

———. *Fées, Bestes et luitons: Croyances et merveilles.* Paris: P.U.P.S., 2002.

Filippo of Ferrara. *Liber de introductione loquendi.* Edited by Silvana Vecchio. Florence: Vallecchi, 1998.

Florentina de getrouwe. Magdeburg: Koch, 1500.

Frank, Emma. *Der Schlangenkuß: Die Geschichte eines Erlösungsmotivs in deutscher Volksdichtung.* Leipzig: Eichblatt, 1928.

Frenken, Goswin, ed. *Die Exempla des Jacob von Vitry: Ein Beitrag zur Geschichte der Erzählungsliteratur des Mittelalters.* Munich: Beck, 1914.

Füetrer, Ulrich. *Das Buch der Abenteuer.* Edited by Heinz Thoelen with Bernd Bastert. 2 vols. Göppingen: Kümmerle, 1997.

Gallais, Pierre. *La Fée à la fontaine et à l'arbre: Un archétype du conte merveilleux et du récit Courtois.* Amsterdam: Rodopi, 1992.

Gaster, Moses. "The Old Hebrew Romance of Alexander." *The Journal of the Royal Asiatic Society of Great Britain* (1897): 485–549.

Gautier le Leu. *Les Sohais.* Edited by Charles H. Livingston in "The Jongleur Gautier Le Leu: A Study in the Fabliaux." *The Romanic Review* 15 (1924): 1–67.

Geeraedts, Loek. *Die Stockholmer Handschrift Cod. Holm. Vu 73.* Cologne and Vienna: Böhlau, 1984.

Geissler, Friedmar. *Brautwerbung in der Weltliteratur.* Halle: Niemeyer, 1955.

Gerald of Wales. *Topographia Hibernica.* Edited by J. F. Dimrock. In *Giraldi cambrensis opera,* vol. V. London: Published by the Authority of the Lords Commissioners of Her Royal Majesty's Treasury, 1898.

Gervase of Tilbury. *Otia imperialia: Recreation for an Emperor.* Edited and translated by S. E. Banks and J. W. Binns. Oxford: Oxford University Press, 2002.

Gonzenbach, Laura. *Sizilianische Märchen, aus dem Volksmund gesammelt.* Leipzig: Engelmann, 1870.

Gottschald, Max. *Deutsche Namenkunde: Unsere Familiennamen.* Berlin and New York: De Gruyter, 1982.

Grange, Isabelle. "Metamorphoses chrétiennes des femmes-cygnes . . . Du folklore à l'hagiographie." *Ethnologie française* 13.2 (April–June 1983): 139–50.

Grimm, Jacob, and Wilhelm Grimm. *Deutsche Sagen.* Berlin: Nicolai, 1891.

———. *The German Legends of the Brothers Grimm.* 2 vols. Edited and translated by Donald Ward. Philadelphia: Institute for the Study of Human Issues, 1979.

———. *Deutsche Sagen.* Edited by Heinz Rölleke. Frankfurt: Deutscher Klassikerverlag, 1994.

Harf–Lancner, Laurence, and Marie-Noëlle Polino. "Le gouffre de Satalie: survivances médiévales du mythe de Méduse." *Le Moyen Âge* 94 (1988): 73–101.

Hartmann von Aue. *Der arme Heinrich.* Edited by Hermann Paul. Tübingen: Niemeyer, 1984.

———. *Gregorius.* Edited by Hermann Paul. Tübingen: Niemeyer, 1984.

Haymes, Edward R., trans. *The Saga of Thidrek of Bern.* New York: Garland, 1988.

Herlem-Prey, Brigitte. *Le Gregorius et la Vie de Saint Grégoire: Détermination de la source de Hartmann von Aue à partir de l'étude comparative intégrale des textes.* Göppingen: Kümmerle, 1979.

Hersart de La Villemarqué, Théodore, ed. *Barzaz Breiz: Chants populaires de la Bretagne.* Paris: Didier, 1867.

Histoire de Valentin et Orson. Troyes: Girardon, n.d.

La Historia del Liombruno. Rome: Silber, 1485.

Historie van Valentyne en Oursson. Amsterdam: Jacobus van Egmont, n. d.

Historie-Liedeken van den Hertog van Brunswyk. Edited by Friedrich Heinrich von der Hagen. *Neues Jahrbuch der Berlinischen Gesellschaft für deutsche Sprache und Alterthumskunde* 8 (1848): 359–69.

Holthausen, Ferdinand, ed. *Beowulf nebst den kleineren Denkmälern der Heldensage: Finnsburg, Waldere, Deor, Widsith, Hildebrand.* Heidelberg: Winter, 1921.

Howlett, Richard, ed. *Chronicles of the Reigns of Stephen, Henry II., and Richard I.* 4 vols. London: Longman, 1884–1889.

Hues Piaucele. *D'Estormi.* In *Nouveau Recueil complet des fabliaux,* vol. I, ed. Willem Noomen and Nico Van den Boogaard. Assen: Van Gorcum, 1983. Pp. 13–28.

Huet, Gédéon. "La légende de la statue de Vénus." *Revue de l'histoire des religions* 68 (1913), 193–217.

———. "La légende de la fille d'Hippocrate à Cos." *Bibliothèque de l'École des Chartes* 79 (1918): 45–59.

Hugo von Trimberg. *Der Renner.* Edited by Gustav Ehrismann. Tübingen: Niemeyer, 1909.

Hyde, Douglas, and Alfred Nutt, ed. and trans. *Beside the Fire: A Collection of Irish Gaelic Folk Stories.* London: Nutt, 1890.

Ilg, Bertha. *Maltesische Märchen und Schwänke.* 2 vols. Leipzig: Hinrichs, 1906.

James-Raoul, D., and O. Soutet, eds. "Les marches de l'au- delà." In *Par les mots et les textes, mélanges Claude Thomasset.* Edited by Danièle James-Raoul and Olivier Soutet. Paris: P.U.P.S., 2005.

Jansen Enikel. *Weltchronik.* Heidelberg University Library, manuscript Cpg. 336.

Jehan de Saint-Quentin. *Dits en quatrains d'alexandrins de Jehan de Saint-Quentin.* Edited by B. Monk Olsen. Paris: Société des anciens textes française, 1978.

Jellineck, Max Hermann, ed. *Friedrich von Schwaben, aus der Stuttgarter Handschrift.* Berlin: Weidmann, 1904.

Johannes de Alta Silva, *Dolopathos, or, The King and the Seven Wise Men.* Translated by Brady B. Gilleland. Binghamton, N.Y.: Center for Medieval & Early Renaissance Studies, 1981.

Johannes Gobi. *Scala coeli.* Edited by Marie-Anne Polo de Beaulieu. Paris: Centre National de la Recherche Scientifique, 1991.

John Mandeville. *Reisen.* Basel: Richel, 1480/81.

————. *Reysen und wanderschafften durch das Gelobte Land.* Translated into German by Otto von Diemeringen. Strassburg: Prüss, 1483.

Jónsson, Guðni, ed. *Þiðrekssaga af Bern.* 2 vols. Reykjavik: Islendingasagnáutgánfan, 1954.

Karadžić, Vuk Stefanović. *Volkslieder der Serben,* vol. 1. Edited by Talvj. Leipzig: Renger, 1835.

Klapper, Joseph, ed. *Erzählungen des Mittelalters.* Breslau: Krappe, 1914.

Klemming, Gustaf Edward, ed. *Namnlös och Valentin: En medeltids-roman.* Stockholm: Norstedt and Sons, 1846.

Köhler, Reinhold. "Zur Legende von Gregorius auf dem Stein." *Germania* 15 (1870): 284–91.

————. "Eine koptische Variante der Legende von Gregorius auf dem Stein," *Germania* 36 (1891): 198–200.

Krappe, Alexander Haggerty. "Guiding Animals." *Journal of American Folklore* 55 (1942): 228–46.

Kuhn, Adalbert, and Wilhelm Schwartz. *Norddeutsche Sagen, Märchen und Gebräuche aus Mecklenburg, Pommern, der Mark, Sachsen, Thüringen, Braunschweig, Hannover, Oldenburg und Westfalen.* Leipzig: Brockhaus, 1848.

Lachmann, Theodor. *Sagen und Bräuche am Überlinger See.* Weissenhorn: Konrad, 1972.

Letts, Malcolm, ed. and trans. *Mandeville's Travels: Texts and Translations.* 2 vols. London: Hakluyt Society, 1953.

Lecouteux, Claude. "Der Drache." *Zeitschrift für deutsches Altertum* 108 (1979): 13–31.

————. "Herzog Ernst v. 2164ff., das böhmische Volksbuch von Stillfried und Bruncwig und die morgenländischen Alexandersagen." *Zeitschift für deutsches Altertum* 108 (1979): 306–22.

————. "Un phénomène d'enlaidissement dans la littérature médiévale: l'évolution de la morphologie du géant." *Revue belge de philologie et d'histoire* LVII (1979): 253–66.

————. "Das Motiv der gestörten Mahrtenehe." In *Vom Menschenbild im*

Märchen. Edited by Jürgen Janning, Heino Gehrts, and Herbert Ossowski. Kassel: Röth, 1980, Pp. 59–71 and 147–51.

———. "Aspects mythiques de la montagne au Moyen Âge." *Le Monde alpin et rhodanien,* (1982): 43–54.

———. "Romanisch-germanische Kulturberührungen am Beispiel des Mahls der Feen." *Mediävistik* 1 (1988): 87–99.

———. "L'arrière-plan des sites aventureux dans le roman médiéval." *Études germaniques* 46 (1991): 293–304.

———. "Le radeau des vents: Pour une mythologie des nuages au Moyen Âge." In *Les Nuages et leur symbolique.* Edited by Jacqueline Kelen. Paris: Michel, 1995. Pp. 193–216.

———. *Mélusine et le Chevalier au cygne.* Paris: Imago, 1997.

———, trans. *La Saga de Théodoric de Vérone.* Paris: Champion, 2001.

———. *Witches, Werewolves, and Fairies: Shapeshifters and Astral Doubles in the Middle Ages.* Translated by Clare Frock. Rochester, Vt.: Inner Traditions, 2003.

———. "Les marches de l'au-delà." In *Par les mots et les textes, Mélanges Claude Thomasset,* Edited by Danièle James-Raoul and Olivier Soutet. Paris: PUPS, 2005. Pp. 483–92.

———. *Mondes parallèles: L'univers des croyances au Moyen Âge.* Paris: Champion, 2007.

———. *Elle courait le garou: Lycanthropes, hommes-ours, hommes-tigres, une anthologie.* Paris: Corti, 2008.

———. *The Return of the Dead: Ghosts, Ancestors, and the Transparent Veil of the Pagan Mind.* Translated by Jon E. Graham. Rochester, Vt.: Inner Traditions, 2009.

———. *Phantom Armies of the Night: The Wild Hunt and the Ghostly Processions of the Undead.* Translated by Jon E. Graham. Rochester, Vt.: Inner Traditions, 2013.

———. *Dictionary of Ancient Magic Words and Spells.* Translated by Jon E. Graham. Rochester, Vt.: Inner Traditions, 2015.

———. *Encyclopedia of Norse and Germanic Folklore, Mythology, and Magic.* Translated by Jon E. Graham. Edited by Michael Moynihan. Rochester, Vt.: Inner Traditions, 2016.

———. *The Hidden History of Elves and Dwarfs: Avatars of Invisible Realms.* Translated by Jon E. Graham. Rochester, Vt.: Inner Traditions, 2018.

————. "Lebenswasser." In *Enzyklopädie des Märchens,* vol. 8, col. 838–41.

Legrand d'Aussy, Pierre Jean-Baptiste. *Fabliaux ou contes, fables et romans du XIIe et du XIIIe siècle, traduits ou extraits,* vol. V. Paris: Renouard, 1829.

Le Roman de Perceforest, pt. III. Paris: Galliot du Pré, 1531.

Liber pontificalis, vol. 2. Edited by Louis Duchesne. Paris: Thorin, 1955.

Lixfeld, Hannjost. "Die Guntramsage (AT 1645A): Volkserzählung vom Alter Ego in Tiergestalt und ihre schamanistische Herkunft." *Fabula* 13 (1972): 60–107.

Luzarche, Victor, ed. *Vie du pape Grégoire le Grand, légende française.* Paris: Potier, 1857.

Luzel, F. M. *Légendes chrétienne de la Basse-Bretagne,* vol. 2. Paris: Les littératures populaires de toutes les nations, 1967.

Madden, Frederic W. *The Old English Versions of the* Gesta Romanorum. London: Shakespeare, 1838.

Maillefer, Jean-Marie. "Essai sur Völundr-Wieland: La religion scandinave a-telle connu un dieu forgeron?" In *Hugur: Mélanges d'histoire, de littérature et de mythologie offerts à Régis Boyer pour son 65e anniversaire.* Edited by Claude Lecouteux and Olivier Gouchet. Paris: P.U.P.S., 1997. Pp. 331–52.

Marbach, Gotthard Oswald. *Volksbücher,* vol. 52. Leipzig: Wigand, n.d. [ca. 1840].

Marie de France. *Die Fabeln.* Edited by Karl Warncke. Halle: Niemeyer, 1898.

Marsan, Rameline E. *Itinéraire espagnol du conte médiéval (VIIIe–XVe siècle).* Paris: Klincksiek, 1974.

Martin of Opava. *Chronicon pontificum et imperatorum.* Heidelberg University Library, manuscript Cpg 137.

Martin von Cochem. *Außerlesenes gar anmuthiges und sehr nutzliches History-Buch: Darin Neben den fürnehmsten, in zwantzig Historien begriffenen und aus den HH. Vätteren etwas erklärten Biblischen Geschichten, Lauter denckwürdige, anmuthig beschriebene, und mehrentheils unbekannte, Alte und Neue, in jetziger hundert-jährigen Zeit geschehene Hundert und zwantzig Historien.* Augsburg and Dillingen: Bencard, 1732.

Matos Fragoso, Juan de. *El marido de su madre.* Barcelona: Sapera, 1770.

Mertens, Volker. *Gregorius eremita: Eine Lebensform des Adels bei Hartmann von Aue in ihrer Problematik und ihrer Wandlung in der Rezeption.* Munich and Zurich: Artemis, 1978.

Mettke, Heinz, ed. *Fabeln und Mären von dem Stricker.* Halle: Niemeyer, 1959.

Meyer, Gustav. "Albanische Märchen." *Archiv für Literaturgeschichte* 12 (1884): 92–148.

Meyer-Matheis, Vera. *Die Vorstellung eines alter ego in Volkserzählungen.* Dissertation, University of Freiburg, 1974.

Micha, Alexandre, ed. and trans. *Lais féeriques des XIIe et XIIIe siècles.* Paris: Flammarion, 1992.

Miller, Nikolaus. "Brautwerbung und Heiligkeit: Die Kohärenz des Münchner Oswald." *Deutsche Vierteljahresschrift für Literaturwissenschaft und Geistesgeschichte* 52 (1978): 226–40.

Misrahi, Jean, ed. *Le Roman des sept sages.* Paris: Droz, 1933.

Montaiglon, Anatole de. *Recueil général et complet des fabliaux des XIIIe et XIVe siècles,* vol. 1. Paris: Librarie des bibliophiles, 1872.

Morris, Alton C. "The Aristotle of Fact and Legend." In *Folklore International: Essays in Traditional Literature, Belief, and Custom in Honor of Wayland Debs Hand.* Edited by D. K. Wilgus with Carol Sommer. Hatboro, Penn.: Folklore Associates, 1967. Pp. 151–59.

Motz, Lotte. *The Wise One of the Mountain: Form, Function and Significance of the Subterranean Smith. A Study in Folklore.* Göppingen: Kümmerle, 1983.

Murdoch, Brian. "Die Bearbeitungen des Hero- und Leander-Stoffes: Zur literarischen Ovid-Rezeption im späten Mittelalter." *Studi medievali* 18 (1977): 231–47.

Nedoma, Robert. *Die bildlichen und schriftlichen Denkmäler der Wielandsage.* Göppingen: Kümmerle, 1988.

Niewöhner, Heinrich. *Neues Gesamtabenteuer,* vol. I. Berlin: Weidmann, 1937.

Noomen, Willem, and Nico van den Boogaard, eds. *Nouveau recueil complet des fabliaux.* 10 vols. Assen: Van Gorcum, 1983.

Oesterley, Hermann, ed. *Gesta Romanorum.* Berlin: Weidmann, 1872. Reprint: Hildesheim and New York: Olms, 1980.

Oldoni Massimo. "Gerberto e la sua storia." *Studi Medievali* 18 (1977): 629–704; 21 (1980): 493–622; 24 (1983): 167–245.

Orain, Adolphe. *Trésor des contes du pays gallo.* Rennes: Terre de Brume, 2000.

Pañcatantra. Translated into French by É. Lancereau. Paris: Gallimard, 1963.

Paris, Gaston. "Le conte du trésor du roi Rhampsinite." *Revue d'histoire des religions* 55 (1907): 151–87, 267–316.

Pasquier, Estienne. *Les œuvres.* the 2 vols. Amsterdam: Aux Armes de la Compagnie des Libraires associez., 1723.

Passional. Nuremberg: Koberger, 1488.

Pétis de la Croix, François. *Les Mille et un jours.* Paris: Pourrat Frères, 1848.

Petzoldt, Leander. *Der Tote als Gast.* Helsinki: Suomalainen Tiedeakatemia, 1964.

———, ed. *Vergleichende Sagenforschung.* Darmstadt: Wissenschaftliche Buchgesellschaft, 1969.

———. *Märchen, Mythos, Sage: Beiträge zur Literatur und Volksdichtung.* Marburg: Elwert, 1989.

Pillet, Alfred. *Das Fableau von den Trois bossus ménestrels und verwandte Erzählungen früher und später Zeit: Ein Beitrag zur altfranzösischen und zur vergleichenden Litteraturgeschichte.* Halle: Niemeyer, 1901.

Piniès, Jean-Pierre, ed. *Le conte de tradition orale dans le bassin méditerranéen.* Carcassonne: GARAE/Hesiode, 1986.

Platten, August von. *Gesammelte Werke,* vol. IV. Stuttgart and Augsburg: Cotta, 1856.

Plenarium, Evangelien unde Epistolen. Lübeck: N.p., 1492.

Pliny. *Natural History* [= *Historia naturalis*]. 10 volumes. Cambridge, Mass.: Harvard University Press, 1961–68.

Prato, Stanislao. *La leggenda del Tesoro di Rampsinite nelle varie redazioni italiane e straniere: saggio critico.* Como: Franchi, 1882.

Predelli, Maria Bendinelli. *Alle origini del Bel Gherardino.* Florence: Olschki, 1990.

Propp, Vladimir. *Morphologie du conte.* Paris: Le Seuil, 1970.

Pschmadt, Karl. *Die Sage von der verfolgten Hinde: Ihre Heimat und Wanderung, Bedeutung und Entwicklung mit besonderer Berücksichtigung ihrer Verwendung in der Literatur des Mittelalters.* Dissertation, University of Greifswald, 1911.

Les Quatre Souhaits de Saint Martin. In *Nouveau recueil complet des fabliaux,* vol. IV. Edited by Willem Noomen and Nico Van den Boogaard. Assen: Van Gorcum, 1988. Pp. 189–216 et 403–11.

Rank, Otto. *Das Inzest-Motiv in Dichtung und Sage: Grundzüge einer Psychologie des dichterischen Schaffens.* Leipzig and Vienna: Deuticke, 1912.

Rastier, Françoise. "La morale de l'histoire: Notes sur la *Matrone d'Éphèse* (*Satiricon*, CXI-CXII)." *Latomus* 30 (1971): 1025–56.

Reiffenberg, Frédéric-Auguste-Ferdinand-Thomas, baron de, ed. *Le Chevalier au Cygne et Godefroid de Bouillon,* vol. I. Brussels: Hayez, 1846.

Röhrich, Lutz. *Erzählungen des späten Mittelalters und ihr Weiterleben in Literatur und Volksdichtung bis zur Gegenwart: Sagen, Märchen, Exempel und Schwänke.* 2 vols. Bern and Munich: Francke, 1962–1967.

Rosenmüller, Ernst. *Das Volkslied: Es waren zwei Königskinder. Ein Beitrag zur Geschichte des Volksliedes überhaupt.* Dissertation, University of Leipzig, 1917.

Ross, David J. A. "Alexander and Antilôis the Dwarf King: A Longer Version and a Hebrew Analogue." *Zeitschrift für deutsches Altertum* 98 (1969): 292–307.

Röth, Dieter. *Kleines typenverzeichnis der europäischen Zauber- und Novellenmärchen.* Hohengehren: Schneider, 1998.

Roussineau, Gilles, ed. *Perceforest: Troisème partie.* 3 vols. Geneva: Droz, 1988–1993.

———. "Tradition littéraire et culture populaire dans l'histoire de Troïlus et de Zellandine (*Perceforest,* troisième partie), version arthurienne du conte de *la Belle au bois dormant.*" *Arthuriana* 4 (1994): 30–45.

Ruelle, Pierre, ed. *Recueil général des Isopets,* vol. III: l'*Esope* de Julien Macho. Paris: Société des anciens textes français, 1982.

Saintyves, Pierre. "Les Jumeaux dans l'ethnographie et la mythologie." *Revue anthropologique* 25 (1925): 54–59.

Saxo Grammaticus. *Gesta Danorum.* Edited by Jørgen Olrik and Hans Raeder. Copenhagen: 1931.

Scherf, Walter. *Märchenlexikon.* 2 vols. Munich: Beck, 1995.

Scheuchzer, Johann Jacob. *Ouresiphoites Helveticus, sive itinera per Helvetiæ alpinas regiones.* 4 vols. Leyden: Vander, 1723.

Schilling, Johannes. *Arnold von Lübeck: Gesta Gregorii peccatoris.* Göttingen: Vandenhoeck & Ruprecht, 1986.

Schmitt, Alfred. "Der gerittene Aristoteles: Ein Motiv misogyner Dichtung bei Matheus von Boulogne." In *Arbor amoena comis: 25 Jahre Mittellateinisches Seminar in Bonn.* Edited by Ewald Könsgen. Stuttgart: Steiner, 1990. Pp. 193–97.

Schröder, Eduard, ed. *Kaiserchronik.* Hannover: Hahn, 1892.

Sébillot, Paul. *Le Folklore de France.* 4 vols. Paris: Guilmoto, 1907.

Een schoone en wonderlyke historie van Valentyn en Ourrsson, Twee edele vroome

Ridders, Zoonen van den magtigen Keizer van Griekenland en Neeven van den Edelen Koning Pepyn, toen ter tyd koning van Frankryk. Amsterdam: Jacobus van Egmont, n.d.

Een schoone Historie Van de twee Gebroeders en vroome Ridders Valentyn en Oursson den Wilden-Man, Zoonen van Alexander keyser van Constantinopelen, ende Neven van Pipinus koning van Vrankryk. Antwerp: Heyliger, n.d.

Ser Giovanni Fiorentino. *Il Pecorone.* Edited by Enzo Esposito. Ravenna: Longo, 1974.

Sichler, Léon. "Légendes russes." *Revue de l'histoire des religions* 19 (1889): 85–94.

Simrock, Karl. *Die deutschen Volksbücher,* vol. 12. Frankfurt: Winter, 1865.

Smith, Karen. "Snake-Maiden Transformation Narratives in Hagiography and Folklore." *Fabula* 43 (2003): 251–63.

Sol, Hendrik Bastiaan, ed. *La Vie du pape saint Grégoire, Huit versions françaises médiévales de la légende du Bon Pécheur.* Amsterdam: Rodopi, 1977.

Splettstösser, Willi. *Der heimkehrende Gatte und sein Weib in der Weltliteratur: Literarhistorische Abhandlung.* Berlin: Mayer & Müller, 1899.

Sprandel, Rolf. "Die *Gesta Romanorum* als Quelle der spätmittelalterlichen mentalitätsgeschichte." *Saeculum* 33 (1982): 312–22.

Stefanović, Svetislav. "Die Crescentia-Florence-Sage: Eine kritische Studie über ihren Ursprung und ihre Entwicklung." *Romanische Forschungen* 29 (1911): 461–556.

Steinmetz, Ralf-Henning, ed. *Historia von den sieben weisen Meistern.* Tübingen: Niemeyer, 2001.

Stephen of Bourbon. *Stefani de Borbone, Tractatvs de diversis materiis predicabilibus.* 2 vols. Edited by J. Berlioz. Turnhout: Brepols, 2002–2006.

Suchier, Walther. *Der Schwank von der viermal getöteten Leiche in der Literatur des Abend- und Morgenlandes: Literaturgeschichtlich-volkskundliche Untersuchung.* Halle: Niemeyer, 1922.

Thomasset, Claude, ed. *Dialogue de Placides et timéo.* Geneva: Droz, 1980.

———. *Une vision du monde au XIIIe siècle: Commentaire du Dialogue de Placides et Timéo.* Geneva: Droz, 1982.

Thompson, Stith. *Motif-index of Folk-literature.* 6 vols. Copenhagen: Rosenkilde and Bagger, 1955–1958.

Thorleifsson, Björn. *Reykjahólabók.* Royal Library Stockholm, manuscript Perg. fol. nr. 3.

Timoneda, Juan de. *Patrañuelo.* Valencia: Albatros hispanofilá, 1987.

Tubach, Frederic C. *Index exemplorum: A Handbook of Medieval Religious Tales.* Helsinki: Suomalainen Tiedeakatemia, 1969.

Ueltschi, Karin. *La Mesnie Hellequin en conte et en rime.* Paris: Champion, 2008.

Ulrich von Etzenbach. *Alexander.* Edited by Wendelin Toischer. Tübingen: Literarischer Verein in Stuttgart, 1888.

Ure, P. "The Widow of Ephesus: Some Reflections on an International Comic Theme." *Durham University Journal* 18 (1956): 1–9.

Velten, Harry V. "Le Conte de la *fille biche* dans le folklore français." *Romania* 56 (1930): 282–88.

Vernaleken, Theodor. *Kinder- und Hausmärchen in den Alpenländern.* Vienna: Braumüller, 1863.

Vincent of Beauvais. *Speculum quadruplex sive Speculum maius: naturale, doctrinale, morale, historiale.* 4 vols. Graz: Akademische Druck u. Verlagsanstalt, 1964 [1624].

Von der Hagen, Friedrich Heinrich, ed. *Gesamtabenteuer.* 3 vols. Stuttgart and Tübingen: Cotta, 1850.

Waitz, Georg, ed. *Pauli Historia Langobardorum.* Hannover: Hahn, 1878.

Wallensköld, Axel. *Le Conte de la femme chaste convoitée par son beau-frère: Étude de Littérature Comparée.* Helsingfors: [Ex Officina typographica Societatis litterariae fennicae], 1907.

———, ed. *Florence de Rome.* Paris: Société des anciens textes français, 1907–1909.

Walter, Philippe. *Canicule, essai de mythologie sur Yvain de Chrétien de Troyes.* Paris: Sedes, 1988.

———. *La Mémoire du temps: Fêtes et calendriers de Chrétien de Troyes à La Mort Artu.* Paris: Champion, 1989.

———. *Le Bel inconnu de Renaut de Beaujeu: rite, mythe, roman.* Paris: P.U.F., 1996.

Walter Map. *De Nugis Curialium/Courtiers' Trifles.* Edited and Translated by M. R. James. Rvised by Christopher N. L. Brooke and Roger A. B. Mynors. Oxford: Oxford University Press, 1983.

Watson, Henry. *The hystory of the two valyaunte brethren Valentyne and Orson, sonnes vnto the Emperour of Grece.* London: Copland, n.d.

Weiske, Brigitte. *Gesta Romanorum.* 2 vols. Tübingen: Niemeyer, 1992.

Wenzig, Josef. "Slavische Sagen." *Slavische Blätter* 1 (1865): 399–410.

Wildhaber, Robert. *Das Sündenregister auf der Kuhhaut.* Helsinki: Suomalainen Tiedeakatemia, 1955.

William of Malmesbury. *Gesta Regum Anglorum.* 2 vols. Edited by William Stubbs. London: Longman & Co., 1887–89.

Wirnt von Grafenberg. *Wigalois, Le chevalier à la roue d'or.* Edited and translated by Claude Lecouteux and Veronique Lévy. Grenoble: Ellug, 2001.

Wright, Thomas, and James Orchard Halliwell, eds. *Reliquiae antiquae: Scraps from Ancient Manuscripts, Illustrating Chiefly Early English Literature and the English Language.* 2 vols. London: Smith, 1845.

Wyssenherre, Michael. *Eyn buoch von dem edelen herrn von Bruneczwigk als er uber mer fuore.* Stuttgart, Württembergische Landesbibliothek, Cod. Poet. Fol. 4.

Zingerle, Ignaz Vinzenz. *Die Oswaldlegende und ihre Beziehung zur deutschen Mythologie.* Stuttgart and Munich: Scheitlin, 1836.

———. "Anteloye und Alexander." *Germania* 18 (1873): 220–33.

Zink, Michel, and Xavier Ravier, eds. *Réception et identification du conte depuis le Moyen Âge.* Toulouse: Université de Toulouse–Le Mirail, 1987.

INDEX

Books of Related Interest

The Pagan Book of the Dead
Ancestral Visions of the Afterlife and Other Worlds
by Claude Lecouteux

Encyclopedia of Norse and Germanic Folklore, Mythology, and Magic
by Claude Lecouteux

Dictionary of Ancient Magic Words and Spells
From Abraxas to Zoar
by Claude Lecouteux

The Tradition of Household Spirits
Ancestral Lore and Practices
by Claude Lecouteux

Traditional Magic Spells for Protection and Healing
by Claude Lecouteux

Dictionary of Gypsy Mythology
Charms, Rites, and Magical Traditions of the Roma
by Claude Lecouteux

Demons and Spirits of the Land
Ancestral Lore and Practices
by Claude Lecouteux

The Hidden History of Elves and Dwarfs
Avatars of Invisible Realms
by Claude Lecouteux
Foreword by Regis Boyer

Travels to the Otherworld and Other Fantastic Realms
Medieval Journeys into the Beyond
Edited by Claude Lecouteux and Corinne Lecouteux

INNER TRADITIONS • BEAR & COMPANY
P.O. Box 388
Rochester, VT 05767
1-800-246-8648
www .InnerTraditions.com

Or contact your local bookseller